Looking Back & Smiling

Looking Back & Smiling
a memoir by **Robert O. Babcock**

Deeds Publishing | Athens, GA

Copyright © 2023 — Robert O. Babcock

ALL RIGHTS RESERVED — No part of this book may be reproduced in any form or by any electronic or mechanical means, including information storage and retrieval systems, without permission in writing from the authors, except by a reviewer who may quote brief passages in a review.

Published by Deeds Publishing in Athens, GA
www.deedspublishing.com

Printed in The United States of America

Cover design by Mark Babcock.

ISBN 978-1-950794-72-0

Books are available in quantity for promotional or premium use. For information, email info@deedspublishing.com.

First Edition, 2023

10 9 8 7 6 5 4 3 2 1

To all my Family, friends, and acquaintances who have shared my life's journey with me, and to those from future generations who care enough to read about one man's experiences from 1943 to 2022. It has been a great life, with more to come.

Now it's time for you to write your memoir.

Preface

I've been thinking for a long time, and decided last year, that it's time to write my memoir. As a publisher, how can I stand on my soapbox and tell everyone over the age of 60 that it's time to start writing your memoir if I, at age 78, haven't yet done it. And as Robert Burns wrote many years ago, "The best laid plans of mice and men, gang aft aglee (often go awry)." From March 2020 through all of 2021 we were fighting the COVID pandemic.

Early in 2021 is when I made up my mind—this is the year I'm writing my memoir. I followed through with that commitment and here it is, released to my layout team on the third day of January 2022, and almost a year later, we published it.

What's special about my writing a memoir—nothing.

I'm just a plain American citizen and patriot who believes that each generation has a responsibility to future generations to record our generation's history. Someone once said, if we don't learn from history, we are destined to repeat it. If anyone can read this and learn a little about a guy they know—either as a relative, a friend, a fellow veteran or IBM retiree, book publisher, Sunday School teacher, or any number of other titles I have worn over the years—then I've done my job.

If you grew up with me in Heavener, Oklahoma, you'll probably remember some of my "growing up" stories. If you served in Vietnam with me, you'll remember some of those experiences, and learn new ones you haven't heard. We IBM retirees love to tell stories, so there are those from my 34-year IBM career.

And I've dealt with a lot of authors over the past 16+ years in my publishing career. Now you can learn a little more about the guy who helped you make your dream of becoming a published author come true.

Plus, others whose paths have crossed mine, whether at church, as a neighbor, through numerous veterans' organizations, as somebody who knows of me but has never met me in person, or as someone wanting to read about how somebody with a passion about everyone writing memoirs wrote his own, hopefully this will help you get started.

I'm writing this to preserve my story for my Family primarily, and then for anyone else who wants to read it. And I challenge each of you to get to work and start writing your memoir—don't wait until you're "old" to write it. As a publisher, I have included an Appendix at the end of this book with my thoughts on "This Year I'm Going to Write My Memoir." You might want to read that first and then see how I applied my thoughts.

A Note to the Reader

This book is an encyclopedia of my life. You can pick it up and read starting anywhere you choose. If you want to read it from front to back, you'll get the whole story of my life as I lived it. If you have a certain part of my life that you participated in or want to learn about, start there. If you get bored with the detail I have included in a section, move to a section that sounds more interesting to you. It's long (close to 110,000 words) so don't feel obligated to read parts that are not of interest. I'm happy if you read part of it. Maybe it will inspire you to start writing your memoir for your kids and grandkids and future generations.

I have two purposes for writing this book—one is to preserve my memories and life stories for my Family, friends, and American history—this is the legacy story of my life (up to December of 2021). The second, as a publisher, is to give an example of how one guy wrote his memoir. I have helped several authors write and publish memoirs. There is no right or wrong way to write a memoir—this is simply a sample of how someone who is passionate about the importance of preserving your life's story wrote his.

This is the second personal memoir I have written—the first covered only my Vietnam experiences in 1966 and 1967, written between 1986 and 1993, published in 2007. Title of that book is, *What Now, Lieutenant?* by Robert O. Babcock. This one covers my life outside Vietnam.

So, dive in—enjoy your reading, and hopefully you will decide this is the year to write your own memoir. You're not getting any younger—quit putting it off.

Contents

Who is Bob Babcock?	1
Birth to High School Graduation, 1943 to 1961	3
Family Trips Worth Remembering	22
Baseball and Wiffle Ball Memories	32
Boys State and Page in Oklahoma State House and Senate	36
Memories of Heavener Football, 1955 to 1960	40
Final Miscellaneous Memories About My Growing Up Years	67
Kansas State College of Pittsburg, 1961 to 1965	82
We're in the Army now, 1965 to 1967	97
Fort Benning and Fort Lewis, August 1965 to June 1966	97
My Vietnam Experiences, July 1966 to July 1967	116
Phillips Petroleum, July 1967 to September 1968	139
IBM Career, 1968 to 2002	149
Early IBM Days, September 1968 to December 1974	149
IBM Industry Marketing Staff Job, Atlanta, 1975 to 1976	168
First IBM Manager Job, Evansville, 1977 to 1981	177
Regional Marketing Manager, Customer Center, 1982 to 1984	190
Atlanta Software Marketing and Operations, 1985 to 1988	204
Kansas City Area Software Manager, 1989 to 1990	214
Tree Hugger, Third and Last IBM trip to Atlanta, 1990 to 2002	219

What am I going to do when I grow up? 2002 to Today	**249**
"Follow your Passion." Supporting our Military and Veterans	249
Reflections on 16 Years as an Author and Publisher	265
Moving to Athens to be close to Ava	282
Reflections on 40 Years with my Special Lady	**295**
A Deeper Dive, Three Stories Worth Writing More About	**307**
Volunteering at the Atlanta Olympics	308
Open Heart Surgery, December 2012	326
Valedictorian Speech, May 1961	341
Random Stories From my 78 Years of Life	**345**
Time to slow down … or not?	**370**
Final Thoughts and Reflections on the Life I've Lived	**373**
This Is The Year I Wrote My Memoir	**383**
Acknowledgments	**395**
About the Author	**397**

Who is Bob Babcock?

After reading the first 100 pages, Jan, my wife, suggested I summarize who I am so people can see from reading my story how I became that. I found that to be an intriguing question—I've never asked myself...who am I?

First, I love my God, my Family, my friends. Second, I see myself as a leader. I've often said, "I don't care what I'm in charge of, just so I'm in charge." Third, although many see me as gruff (because of my voice), I'm a big teddy bear in reality—a man with compassion. Fourth, I'm an American patriot who loves our country and will never forget what the bracelet I've worn every day since early 2006 says, "Freedom Isn't Free." Every American must understand that we live in the greatest place God and our forefathers ever created; it is our responsibility to preserve it for future generations. Fifth, I love sports, especially football and baseball—and I love rescue dogs, which we always have one or more living with us.

I also love history, especially military history, and never get enough of sports or history. Finally, I love to help others make their dreams come true—whether it is to become a published author, to move up the ladder of the career they have chosen, and to be a positive influence they can come to for help when they need it. I'm a half-full, not a half-empty person, always have been and plan to always keep that positive view of our world. I have mentored several during my IBM career who have far surpassed my success there. I loved doing that then, and think I am still able to do it today. Even though my views and experiences come from days gone by—they are still true in dealing with humans.

IBM's basic beliefs, which I have lived by since I joined IBM in September 1968, are still my basic beliefs—Respect for the Individual, Provide the Best Customer Service, and Strive for Excellence in all that you do. To those Basic Beliefs that IBM founder Tom Watson started, I have added Integrity, a trait that too many in today's world do not have. These four basic beliefs are what I (and our company, Deeds Publishing) live by every day.

Enough about answering Jan's question of who I am—read on and see if you remember living some of these experiences with me…

Birth to High School Graduation
Heavener, OK — 1943 to 1961

My first memory in my life, one that never wavers as my first memory, is one evening in 1949 when the new educational building at the First Methodist Church in Heavener, Oklahoma was dedicated, and the cornerstone put into place. It is still there today.

I can't for the life of me come up with why that is so indelibly imprinted in my brain. Before that, I have nothing I can bring up. After that, I have a lot. It is interesting to me that my first memory comes from my time at the Methodist Church. I have been a Methodist all my life and will likely be the rest of my life. My favorite Bible verse is Proverbs 22:6 — *Raise up a child in the way he should go, and when he is old, he will not part from it.* I am so happy my parents brought me up in the Christian faith.

August 30, 1943, in the front bedroom of the two-bedroom and one bath home that my dad built in the early 1940s in Heavener, Oklahoma (pronounced He (long e, silent a) ven er — Heven-er — but spelled Heaven with an er on it) is when and where Robert Owen "Bob" Babcock (me) came into this world. It was my brother Bill's fifth birthday. He has always claimed me as his best birthday present ever.

My birth certificate says I was born at 8:40 AM and weighed in at 8 pounds, 12 ounces — a big boy. Dr. John Harvey was the doctor and Mrs. Carter was the midwife. Back in those days, being born at home was normal. I was the third boy in our Family — James Hermann "Jim" Babcock was born on November

12, 1936, William Bert "Bill" Babcock on August 30, 1938. Two years after me, on November 3, 1945, the fourth brother, Joseph George "Joe" Babcock, rounded out our Family of six. Mother remembers Dr. Harvey saying, "Oh, no…" when Joe was born. She didn't think anything was wrong, she just knew it was another boy (she had always wanted a girl, and never got one).

From early in my life, I've heard the story about Jim, Bill, and two neighbor kids going door to door in the neighborhood the morning I was born and told them about Bill's birthday present.

My mother, Dorothy Davidson Thompson Babcock, was born on September 2, 1912, in the same town, Heavener, Oklahoma, where I was born. She lived there all her life except for a short time living in Kansas City after she and my daddy were married. Her parents were Jeff and Annie Thompson. Her sister, born just over a year before her, was Loucille. As I grew up, and through my college years, they lived across the alley and two houses down from where our Family lived. It was nice having grandparents so close during all my growing up years. And, my Auntie Lou had a son, my first cousin Bud Thompson, who lived with our grandparents and her.

Living so close to my maternal grandparents was a great experience. My granddaddy loved to work his garden on railroad land across the highway from their home. He also loved his flower garden in their front yard. He would get frustrated when someone would tell my grandmother how pretty her flowers were—she wasn't a gardener. I also have fond memories of when in high school, I would take him for a ride, just to see the surrounding countryside and get him away from his home. Although he had a car at some point, he never had one in my memory. After Phyllis, my girlfriend, and I would take him for a ride, he insisted that we stop at the Phillips 66 gas station near where he lived and he would buy us three or five gallons of gasoline, even over our protests. The gasoline pumps from his days were different from today—you told them then how many gallons you wanted, not how many dollars' worth.

I also remember many times sitting in the glider swing in the shade of their front yard simply watching the world go by. We would talk, we would be silent, and he constantly had a fly swatter in his hand. He would say, "Bob, be still." I would and he'd kill another fly that was somewhere on me. The only off-limits place to kill a fly was on my face. No telling how many hundreds of flies we killed sitting in front of his home, a typical 1950s experience in the days before air conditioning.

My daddy, Joseph Hermann Babcock, was born in Pittsburg, Kansas on October 9, 1913, the youngest of four born to Bert and Nora Babcock. My middle name came from his brother, Owen Babcock, who died of a fever when in his 20's. My dad's two sisters were Leona and Opal, both lived into their 90s. Opal and Byron Mason had a son, Mike Mason, my other first cousin. A year older than me, Mike and I got closer as we went to college together in Pittsburg, Kansas.

Daddy went to college for two years at what was then called Kansas State Teachers College in Pittsburg where he learned to be a printer (the same college, different name, that I went to). He worked in the 1930s at a print shop in Kansas City and later at the Heavener Ledger newspaper after he and mother married and moved from Kansas City to Heavener. In the early 1940s, he went to work as a fireman on the Kansas City Southern (KCS) Railroad, where both my grandfathers worked, and retired from the KCS after 36 years of service. We were a railroad family, living in a railroad town. The largest employer in Heavener as I was growing up was the KCS railroad.

Bert Morgan Babcock, my grandfather on my dad's side, was

part of the Army's 20th Infantry Regiment in the late 1890s. After he got out of the Army, he worked in train service for the KCS, had an injury at work (I never knew how it happened) and lost a leg. I understand he walked with a wooden leg (long before today's magical prosthetics) and at one time I saw one of his crutches. The KCS moved him to roundhouse service in Pittsburg, Kansas where he worked until he died too young, January 21, 1923, of rheumatic fever at age 46. My daddy was just nine years old when his dad died.

My Grandmother Babcock, Nora Scott Babcock, took charge of her Family when her husband died. I remember her as being always smiling, loved her grandkids, and was also taken from us too soon. She died of a heart attack on September 19, 1949 (age 65) when I was in the first grade.

In a nutshell, that is my background and direct ancestors. I'm sure my brother Bill and his wife, Joan, have much more details on our entire Family background if you want to ask them about it. They are the genealogy people of our Family.

* * * * * *

My boyhood memories are pleasant. We lived two blocks from the mainline of the KCS railroad. The sound of trains, both passenger and freight, are a big part of my growing up memories. Even today, I love the sound of trains passing by. And another block east, beyond the railroad tracks, was downtown Heavener. Almost everything anyone would ever need could be bought there (at least that's what I thought). If they didn't have it, we regularly received catalogs from Sears, Spiegel, and Montgomery Ward—especially at Christmas time with their special Christmas catalogs. It was an exciting time to broaden the possibilities of toys that weren't stocked in our downtown stores. We would circle what we wanted in the catalog and wish for it on Christmas morning.

As was normal in those days, my mother was a stay-at-home mom. She was always there for us, and I was very close to her. With Daddy regularly traveling as a fireman, and later engineer, on the KCS railroad, Mother was the one who kept the home fires burning. And speaking of burning, Daddy had strong and muscular arms from shoveling coal as a fireman on the old coal-fired steam engines he worked on.

We didn't have an automobile in my early years. Traveling beyond our small area where we lived wasn't something that many people did. I remember some train rides (free passes for families of those railroaders who worked for the Kansas City Southern railroad) to Pittsburg, Kansas to visit my dad's two sisters and his mother while she was still alive. Beyond that, my young years were pretty much all spent within a few blocks of where I was born. Walking to where we needed to go was the norm—school, church, grocery store, etc.

Then my second oldest memory comes to mind…in 1950 my Daddy bought our first car, a brand new green 1950 Buick. I was surprised when he showed up in it one day, had no idea we were going to get a car. The whole family of six loaded into it and took what I thought was about the longest drive that anyone could ever take. We drove five miles north to the next little town of Howe, and then back home. I still couldn't imagine going that far—and I still smile at how I remember that seeming to be such a long, long drive. I think we had that car for four years, then he bought a 1954 and then a 1956 Buick—always a new car and he was absolutely a Buick man. It seems the 1956 Buick was a "lemon" and he switched to Chrysler products after that and I think stuck with them until he died, maybe a Ford mixed in occasionally.

Of course, the new 1950 Buick couldn't be left out in the rain, heat, and cold, so he built a stand-alone garage in our backyard for the car, which still stands today, although it has had several alterations over the years. In the later years of his life, it was the "parlor" where he had his trophy and engraving business set up—garage door replaced, window air-conditioning installed, and always a small refrigerator full of soft drinks. Drink what you want, but woe be unto you if you didn't drink all of what you opened.

Daddy was a woodworker as a hobby and had built our home in the early 1940's, before I was born. The original house had two bedrooms, one bath, a kitchen, and a living room. Also included was a screened in porch that I remember playing in when the weather was warm.

A third early memory was when Daddy expanded our home. This wasn't a time of hiring somebody to do it for you and have it done quickly, this was a long project that Daddy and a couple of friends worked on when he wasn't shoveling coal on a steam-engine locomotive on his railroad job. The expansion brought us a much bigger kitchen, the old kitchen being remodeled and included into the living room, a dining room where the screened in porch had been, and an upstairs bedroom big enough for all four of us boys to sleep. Stubbed in between the upstairs bedroom and the attic was a second bathroom, which was still unfinished when we sold the house in 2006—always a one-bathroom home. He also included a wood-burning fireplace in the old kitchen area that had become part of the living room.

One December night when I was in second grade, my brother Bill woke up, smelled smoke, checked it out, and saw the fireplace was on fire. He woke everyone up and I remember running out the back door, barefooted, and across the alley through the snow to our neighbors, the Ledbetters. Of course, Daddy was out of town on his railroad job, so Mother had to take care of everything until he got back home. The volunteer fire department came, put out the fire before it caused too much damage, and we all lived for a long time with no desire to ever have a fireplace again.

Elementary School Days

We lived two blocks from Westside Elementary School—the only elementary school in Heavener, a town of around 2,000 residents. It was an easy walk, which I did from first through sixth grades (we did not have kindergarten back then). I don't recall mother ever walking with me, we neighborhood kids all seemed to head to school about the same time and we had zero concern about anyone bothering us. Rather than take lunch to school, we went home for what we called dinner—back then meals were called breakfast, dinner, supper. Lunch was something you carried with you and supper was the evening meal, not dinner as it is called now.

My elementary school memories are universally positive. We had excellent teachers, my two older brothers had gone to the same school before me, mother had grown up with some of the teachers, and two of them lived close to us—Mrs. Faye Moore, my fifth-grade teacher, directly across the street and Mr. BJ Keller, my sixth-grade teacher, halfway between us and school. There were no strangers in small-town Oklahoma in the 1950s.

I was a good student from the beginning—the only "C" grade I ever made was the first six weeks of first grade, in penmanship. I learned to improve on that and made straight "A's" all year in third grade, only time I accomplished that. As you would guess, Miss Himes, my third-grade teacher was a favorite.

Anyone who knows me understands that I have a loud bass voice. That has always been there and started serving me well in elementary school. In school plays, I always had speaking parts because I could be heard. Those were the days before portable microphones, we probably didn't have a single microphone or loudspeaker in the school. In the sixth grade, I was Santa Claus in the all-school Christmas play—moderator of the play, had lots of speaking parts, could be heard in the audience. That made me realize that being able to be heard was an asset. One of the younger kids came up to me after the play and asked how I could remember all the speaking parts I had. I showed them the script that was printed in the play book that sat on a box hidden behind the cardboard silhouette of Santa's sleigh that I sat on.

All in all, elementary school was the beginning of my very positive memories of my education and growing up years in Heavener, Oklahoma. I like to tell people that our class took three decades to complete school—we started in 1949 and graduated in 1961.

Third Grade, broken arm

During August between 2nd and 3rd grade, we were visiting our Aunt Elma and Uncle Charlie on their farm outside Cove, Arkansas. We loved to go there; it was truly an old-time farm full of memories. They had no electricity, cooking was done on a wood-burning stove, water was pulled from a well, and the "outhouse" was 50 yards or so behind the house. Aunt Elma was a great cook and I picture her dripping with sweat as she fried freshly killed chicken on the hot stove in the heat of August (no fan, no air conditioning, just hot). They had two plow horses, Silver and Bess, that Uncle Charlie used to work his fields. Silver was white and Bess was brown. Both were tame and old. We loved to ride them.

There were no saddles, so somebody filled a tow sack (as we called it, others called it a gunny sack) with hay to soften the hard back of the horses. I was riding Bess and she stopped to eat some grass, nothing out of the ordinary, but as her head went down, I slid off her back and landed on the rock-hard ground on my left elbow—and broke it. It was serious business, and the closest hospital was in Fort Smith, Arkansas, about 100 miles away on two-lane roads. I do remember that I lay across the back seat, with my head in mother's lap. I don't recall if my three brothers also went with us or what happened.

Net is, my left elbow was operated on, I still have a scar, and the smell of ether is a memory that I never want to deal with again. I started third grade with my arm in a cast and kept the elbow part of the cast for many years as a souvenir. My elbow healed well and has never caused a problem. The one after-effect I still live with…I refuse to eat coconut. I believe the smell of ether and coconut are too similar.

Fifth grade, end of Korean War Welcome Home, 1953

John M. "Patch" Patton, Heavener football star in the late 1940s, was released from the prisoner of war camp he had been held in during the Korean War. The town turned out for a parade and a big party on the high school football field. Each class had a float—our class had Uncle Sam (me) and the Statue of Liberty (Judy Gail Summers) riding on it. I remember the band playing, and the crowd singing, "When Johnny comes marching home again, hoorah, hoorah…" That song fit him well since his name was John and he was a hometown hero even before he went off to war. Interestingly, I just learned in December 2021 from the 70 years ago section of the Heavener Ledger, that Patch Patton had been declared killed in action (KIA) in Korea before his parents received a letter from him in December 1951 telling them he was in a POW camp.

Those were days when patriotism was the norm in our country—a much different experience than for those of us who returned from Vietnam 13 to 20 years later and were ignored. Sadly, the Korean War veterans have also been ignored, with the Korean War now having the nickname of "The Forgotten War."

Playing Army—a passion for many years

Why I have such a strong interest in the Army, I can't explain. Other than my oldest brother, Jim, who served with the 2nd Armored Division in Cold War Germany in the mid-1950s, nobody in my Family served in the military, except my Grandfather Babcock who died long before I was born. But from as early as I can remember, I loved to play Army. We played with sticks for rifles at times, but a plastic rifle I got for Christmas one year was my most prized possession. John Tatum, my neighbor who was two years older, had the same passion I did. We fought the Japanese, the Germans, the North Koreans, the Chinese, anybody who was or had been an enemy of the United States.

To make us even more official, Daddy stopped at an Army surplus store in Fort Smith and bought an Army surplus helmet for my cousin, Bud, my brother, Joe, my friend, Charlie, my best friend John, and me. To make it easy to know whose helmet we were wearing, he painted our initials on the back of each one—PDT, JGB, CCO, JET and ROB. John and I thought we were big shots since our initials spelled something and the others didn't.

When we weren't running through the neighborhood playing Army, we were in the dirt in our back yard playing Army with our toy Soldiers. I played for hours at a time, as did John, with those Soldiers. You could buy one for a nickel at Towery's 5 & 10 cents store, and we saved our money and kept ourselves supplied any time a new and more action-oriented Army man came into stock.

To make my passion for the Army even greater...during the Korean War, we regularly had troop trains come through Heavener. As a key terminal and maintenance area for the railroad, they would stop for an hour or so while refueling and adding water to the train. The troops had time to get off and stretch their legs along the side of the train. Living with a clear view of the railroad tracks, I always stopped what I was doing and simply watched the Soldiers, dreaming about how one day I hoped to be one. Freight trains came through regularly carrying military supplies—tanks, trucks, jeeps on flat cars—heading to the port of New Orleans where they would be loaded on ships to traverse through the Panama Canal, headed for Korea. And it was during this time that I became a regular newspaper reader. We got the Tulsa World in the morning and Fort Smith Times Record in the afternoon. As soon as the afternoon paper was thrown into our front yard, I would grab it and look for pictures of our Army fighting in Korea and read the articles about our progress. (I got my sports news from the Tulsa World.)

Playing Army was my favorite activity as a child, followed by lots of time playing wiffle ball as I got into later elementary through high school. I was also a baseball fan and became an avid Brooklyn Dodgers fan. Even today I can tell you the starting lineup of the Dodgers in the mid-1950s. By the time I was in junior high school, I found there were other things, like girls and football, which made playing Army drop out of the way I spent hours and hours of my time.

Junior High and High School Memories

After having walked the two blocks from home to school for six years, it was time for me to leave that comfortable place and head to the combined junior and senior high school. As with most things built during the 1930's, our high school was built by WPA (Works Progress Administration) to help our country come out of the Great Depression of the 1930s. The school was always there during my time in Heavener, and I have no recollection when it was built—before my time, sometime in the late 1930s is my guess. It was replaced with the current high school building a few years after I graduated.

During my 7th grade year, my brother Bill was a senior and was my ride to school, and home for lunch (we called it dinner) in the middle of the day. Getting home after school was up to me—Bill either worked or had other things to do that precluded him worrying about his little brother's transportation.

Living in small town America, and that includes Heavener, nothing is very far away. With elementary school being two blocks away, high school (we never called it junior high and high school, it was simply high school—grades 7 through 12—so I'll keep calling it that) was maybe ten blocks away, all the way on the east side of town.

I don't recall a lot about junior high school. I continued as a good student, made good grades, continued as a leader, became a water-boy and batboy on the high school teams, and generally had a great life.

I remember in English class in 7th grade, we had to memorize the poem, *Stopping by Woods on a Snowy Evening* by Robert Frost. I memorized it, likely made an A by reciting it, and decided then and there that, even though this was a fine poem, I had zero interest in poetry. I cover that minor event here for one reason...often in my life and career as a publisher, people have come to me with books of poetry to publish. I quickly tell them this story, add that I have no value to add in editing their work since I have no love of poetry, and then tell them I'm not interested in publishing their poetry book. That's my story and I'm sticking to it...

What I do remember very well from junior high school, is the girls I had grown up with suddenly started looking much better and I had a lot more interest in them. One girl in particular, a blonde who I determined was the most beautiful girl I had ever seen. It's amazing how junior high school changes your priorities. Suddenly playing Army all the time wasn't nearly as much fun as hanging around with girls at the T&M Pharmacy after school. That beautiful blonde girl's name was Phyllis Campbell. She was my first date, soon to be my steady girlfriend, and before our senior year in college became my wife.

I was bashful with girls but was bound and determined I was going to ask Phyllis for a date to go to a movie. I finally built up my courage, called her on the phone (her phone number was 208 and ours was 348—and an operator connected us), asked her to the movie, and on January 24, 1958, I knocked on her door and we walked to the movie. I don't recall what movie we saw, what the weather was, but do know that as I walked the six blocks home after the date, I was walking on air. More dates followed, can't recall the frequency, but I never once considered asking anyone for a date but Phyllis.

By the time our sophomore year came around, we were seeing

a lot of each other and before long we were "going steady." When I earned my first letter jacket in football, I wore it a few days and then gave it to Phyllis to show we were going steady. (My mother didn't like that, but it was the thing we did in those days in the 1950s). We were together so much in high school, that "Bob and Phyllis" or "Phyllis and Bob" needed no last names, our small school and town knew who we were. One time when we were home from college for the summer, I got a letter in our Babcock family mailbox addressed simply to, "Bob and Phyllis, Heavener, Oklahoma." Even the post office knew us as a couple. The letter was from my Aunt Opal in Pittsburg, KS.

As we were walking down the sidewalk in front of Tate's Store one afternoon of our sophomore year, headed to the T&M Pharmacy for a Coke, Bob Tate, one of the store owners came out and stopped us. He looked me in the eye and said, "Bob, don't you know that a gentleman never lets a lady walk on the outside of a sidewalk, near the traffic?" I replied, "No, I didn't know that." He then went on to explain how in earlier times, gentlemen walked next to the street to protect their lady from being splashed by mud from a passing horse and carriage, or from somebody in any way abusing the lady.

From that day forward, and until the day I die, I have never walked on the inside of the sidewalk when walking with Phyllis or any other lady, and never will. Even during the women's lib movements of the '70s and '80s, when an IBM women's libber protested my walking on the outside, I simply dropped back behind her and let her walk alone. Bob Tate taught me a very valuable lesson that I have taught to my sons and grandson. Sadly, that act of chivalry seems to have not been taught to most of the current generations. I cringe as I see young men walk on the inside of young ladies each day as I drive by the University of Georgia.

Dating in Heavener was typically made up of a movie, cruising up and down the highway and main street, stopping at the drive-in Dairy Queen type place (can't remember its name) and, of course, parking. We frequently double-dated with Wayne Kelley and Ann Vickers. Wayne and I both worked and were proud that our girl friends were dating us, not our dad like those who provided date money for some of our friends who never took it upon themselves to get a job. (By the way, for the younger generation, a movie date cost $1.00—that bought two admissions for 40 cents each, a box of popcorn to share for a dime, and two small cokes for a nickel each—and I swear that is the truth from the late 1950s in Heavener, Oklahoma).

Reflecting on my junior and senior high school days, always being with Phyllis when I could, playing football during the season, being active in other school activities (as a leader) and sports, working as a janitor at State National Bank and as a trophy parts maker at Babcock & Sons Hobby Shop filled up most of my time. I attended Sunday School and church every Sunday (a rule in my Family which I never tried to go against) and overall lived a simple and carefree life. You will notice that I didn't mention studying, that was never high on my list. I did well in school without studying much and would pay for it when I got to college, but that's another story for that section of this book.

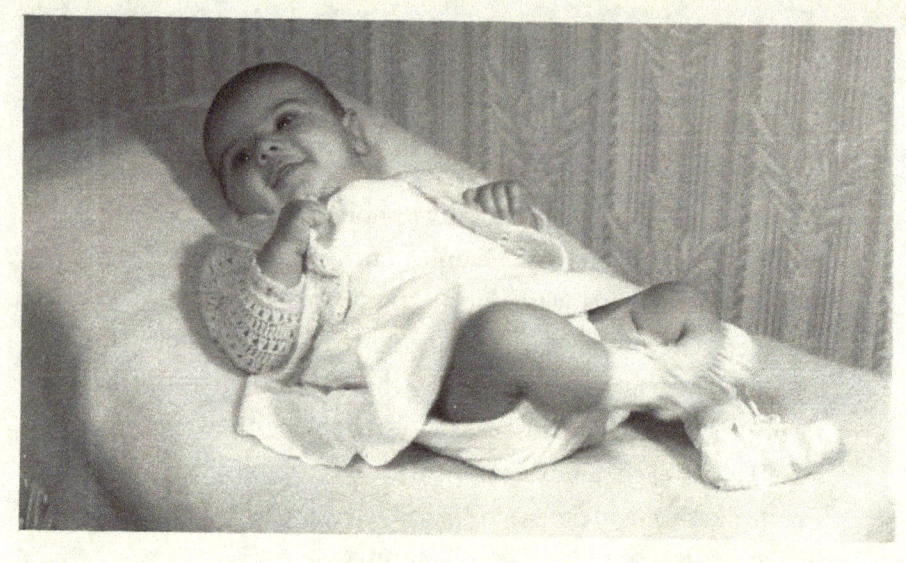

BILL 5   BOB 3-Mo.   JIM 7

Howdy Folks!

☆

*May we come in long
enough to wish you a
Merry Christmas
and a
Happy New Year*

☆   *The Babcocks*

Babcock Family visiting Pittsburg, KS — 1946 or 1947

301 West 2nd, back of home, late 1940s

Elementary school picture, probably 3rd or 4th grade

My first formal picture

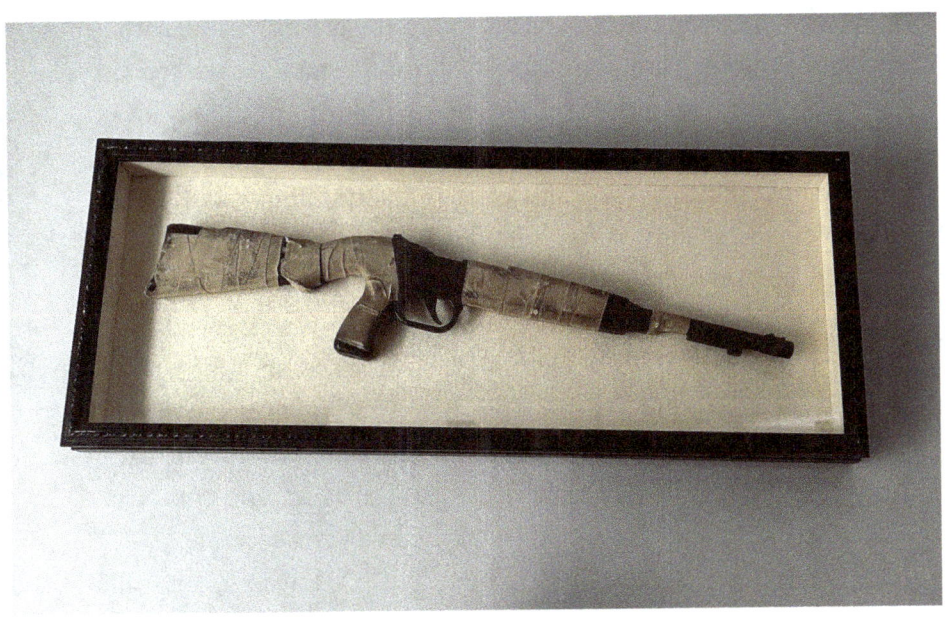

My boyhood Army rifle, now hanging on our wall

Family Trips Worth Remembering
Family Vacation to Carslbad Caverns
New Mexico — 1954

The only vacation I remember the whole Family taking was when all six of us piled into our 1954 Buick and headed out to New Mexico to visit Carlsbad Caverns, Santa Fe, and Bandelier National Monument. Why my parents picked that destination, I never knew or asked — but it was a memory that sticks with me. Being less than wealthy, we went on the economy plan. We would stay in a motel one night, and the next night we would camp out. Most meals were picnic style — sandwiches eaten along a place to stop on the highway, not a full-blown restaurant meal for six.

    A basic cartop carrier was affixed to the top of the car with a tarp to keep the camping gear dry in case of rain. As we started our adventure, we made it to the first pullout from the highway north of Heavener for Daddy to have to stop and fix the flapping of the tarp and make sure it was tight and nothing would fly off. Never again, as long as he lived, did I ever know of him to have any problem with packing a car on any trip he took.

    Camping was easy for Joe and me — we were the youngest and smallest so one of us slept on the front seat and one on the back seat of the car (long before bucket seats were common). For the other four, they weren't as comfortable as we were. I remember complaints about how cold it was as we got into New Mexico, but that is just a blur memory, I was comfortable.

    Three things stuck out to me at Carlsbad Caverns, the walk

down into the cave was a great sight to see. Stalagmites and stalactites, formations of minerals from thousands of years were growing upward from the floor of the cave (stalagmites) and downward from the ceiling (stalactites). Truly amazing—not sure I ever saw either one again but that made a great impression. And, at one time when we were deep into the cave, they stopped us, told us not to move, and they turned the lights off. It was the darkest dark I have ever experienced, before or since. You truly couldn't see your hand in front of your face. (I probably had Mother's hand with my other hand, so I wasn't afraid at all). Then at dusk that evening, we went back to the entrance of the cave and watched thousands of bats fly out of the cave to start their nightly mission of finding insects to eat and keep them sustained as they slept in the cave during the day and flew through the night.

Santa Fe, the capital of New Mexico, was an ancient city with buildings that dated back many years and Bandelier National Monument (Frijole Canyon) was a place where Indian cave dwellers had carved small caves into the sheer sides of volcanic cliffs and lived safely above predators. Rustic ladders (reproductions when we were there) was how they got to their dwellings.

I guess what makes it memorable and worthy of me including here is it is the only vacation where all six of our Family members took part. Jim graduated high school in 1954, went off to college at Oklahoma A&M (now Oklahoma State) for a semester, didn't like it, and joined the Army in early 1955. That led to our second Family vacation, to attend his Basic Training graduation at Fort Carson, Colorado.

A tradition that started on this trip, that continued as long as I took trips with my parents...at the state line of each new state we entered, we would stop and take a picture of the boys standing by the "Welcome to (whatever State)" sign. On this trip, we added Texas and New Mexico to our new states. Up to then, I had been in Oklahoma, Arkansas, Kansas, and Missouri.

Colorado vacation for Jim's graduation from Basic Training—1955

As you can imagine, it was traumatic for the first son to leave home and join the Army. When he graduated from his eight-week Basic Training, the whole Family again piled into our 1954 Buick and drove to Fort Carson, south of Colorado Springs, Colorado. Of course, we stopped and took a picture at the state line of Colorado—now up to seven states I had visited in the first eleven years of my life.

I was extremely happy to be on an Army post, to see all the Soldiers and military equipment. And to see my big brother in uniform, I was over the moon in being proud of him. I have been to Fort Carson many times since then (the 4th Infantry Division that I served with in Vietnam is stationed there now). Each time I go on post, I think about that first trip in 1955.

Other highlights were Garden of the Gods, Royal Gorge, and Pikes Peak. The winding road going to the top of Pikes Peak scared us all to death (Daddy was more of a sightseer than we were comfortable with as he drove on that narrow road). Plus, at the high altitude of something like 14,000 feet above sea level, we all became semi-sick and couldn't wait to get down off that mountain. In all my subsequent trips to that area, I have never been tempted to go back up Pikes Peak—been there, done that.

Third year in a row — another vacation trip Cleveland, Ohio — 1956

Daddy was the secretary and treasurer of the Heavener chapter of the Brotherhood of Locomotive Engineers (B of LE). He was selected to attend the national convention in the summer of 1956 in Cleveland, Ohio and decided to take all of us with him. By then, my brother Bill had graduated from high school in May 1956. On graduation night, he, and a bunch of his buddies (Mike Sullivan, "Salty" Self, Ken Bishop, Bill and a couple others whose names escape me), left at 10:00PM on graduation night to drive to California to make their fortune. You can imagine how Mother was worried to death — but that's a story for Bill to tell.

The trip to Cleveland was an almost summer-long adventure. We left about a week before we had to be in Ohio and drove through the South to see the sights before we wound up in Cleveland. We drove across Arkansas to Tennessee, spent a day or so at Gatlinburg, Tennessee (most people now think of it as Dolly Parton Land, but we were there long before she became a singing star). We next cut across North Carolina and drove up through the Great Smoky Mountains. I still think of that part of North Carolina as the prettiest place I've ever been. It was not unusual to see deer and bears along the side of the two-lane highway (again, long before the Interstate highway system was everywhere). We crossed Kentucky and on up to Cleveland — quite a road trip seeing new parts of our great country.

The convention headquarters was in the Manger Hotel in downtown Cleveland — where we stayed for six weeks. Highlights of this adventure were seeing Bob Hope perform in a theater in his hometown of Cleveland (I didn't get to see him in Vietnam but at least can claim that I saw him in person once).

We also went to several Cleveland Indian baseball games. Joe and I would ride the bus to the old Municipal Stadium, near Lake Erie, in time to watch batting practice and then the game. Bob Feller, Early Wynn, Sal Maglie, Herb Score, Rocky Colavito, Bobby Avila, Vic Rosen were some of the players we loved to watch. We roamed around downtown Cleveland by ourselves (something that was not unusual for an almost 13-year-old and almost 11-year-old boys to do in those days when big cities were much safer than they are today).

The highlight was when Daddy took Joe and me up for our first ever flight—and it was in a helicopter. We had a 20-30-minute flight over the stadium, downtown Cleveland, out over Lake Erie, and back to land on the shore of Lake Erie, near Captain Frank's Seafood House—our favorite dining place that summer.

As an official function of the B of LE convention, they chartered a train to take the delegates and their Family members from Cleveland to visit Niagara Falls. Not only did we take the Maid of the Mist boat down under the Falls; we also landed in Canada to observe the Falls from the Canadian side. It was a great day for this young boy. On this day we picked up two new states that we had been in, Pennsylvania and New York, and our first foreign country—Canada.

Two more memories of the summer of 1956…In late July, Egypt nationalized the Suez Canal, causing a world crisis since that was the way oil and other essentials moved from the Middle East to Europe and the US. By then, my oldest brother, Jim, had finished his Army training and was assigned to the 2nd Armored Division in Germany, as part of a tank platoon. It was announced that his unit had been deployed down to Italy to be ready to strike if the situation called for it. I remember nights hearing Mother crying in our hotel room as she worried about Jim's potential to go into harm's way. Little did we know then that ten years later, she would be worrying about me as I served in Vietnam.

After six weeks living in a hotel, Joe and I were getting tired of that adventure. We were ready to go home, and the convention had two more weeks to run. Fortunately, our grandparents lived across the alley from us and were more than happy to have us come back home. They would take care of us. Thus, in early August, we boarded a train in Cleveland and rode for the better part of two days and nights to get home.

It boggles my mind that our parents agreed to let us do that, but again, life was much simpler and safer in 1956 than it has been the past many years. As a yet to turn 13-year-old, I took responsibility for Joe and me and we headed home. I don't recall how many train changes we made, but probably at least two. The beauty of railroads back then was we rode on free passes. It cost nothing for us, as railroad Family members, to get from Cleveland to Heavener. We didn't have a Pullman berth to sleep in so we slept as best we could in the seats of the train.

We also picked up two new states that we could claim we had been in—Indiana and Illinois. By the end of the summer of 1956, I was proud that I had been in 15 of our United States, plus barely into Canada, my first foreign country.

We resumed our life in small town Oklahoma and were very happy to see our parents when they arrived home two weeks later.

Camping trip with the Franklins North of Noel, MO

I don't remember the specific year, but I very well remember the event. I was probably in junior high school. We camped along the banks of the Elk River north of Noel, MO. The Franklin Family were with us—Reese, Joann, and their three girls, Jean Ann, Janis, and Nancy. Mother and Daddy, Joe and I were the ones from our Family. And Bill rode a train to get to Noel (he had returned from his big adventure to California). None of us were experienced campers. I can't recall why our parents wanted to do it, but we did. We camped along the river, rudimentary camping gear at best. I don't remember tents, probably slept under the stars.

We swam in the river, fished, and put out a trot line to see if we could catch some big fish. We didn't have a boat and Bill swam across the river, pulling the trot line to secure it to the other bank, just below the KCS railroad line. The next morning, Bill got on a blow-up raft and went across the river, checking the trot line. As he checked the hooks, all were empty until he got to the far side of the river where he yelled, "We've got a big fish here!" Everyone ran to the bank to see what he was yelling about. We were skeptical (he kidded a lot). But when he got to the far bank, he tied the end of the trot line to his small raft and told us to run up the bank with our end of the trot line. We did it, and Bill swam along watching that the fish didn't get away or the trot line came loose from the raft.

Just as we got the fish into shallow water, the hook came loose from its mouth. Bill, staying close behind, moved forward and grabbed it and ran ashore. We came back and were shocked at the size of the catfish. Bill and the fish made the front page of the Heavener Ledger the next week—a 34-pound catfish. I think we kept it and ate it, don't recall, but will never forget pulling that trot line up the riverbank and Bill catching the fish when it got loose.

This fall of 2021, I talked on the phone to Jean Ann and Janis Franklin. Both fondly remember that camping adventure, just as I do.

My last vacation trip before leaving home
West Coast, 1961

After I graduated from high school, we took our last Family trip. It was just Mother, Daddy, Joe, and me; we were headed to the West Coast. It was new territory, and we were excited about the opportunity. Keep in mind—Interstate highways were being constructed, far from complete in 1961. Most cars did not have air-conditioning, and quality of cars was not as good as today. With that as a backdrop, let's start the trip.

We hadn't left the state of Oklahoma when we had our first tire blowout, the first of four or five on the trip. Western Oklahoma, Texas, New Mexico, Arizona are not the most beautiful or comfortable places to drive in the summer without air conditioning. But we were on an adventure, and we kept plugging along. We were constantly switching between the old US Highway 66 and the under-construction Interstate Highway 40 going across the country.

Our first stop was the Grand Canyon, didn't go down into it but looking at it from the rim was awe-inspiring. We then stopped at Las Vegas (or maybe it was reverse order—not sure) where Joe and I were too young to go into the casinos, so we stood outside while Mother and Daddy tried their luck at slot machines. From there we spent a night or two with Family relatives (distant—can't remember the connection or their names) in Los Angeles, and then took a two-day trip through San Diego into Mexico (our second foreign country). We spent some time being tourists in Tijuana (again, keep in mind, the world was different in 1961 than it is today) and on down to Ensenada, a 70-mile drive down the coast. It was a great trip, we saw a totally different country, we saw conditions that made us appreciate what we have in America, and we picked up some cheap souvenirs to take home. It was a real eye-opener for this small-town Okie boy. Glad we took the trip, love the memory, and for the past 20+ years there is no way in hell that I would ever drive over the border into Mexico.

We drove up the Pacific Coast Highway to Monterrey, Carmel, San Francisco (ate on Fisherman's Wharf and saw all the tourist spots—Alcatraz prison, Golden Gate Bridge, etc.) and then over to Yosemite National Forest as we headed back toward home. We were in awe of the herds of wildlife and other beauties in Yosemite, but I had my first confrontation with my Daddy—and I won it. The roads were narrow and winding, the drop-offs from the road were steep and close to the road. Keep in mind, Daddy was a locomotive engineer. The trains he "drove" followed the railroad track and he didn't need to keep his eyes on the road like you do on a winding, narrow road.

Finally, with Mother, Joe, and me all about to go crazy that he was going to wreck the car, I took control. "Stop!" I said when we got to a pullout place. Mother agreed with me. I told him, "I'm driving, you sit in the passenger seat and sightsee all you want to. When I have a son of my own, I'll have him drive and then I'll get to see the beauty of Yosemite."

Mother and Joe were with me, all of us were ready to walk if he didn't let me drive. I'm sure he was upset but he was outnumbered and turned the driving over to me, which I did and kept my eyes on the road. No harm, no foul. Daddy got over me standing up to him and nothing further was ever said about it until now. Thus far, I have not been back to Yosemite. One of these days I'll get one of my kids or grandkids to drive me through there. I hear it is a beautiful drive.

Pointing the car back to the east toward Oklahoma, we headed across Utah, another new state for us. What I remember about Utah is miles and miles of straight road for as far as the eye can see. We would go for many miles without seeing another car, and then we had another blowout! This made the third to fifth tire we had lost on the trip (worst tire experience of my life—turned out they were faulty, and Daddy got reimbursed for the cost after we got home).

It was getting toward evening with us sitting by the side of the road, no spare tire, and Daddy had spent all his travelers' checks while Mother still had most of hers (this was before credit cards were popular). Thus, when a car stopped to help us out, she had to ride with them to the next town, some 25 or more miles away. They only had room for one passenger, so we had no choice but to let her ride off with total strangers while Daddy, Joe, and I sat out there in the middle of nowhere with darkness quickly approaching. After a couple of hours sitting along the highway in the dark, we saw lights in the far distance to the east (you could see forever on those straight roads). We were thankful to see mother drive up in a tow truck and we all breathed a sigh of relief. The rest of the trip was uneventful.

That was the last long trip I remember taking with my birth Family. I soon left for college and the boy growing up in Heavener, Oklahoma phase of my life had come to an end.

But my writing about growing up in Heavener is not ending. If you are still interested, I have another 50 pages of my growing up memories after this. Skim them, read what sounds interesting, or skip down to the next section…

Baseball and Wiffle Ball Memories

I have many fond memories of baseball from my growing up days in the 1950s. There was no question that baseball was the national pastime then. The Major Leagues had eight teams each in the National and American Leagues, mostly clustered in the northeast. The furthest west teams were the St. Louis Cardinals, Chicago Cubs, Chicago White Sox, and Milwaukee Braves. Rather than pick one of those teams as my favorite, I became an avid Brooklyn Dodgers fan (I don't remember why but I followed them religiously until they moved to Los Angeles in 1958). My cousin, Bud, loved the Cardinals and my great friend, John Tatum, was a Milwaukee (now Atlanta) Braves fan. Every morning during baseball season I would grab the Tulsa World newspaper to see the baseball scores and check the statistics of my favorite Dodger players.

The closest radio station (KFSA in Fort Smith, Arkansas) carried all the St. Louis Cardinals games, announced by Harry Carey and Jack Buck. I spent many evenings sitting on the screened-in porch of our across the alley neighbors, Fred and Kate Ledbetter, listening to the Cardinals baseball broadcast. Although the station was less than 50 miles away, it was common to have to listen through the static if it was the least bit cloudy or if heat lightning was near. It was an especially good evening when the Dodgers played the Cardinals.

When I was in late elementary school, my grandparents took Bud and me to St. Louis to watch a three-game series of the Cardinals playing the Dodgers. We rode a train from Fort Smith to St. Louis, slept in a Pullman car berth, and stayed in a hotel in downtown St. Louis—all new things for this small-town boy (this was before our Cleveland trip in 1956). We showed up early for all three games and watched batting practice and hung around begging for autographs and got some good ones from both teams. One we didn't get was Stan Musial. He never slowed down or looked right or left as he left the field and headed for the dressing room. It made my Granddaddy furious that he wouldn't, "Stop and give these boys an autograph." I don't think he ever forgave "Stan the Man" for giving us that disappointment.

Another memorable trip was when my brother Joe and I rode the KCS train to Kansas City to watch the All-Star Game in July 1960, played in the old Municipal Stadium, home of the Kansas City Athletics (before they moved to Oakland in 1968). We left Heavener on #16, the train that left about 11:00PM and arrived in Kansas City around 6:00AM the next morning. We hung around the Kansas City Union train station until mid-morning (per instructions from our parents) and then caught a bus to the stadium to watch batting practice and the game. The one play that stands out with me was Willie Mays making one of his famous "basket catches" out in centerfield after a long run. After the game we rode the bus back to Union Station (as instructed) and caught #15 which left sometime around 9:00PM and got into Heavener around 6:00AM the next morning. Two nights of sleeping in a seat on a railroad car, but well worth the adventure for Joe and me.

When I moved to Kansas City with IBM the first time, the Kansas City Royals were an expansion team that played their first season in 1969. I was in the Army Reserves, and among the troops in my unit was Lou Piniella, who was Rookie of the Year for the American League that year, before going to the Yankees a few years later and finishing his long baseball career as the Yankees manager. I must say, Lou Piniella made no attempt to even act like a Soldier—he was a sorry excuse, but by joining the unit he missed the draft and Vietnam. The battalion commander of the unit was a baseball nut and never put any pressure on Lou to act the part of a Soldier.

Another baseball legend that served in my unit was John Schuerholz, the assistant farm director of the Royals at the time. He was as good a Soldier as Piniella was bad. John was great to be around, always put out a lot of effort and quickly made Staff Sergeant. Later he won the World Series for the Royals as General Manager and then moved to Atlanta as General Manager where he led the Braves from their worst to first record in 1990 and into the playoffs for 15 years in a row.

A staple during my growing up years was an almost continuous Wiffle ball game being played in our side yard. I always had the Brooklyn Dodgers as my team and knew the batting order and batted both right and left-handed, depending on who I was batting for. For a normal right-handed hitter, I became a decent switch hitter because of the seemingly thousands of games we played over the years. Russell Walker, who lived next door to us was several years younger than me and would come and watch us every day, shagging foul balls. He was very patient, never complained, and towards the end of our playing, we'd let him bat a few times. I still feel bad how we took advantage of his enthusiasm for chasing foul balls and he got so few turns at bat in return.

When it came time to select a position to play on the high school baseball team, I played catcher because I didn't have a lot of talent and knew most people didn't want to play behind the plate. If someone else was catcher, I played enough in the outfield to earn a letter in baseball each year.

My senior year in high school, Coach Collins asked me to coach the junior high football team during their spring practice. He assured me that, even though I never practiced baseball, he would play me enough during the games to earn a letter. He was good to his word, I coached football for him and earned my letter in baseball at the same time. It was amazing how much we asked of high school coaches during those days in small-town Oklahoma—one coach coaching every sport. This was before Title IX. The only high school sport for girls was girls' basketball.

Boys State and Page in Oklahoma State House and Senate

I was very fortunate to have had three unique opportunities during my high school days. During my sophomore year, in the spring during the Oklahoma House of Representatives legislative session, I was selected by Ralph Vandiver, our district representative, to spend a week in the Oklahoma State Capitol in Oklahoma City as a page. At the end of my junior year, I was selected to attend Oklahoma Boys State, sponsored by the American Legion, and my senior year, Clem Hamilton, our high school superintendent, and member of the Oklahoma State Senate, selected me to be a page in the Oklahoma Senate.

My Boys State experience was a disappointment. Jim, my oldest brother was getting married on the Saturday at the start of Boys State. Of course, I both wanted and was expected to be home for the wedding. If memory serves me right, Boys State started on Friday and ran until the following Friday. Someone took me to the military barracks outside Norman, home of the University of Oklahoma, where Boys State was held. (I believe that is where it was—can't be sure this many years later). I barely introduced myself to those in my immediate dorm vicinity when I had to leave to head home late Friday for the wedding. It was a 200+ mile trip on narrow two-lane roads, but we made it fine.

The wedding went off without a hitch and I headed back late on Saturday to retrace my trip to Norman. All the Saturday activities at Boys State were over by the time I returned, and it was time to go to bed when I checked in. Elections for all the state and local offices were on Sunday. Because I wasn't there to campaign during the big campaigning time on Friday night and all day/night Saturday, I ended up as dog catcher or something as innocuous as that.

The rest of the week was somewhat a blur since I didn't have a key job. I was pleased to have had the honor to attend, but as I look back on it these many years later, the only thing that comes to mind is the wedding and the disappointment of not having campaigned for a job I would have enjoyed. I missed out on what most likely would have been a more memorable experience had I been there that key first day and a half. I learned early in life that I love being a leader. I've often said, I don't care what I'm in charge of, just that I'm in charge.

I did have a good time in high school as a page in both the Oklahoma House of Representatives (sophomore) and Senate (senior year in high school—back then Oklahoma's legislature just met every other year).

I was a page in the House during the week that Oklahoma repealed prohibition in 1959. We and Mississippi were the last two totally dry states in the nation. As a small-town boy whose parents nor any of their friends ever drank, I was appalled that Oklahoma was going to change that law. (I had my first ever drink my junior year in college, on Phyllis' 21st birthday—just a few months before we got married). The major ones against the repeal were the Bible belt small town Baptists (I am a Methodist but still was against drinking) and the bootleggers. Bootleggers made lots of money in those days.

The whole process was an eye opener and a big disappointment to me. I envisioned those who represented us to be focused and always serious. During this tumultuous week in the Oklahoma House, any sense of decorum or getting along was thrown out the window. (Not unlike how the US Congress appears to operate regularly the past many years). During this key vote, I saw the first live TV cameras I had ever seen, bright lights everywhere, noise, and excitement. In 1959 Oklahoma, this was an extremely hot and emotional topic.

As I watched, the big city representatives ran rough-shod over the Bible belt small town representatives. It was a real education on some of the tactics they used, and the disrespect shown by those on opposite sides. The team for repealing prohibition knew they had the advantage and they sat in their seats talking to each other, reading newspapers, or walking out of the meeting room to do who knows what.

Those against repealing prohibition tried to amend with the most minute word changes, just to delay and try to kill the bill. While some small-town representative stood up, probably for the first time ever in front of a TV camera, pleading his case about how the bill needed to be rejected, or at least amended to neuter it, the opposing side continued reading their newspapers, talking with no respect shown to the one who had the floor, and totally made this small-town Okie boy see that those in our state legislature were not nearly as dignified and serious as I had expected them to be.

Every proposed amendment required a House Roll Call. As the guy with the booming voice, each time a roll call was ready to be voted on, I was always instructed to walk the halls where all the individual representatives' offices were located, blaring out "House Roll Call. House Roll Call. House Roll...." (I was saying it in my sleep by the time the week was over). A great memory and a great education. The prohibition bill passed, Oklahoma has survived with the evils of alcohol being sold legally in the state, and maybe that week's experience is why I have limited respect for politicians ever since.

My senior year as a page in the Oklahoma State Senate

showed me a more dignified place than what I had observed two years earlier. There were no controversial bills brought to the Senate that week. I think, overall, a state senator is a step up in civility from those in the House at the other end of the State Capitol building. Once again, my deep, loud voice caused me to be quickly singled out to be the one walking the halls calling out, "Senate Roll Call, Senate Roll Call, Senate Roll…" (For those not from Oklahoma, we were the only state in the Union to not have a dome on the capitol building…and the only one to have a working oil well on the grounds of the state capitol).

Memories of Heavener Football
1955 to 1960

Some of the greatest memories of the early years of my life relate to football and Heavener, Oklahoma. Other than the time I spent in the Army and in Vietnam, I probably reflect on my football days as much as any of my life's memories, especially in the fall when my weekends are focused on football. *This is the longest story in this book—if you love football like I do, you will enjoy this. If not, skip it and go on to the next section.*

Growing up during the time when Bud Wilkinson and the Oklahoma Sooners were building their still unbroken 47 game winning streak, I became an avid football fan during my grade school years. That love for football continues through today, still focused on college football. OU remains my favorite college team, with University of Georgia Bulldogs as my second favorite. I will watch NFL games; despite the disrespect many players show to our National Anthem and flag. (I just wait to tune into the game after it has started). The Kansas City Chiefs are my favorite pro team, has been since their earliest days. (I had season tickets during the 1972 thru 1974 seasons, was there at the first game ever played in Arrowhead Stadium.)

My early memories are of playing football on the school grounds of the old Westside Elementary School. Unlike today with coaches, officials, parents, and full uniforms, we played with whoever showed up and with whatever equipment we had. It was not unusual to have a game going on at the school grounds with boys from an age span of ten years from the oldest to the youngest. Equipment also was all over the map—many played with no equipment, a few would have shoulder pads with no helmet, or a helmet with no shoulder pads, and I believe Fred Sonaggera showed up with almost a complete uniform when he played. We played until it got dark or until we knew that we would get in trouble with our mothers if we didn't get home in time for supper. I don't ever recall seeing an adult sitting around watching or supervising us—we were just boys having fun.

The next memories come from games in John Council's side yard. John, Jim Scrivener, Mickey Wynn, and I were the only Methodist boys of our age in a town full of Baptists. At Sunday School in the fall during our junior high years, we would put together a football afternoon and assemble in John's side yard and play two on two tackle football, no pads—great memories. John's dad, Howard, would come out and watch us. We played until we wore out or had to go home, it was always fun—no greater way for young boys in junior high to spend a Sunday afternoon. This was long before sitting in front of the TV and playing with video games became the thing young boys do. On many occasions we had others join us and we played with more players—never with pads, just tackle football in jeans and shirts. The four players that seemed to always be there were John, Jim, Mickey, and Bob, the small contingent of Methodist boys in our timeframe in Heavener.

Junior High and Water Boy Days

Coach Carl Twidwell (everyone called him Twid) came to Heavener, replacing Coach Kester Trent (if memory serves me right, there could have been another coach between Trent and Twid). Twid rented a house just down the street from where we lived, across the street from John Inman on West 2nd Street. I'm not sure how it happened, but I volunteered to become the HHS water boy for Twid. Once my brother, Bill, graduated from high school in 1956 and went to California to earn his fortune, I probably rode to and from school more days than not with Twid, in his old Hudson automobile.

In at least two of his early years as Coach, Twid took the team in early August (before practice could legally begin) to a football camp somewhere out in the country, near Clayton as I recall. The field was basically a farm field, but Coach wanted to get a head start and we spent several days practicing before coming home to practice openly in public after the official practice start date arrived. I do remember that as one of my first water boy times—not a lot of memories there but do recall that the illegal football camp was one of the early indications of how important football was in small town Oklahoma. We were never caught—no harm, no foul.

I loved being the water boy. Like all water boys, I took good natured abuse from some of the football players, but never anything that caused me to want to quit. I think my first full year as water boy was when Jim Monk, Bruce Smith, Chock Manley, Paul Stewart Johnston, Bill Hines, Don Cron and others whose names escape me played. One of the highlights of game nights was to run out onto the field after each of our kickoffs to retrieve the kicking tee—that was a big deal to a young junior high boy. And my second year as a water boy, Don "Oscar" Sullivan joined me. We were a great pair and took good care of the equipment and our players' needs.

Bethany

Coach Twidwell scheduled a game with Bethany, a suburb of Oklahoma City. Since none of our school buses were good enough to make the trip, the team went to the game in automobiles and trucks. Twid drove a pickup truck with the equipment. He made the decision that me, the water boy, would stay at home. Heartbroken, I went home and broke the news to my mother and daddy (neither were football fans). Unknown to me, my daddy went over to talk to Twid and offered to pay for him taking me to the game. I had never missed a game, dating back to my first one as the water boy (and never missed one until I graduated high school). Twid understood and told me I would be going to the game and assigned me to a car. When the game was over, which we lost, I hung around Twid and ended up missing my ride home. Coach was really upset, the pickup he was driving had three in the cab already. He added me to the pickup, and we headed back to Heavener. Every time I dozed; he would shake me—no way was he going to let me sleep since I had screwed up.

Gauntlet

One of Coach Twidwell's favorite punishment drills was the gauntlet. If he got mad at not enough effort in practice, or on the Monday after a bad game performance, the team could count on a half hour or so of the gauntlet. The gauntlet consisted of putting a player every ten yards down the length of the field, laying down blocking dummies to limit the width of the field, and then giving a football to a player to run through the gauntlet. Poor effort on the runner's part meant laps, and poor tackling on those manning the gauntlet meant they would be running laps. I don't recall anyone ever getting hurt in this drill, but no one ever seemed to enjoy it—it was, in my view, purely for punishment for bad efforts. I know when I played for Twid, I never enjoyed the gauntlet but participated whether I liked it or not.

I have no vivid memories of game scores, or even season records when I was the water boy at Heavener. I know we never made it to the playoffs, but we also never had a losing season.

One other memory from my water boy days...this relates to baseball, where I was also the bat boy. During intra-squad practice games, I was typically the behind the plate umpire. Bob Hall, a great knuckle ball pitcher, typically pitched for one squad while Twid was the pitcher on the other squad, saving our real pitchers for game days. When they didn't like my ball and strike calls, they would storm the plate and argue with me. I stood my ground, listened to their abuse, and the practice went on.

It was comical when Bob Hall came up to argue, even as a senior in high school he was shorter than I was as an 8th or 9th grader. I towered above him while he ranted and raved about how bad my calls were. Another baseball memory—during real games, I was usually the third base coach. One time a line drive came screaming at me and I couldn't duck in time, it caught me square in the throat. I went down like a rock, scared that I had been seriously hurt, and Twid came running out to check on me. I soon recovered and my deep voice was not affected, just another pleasant memory of my days with Heavener athletics.

8th and 9th Grade Football Game

Twid figured out early that the class behind mine, the HHS class of 1962, had lots of talent in it. In those days, there were no coaches or money for junior high football programs, but Twid put together a program for the 8th grade class, the HHS class of 1962 who ended up going to the state semi-finals their senior year. We a year older were left out, we didn't have as many talented players as they did. However, they wanted to play a game at the end of their spring practice and needed someone to play against.

Coach came to me and asked me to put together a team of 9th graders. I was a great student of the game, knew all the plays, and had good leadership abilities. The only stipulation was that Jerry Johnston, who, as a freshman, was playing on the high school team, could not play in the backfield against the 8th grade.

That was a great opportunity for me. I knew the plays, had always wanted to play quarterback, so took on that role and got enough 9th graders to volunteer to practice a little and suit up and play a week or two later. Jerry Johnston was relegated to playing tackle, probably the only game he ever played in the line (and it was the only time I ever played in the backfield).

The game was played on a Thursday night, right after the weekly Heavener Ledger was published. Unknown to me, the starting line-ups were published in the paper. My stomach came up into my throat—I was in trouble. My mother would not allow any of her boys to play football. She remembered when Bill Rockwell was hurt playing football back in the 1940's and ended up losing his leg. My two older brothers, Jim and Bill, both better athletes than I ever was, were forbidden to play football by my mother, and she was backed up by my daddy who never cared much about sports. That was a kiss of death in the social circles of small-town Oklahoma in those days—virtually every boy played football.

As I rode with my mother to the post office to pick up the Heavener Ledger that afternoon, I told her there was something in the paper she wasn't going to like. She asked me what, and I told her. She said, "You're not going to play football!" For the first time ever, I stood up to her and told her that, "Yes, I'm playing football tonight and there is no way you can stop me." For a boy who had always been totally compliant with parental instructions, that was a big step for me. Mother seemed to get it — and didn't push the issue, she didn't approve but didn't get my daddy involved to keep me at home that night.

We played, it was a fun game, and I scored the only touchdown, a quarterback sneak, in a 7-0 9th grade win over the 8th grade.

Sophomore Football — first season of high school football — 1958 Season

When summer started coming to an end and football practice was about to start, I again had the conversation with my mother. I very strongly told her, "I'm playing football — or else." She asked me what I meant with "or else." I told her my grades would drastically fall if she didn't let me play. She understood my love for the game, and despite her fears, she consented for me to play.

Going out for football as a rookie meant you had to decide what position you wanted to play. I was among the biggest of my age group (at a huge 160-165 pounds), and one of the slowest. There was no question that the backfield was not where I was going to end up, I was born to be a lineman. As I scoped out the 1958 team, dominated by 11 senior starters, I sized up what my best options were. My cousin, Bud Thompson, was the center. I knew they would need two centers on the traveling squad, so I decided that is my position. No one particularly wanted to play center and that was a sure way for me to make the traveling squad. I immediately became the second-string center and was on the traveling squad.

We started the season and were winning. I was included in the traveling squad for away games, even though I seldom got to play. In the fifth game of the season, against Spiro at home, Bud Thompson, our kickoff man, and center, was blocked and blew out his knee on a kickoff. They carried him off the field and Twid came to me and said, "Babcock, get ready to go in when we get the ball back." My heart immediately went up into my throat—I was thrilled, scared, and hated it that my cousin had been hurt in his senior year.

When the offense went back onto the field, there was Bob Babcock, the only sophomore on a team full of seniors. I did okay, don't recall any mistakes, but we didn't score and ended up with a 4th down punting situation. There was one minor problem. I wasn't any good at snapping on a punt. John Tatum, our center the previous two years, who had moved to fullback his senior year, said he would snap the punt and I could fill in for him at fullback. When the ball changed hands, I left the field, replaced by Jerry Johnston who was the only sophomore on the defensive team (ten seniors never left the field of play, back in the days when many players went both ways, and, in our case, all but one of them did that).

The next week we went to Broken Bow and lost our first game, a big disappointment and one that we really shouldn't have lost. As in the Spiro game, John Tatum snapped punts and I played in his fullback slot on those punting situations.

On Monday after the Broken Bow game, with Twid still upset about the loss, he told me that if I couldn't learn to snap punts, he would find someone who could. That, of course, got my attention. I took a football home with me and worked until dark after I had gotten home from practice, snapping punts to my brother Joe. If memory serves me right, John Inman and Russell Walker, two neighbor boys younger than me, might have been out there taking some of my snaps.

I broke the code and learned how to snap for punts. The next game, I was the punt snapper and never had a bad snap during all my time as a starting center (but I must admit, Jerry Johnston saved me in the Poteau game of our junior year when my snap got caught up in the fierce icy north wind that was blowing like a gale. Jerry stepped up, grabbed the snap, and got the punt off, keeping my record safe).

I continued to keep my starting center job through the end of the 1958 season. As the youngster in the huddle, some of the guys looked out for me, some gave me a hard time. We continued with the same alignment, I was the one player who came in on offense, Jerry Johnston replaced me when on defense, as a safety. The rest of the senior starters played both ways. Occasionally, if we got far enough ahead, Twid would put in some second stringers, but building a team for the next year didn't seem to be a priority for him. We won the 10-B conference championship and were slated for the state playoffs for the first time in my memory.

Let me digress and see if I can remember that 1958 team's starters: Hal Dowden at quarterback, Jim Davis and Roger Webb at halfbacks (Ron Cagle also got playing time at halfback), John Tatum at fullback (later a three-year starter at OU). On the line, we had Will Bennett and Don Frost at ends, Glen Lazalier and Robert Rockman at tackle, Larry Pyle and Don Huie at guard, and Bob Babcock at center after Bud Thompson was hurt. Co-captains were Don Frost and Will Bennett.

A side bar—in later years, when watching Big 8 or Big 12 football games on TV, when I would see Hal Dowden on the field as the referee. I would tell my sons, "That referee has had his hands on my butt more than just about anyone you know." Of course, the first time they heard it, they looked at me in shock, and then I told them that Hal had been the quarterback when I was a sophomore center. I always enjoyed watching Hal as a Big 8 / Big 12 referee.

We played Poteau, our archrival, on a muddy field, at home at the end of the regular season. In most seasons we lost, but that year we won. It was a real high, we had confidence going into the first round of the State playoffs.

Our first-round opponent was Idabel Washington, back in the days when schools were still segregated. With no black kids on our team, and very few that we had played against during the regular season, this was a new situation for us. My grandad, an old timer from Texas, told me, "Bob, just kick them in the shins and they'll quit." He was a great man, but integration and the civil rights movement were still in the future of America. We played a tough game against them and won. The quarterfinal game, played in the sleet on Thanksgiving Day, at home, was against another all-black team, Okmulgee Dunbar.

Okmulgee Dunbar had an All-State linebacker, Laron Dozier. He may have played offense as well, but my experience was with him as a linebacker. It was a hard-fought game, we ended up losing, but my memories go back to two specific plays. On one of our punts, which our punter got off fine, I ended up with a good blind-side block on Laron Dozier, I knocked him on his butt. It was such a good hit that Martin Tate, the public address announcer, made a big deal about Bob Babcock's great block. Unfortunately, Dozier got my number.

The next time we punted, he lined up about ten yards deep, right over center, and started running, crossing the line of scrimmage just as I snapped the ball. He hit me and knocked me five yards into the backfield, one of the hardest hits I ever got on a football field. The next time we punted, I was gun shy, got off a shaky snap, but he had decided to leave me alone and not punish me again—thank goodness. We lost that game and our quest for a state championship, ending our season with a 10-2 record.

Sadly, as the school year ended, Carl Twidwell announced he was leaving Heavener and going to become the head football coach at the new Star Spencer high school in Oklahoma City. As a boy who had worshipped Twid since my junior high school days, I was devastated. How could we ever replace him—he was the best, and only, coach I had ever known. And we had two more years of football before I got out of high school. It was a dark day as Carl Twidwell drove out of Heavener to start his new career at Star-Spencer high school, a much bigger school that he did well in and retired from.

Part of the summer between my sophomore and junior years was spent in Tulsa. My brother, Jim, fresh out of the Army, was a student at Spartan School of Aeronautics. He owned a blue Taylorcraft single engine airplane and lined up a job for me at Harvey Young Airport where his plane was based. I lived with Jim and my job was to gas airplanes, clean windshields, run the snack bar, and do whatever else Harvey Young told me to do, including a lot of grass mowing. One of the perks I was going to get that summer was to get my pilot's license. Jim had arranged for a friend of his, a qualified instructor pilot, to give me free lessons, with Jim providing his airplane and the gas to fly it—a sweet deal that I would never have happen again.

I took my first lesson or two, and then, while home on a weekend, found out that our new football coach, Bob Collins, had arrived in town and was having informal football practices with anyone who showed up at the football field every afternoon. I had a major decision to make—what was I going to do. What was the most important to me, getting a pilot's license, or football? It was an easy decision—for a boy from Heavener, Oklahoma in 1959, football won, hands down.

Much to the dismay of my brother, I quit my job at Harvey Young Airport, gave up on my flying lessons, and headed home for football practice (plus, I was missing Phyllis, my girlfriend—that also played into my decision). To this day, I wish I had finished those free flying lessons, but I can't say that I wouldn't make the same decision again if given the chance—that's how important football was to me.

I showed up for football practice and met Coach Bob Collins. He had us sit in a circle in the north end zone of the football field and walked around the circle talking to us and laying out his rules. As he walked around, he stepped on the hand of Jim Pybus. Jim, a free-spirited player, said, "Hey, Man, you're standing on my hand." Coach Collins stood there, looked down at Jim, foot still on his hand, and calmly said, "My name is Coach, not Man." Then he walked on and continued his talk.

Wow—that made an impression on me, and probably everyone else sitting in the circle. I'll never forget that experience. Who was this new guy that was going to be our coach? He had a buzzed haircut, wore a white football jersey with a red X painted across the front of it, and had a totally different personality than Carl Twidwell. I wondered what we were in for.

Junior Year—Second year of high school football
1959 season

With only two starters returning, Jerry Johnston on defense and me on offense, the outlook for the 1959 season was dismal. Few of our seniors had much playing time the previous year, fewer of my junior class, other than Jerry and me, had played much, and we had a new crop of sophomores who had never played high school football before. No one knew what the 1959 season would hold for us, but we were ready to give it a shot. Our enthusiasm for the game of football had not waned, even with a new coach leading us.

Again, let me see if I can remember our starting lineup for the 1959 season. In the backfield, Jerry Johnston was our quarterback, Clarence Raines was fullback, Tony Gregory was one halfback and Homer Jones was the other, a sophomore. In the line, Jerry West was one end, can't recall our other end (was it Kenny Ames), Jim Norwood and Don Wheat were our tackles, Wayne Kelley and Ron Campbell were our guards, and I was again at center. Co-captains were Clarence Raines and Don Wheat.

We started with a win in our first game, against Vian. Then we won again the next week against Muldrow. In that game, we played against a fullback who was destined to be a starter at OU, Glen Condren. We won by 6-0 in a hard-fought game. Before we took to the field, in an away game, Glen Condren was standing outside our dressing room with his hand under his arm, making his big muscles bulge even more, trying to intimidate us as we got off the bus and went into the dressing room. A memory that will never leave me is a play when Ron Campbell made a classic tackle on Condren, hit him head on, picked him up, and slammed him to the ground. I had a ringside seat; I was laying on the ground watching the whole thing after being blocked.

The next week we beat Panama, which we always won, and played Eufaula in a driving rainstorm the following week. An interesting aspect to that game was that we showed up in our purple jerseys, with gold helmets, and Eufaula was in maroon jerseys with white helmets. With the rain and mud, all the jerseys looked the same—the only way to be sure who you were hitting was to look at the helmet color, and some of our guys also were wearing white helmets (in those days, our equipment wasn't as good as it is today, we made do with what we had).

Tony Gregory made a great memory when he ran through the end zone chasing a pass thrown by Jerry Johnston and disappeared into a deep ditch full of water. He came up sputtering and spitting out water. We pulled him out to continue the game. If memory serves me right, we won that game 8-0. We weren't a high scoring team, but we were a winning team — four wins and no losses were beyond anyone's expectations.

The following week we played Spiro to a tie, and then came back with a win against Broken Bow, putting us at 5-0-1 with four games to go. Then the floor fell out, we lost the last three games. I have never been beaten as bad as we were in the next to last game of the season, Stigler beat us something like 50-6. Fortunately, I was blocked on a kickoff early in the first half and sprained my ankle and was out for most of the game. I watched from the sideline, sorry I couldn't be out there playing, but glad I wasn't having to take the physical beating that we got.

We ended the season on a cold, windy night in Poteau, where they beat us pretty bad after we held them even early in the game. I had returned to play, although still a little hobbled with my ankle. With the season ending, and no playoff games ahead of us, we had a 5-4-1 season, better than anyone expected, but a big disappointment after the great start we had. Coach Collins and those interested in basketball started that season the following Monday, I had no interest in basketball so started thinking about the next football season. I was a strong supporter of Coach Collins, respected and admired him as much as I had Coach Twidwell, and was ready for our senior season.

Senior year — third year of high school football 1960 season (undefeated)

We had a strong team coming back for the 1960 season, my senior year. The largest number of players ever, at least since I had been associated with the program, turned out — I think we had 42 or 43 players suit up, just short of four full teams. I could remember years when I was a water boy where we had a hard time having 22 players to run a full scrimmage during the week.

We had lost a few players to graduation but had plenty more to fill their shoes. Remember, we now had the Class of 1962 as juniors, the same class that Carl Twidwell had noted back when they were in junior high school as the next strong Heavener team. Those guys filled in with those of us who were seniors and did a superb job.

A New Playing Field — Complete with Chicken Manure

The HHS football field always had a downhill slope on it, from the hill to the southeast down toward the street on the northwest corner of the field. I'm sure some coaches selected an end of the field to attack or defend based on downhill slope, not necessarily on wind direction. That was changed during the summer between my junior and senior years of high school.

Clem Hamilton, HHS superintendent (and State Senator), used his political clout to get the county road crews to level the field, which they did in a quality manner. The only problem was, when they finished, there was no grass left on the field.

On his own, Coach Collins took on that challenge. All summer long he could be seen, early morning, noon, and late evening working on the field, seven days a week. Watering hoses had to be moved, grass seed had to be planted, and the field had to be fertilized. With no pay for himself for tackling the project, and probably a budget of zero to work with, he solved the fertilizer problem by going down south of town and getting a local chicken farmer to deliver his chicken manure to the football field, which Coach methodically spread across the field. Several players, including me, volunteered to help spread the chicken...

Once the water hit it, the stink engulfed the entire east side of town! No one could miss the smell, it was the talk of the town, especially when the wind blew from south to north. Eventually, the smell abated, and the grass started growing in with a lush green color, all was looking great for our team to have the best playing field ever during my senior year.

Sometime before football practice started, someone raised the question of safety for players who played on the field. The question was, will the chicken manure infect the boys when they get cut during a football practice or game. The rumor even became rampant that we would have to play all our games that season as away games, never something a team wants to do. Without knowing the details of who figured the solution out, Doctor Joe Looper, our team doctor (and only doctor in Heavener) gave each player on the team a tetanus shot, and I even heard that HHS paid for tetanus shots for all the teams who would be playing on our field that year.

All's well that ends well, and we started the 1960 season on a field that was far better than anything our town had ever seen.

Again, let's see if I can remember our starting lineup: Jerry Johnston was again at quarterback, although John Council played almost half the time, with Jerry moving to halfback. Mickey Wynn was fullback, Tony Gregory again was one halfback, and again I can't remember who our other starting halfback was (maybe Jim Gore). In the line, Jerry West was one end,

John Titsworth, a freshman (later a four-year starter at OU and on a National Championship team), and Ray Gaskin, a sophomore, split duties (and ran in plays each down) at the other end, Bennett Childers and Kenny Ames were our tackles, Don Bentley and Homer Jones, moved from halfback to the line, were our guards, and, for the third year, I was the starting center. Tri-captains were Jerry Johnston, Don Bentley, and Bob Babcock.

The whole town was fired up, knowing this could be a great year for us. For those who have never lived in a small town in Oklahoma in the 1950's and early 1960's, you've missed something. Back in those days, there were two sports in Oklahoma—football and spring football.

Monday Challenges—"A Full Titsworth"

Coach Collins had a policy that any player who thought he could beat out a player above him on the depth chart could challenge the one above him as the first order of business in practice each Monday. I don't recall how the challenge system was handled for backs, but for lineman it was very simple and straight forward. The two players would line up head-to-head with each other, one on offense and one on defense, a young player was given the ball, Coach would blow his whistle, and whoever did the best got a full point or a half point. If the ball carrier got by the defensive man, the point went to the offensive player, and vice versa. If it wasn't clear-cut, a half point might be awarded. This was repeated, with players alternating between offense and defense, until one of them got five points. If the lower-level player won, he moved up and took the place of the player he beat. If it was someone challenging a starter, that meant he started the next game.

Each week there were challenges, usually the higher placed player held his position, but occasionally he was beaten out. That always raised his level of practice and commitment, waiting until the following Monday to try to regain his position.

One day, John Titsworth, a tall, lanky freshman who was already one of the starting split ends, decided he wanted to also play on defense. I forget who it was he challenged (not me). The team stood around watching the challenge, Coach blew his whistle, and John handily beat his opponent. Coach, in his normal stern manner, matter-of-factly declared, "That's a full Titsworth." The whole team cracked up with laughter, Coach realized what he had said, blushed, and continued with the drill. From then on, when Titsworth won a point, Coach declared it as, "That's a full John." I can't remember if John ultimately won the challenge or not but will never forget Coach's "full Titsworth" comment.

Our Undefeated Season

We started against Vian, beating them easily, scoring 54 points. Our next game, against Muldrow, we also scored 54 points, holding them scoreless. If memory serves me right, we scored a touchdown on the first or second play of both games, one being a pass from Johnston to Gregory, right down the middle of the field. We played Panama and were ahead of them so much by halftime that Coach Collins took mercy on them and wouldn't let his starters play much in the second half. Our second team, almost as strong as our starting team, and who played about as much as we did during the season, kept scoring. As we entered the fourth quarter, Coach decided to punt on first down, not wanting to run up the score. He also let Jerry West try kicking a field goal on first down, which he missed. In that game, I had a thrill that centers seldom get. I talked Coach into letting me play end on an extra point and caught a pass to score a two-point extra point. Again, we scored 54 points, holding them scoreless, the second week in a row not to be scored on.

The next week, at home without the rain we had the previous year, we again ran up 54 points, beating Muldrow handily, holding them to 8 points. On Sunday morning, the Tulsa World had a piece in the sports section saying something like, "Heavener is in a rut—scored 54 points in each of their first four games." We were on a roll and loving it.

The next week, again at home, we played Spiro. By halftime, we were ahead 28-0, expecting another high scoring game. But we must have gotten a little too sure of ourselves, or Spiro reached down to not be humiliated, and they held us scoreless in the second half, with us winning by a 28-6 margin. That was a letdown for us, but we were still proud and confident. We were ranked in the top 5 in Class B across the state, real heady stuff for high school boys.

With the season half over, we had the tougher part of our schedule ahead of us. Broken Bow, a Class A school, played on their field, was a tougher win, but we won without much problem, beating them 42-6. Wilburton, our opponent the next week, was typically a tough opponent. This year, however, it was a disaster...for them. We beat them 78-14, one of the most fun games I had ever played in. The previous year, they had handed our heads to us. Revenge was sweet.

This brought us to our last two games that would determine whether we made it into the playoffs or not—Hartshorne and Stigler, both games played on their fields. Both were highly ranked in the state, as were we. Both games were viewed as toss ups before we played—and both were everything that was expected.

Hartshorne was a hard fought 14-0 win for us. A funny sidebar...I was hit in the nose with a forearm shiver and bled like a stuck pig. Wearing our white jerseys, I was quite a sight out on the field, looking like the wounded warrior. It didn't hurt that much, and I kept playing. The next day, on Saturday, we were to take our ACT tests for college entrance. I sat through the morning of testing with a handkerchief to my nose, with some blood still seeping from that well placed shot I had gotten the night before. But I was happy, we had won and were going into the state playoffs—and I did great on the ACT exam as well.

The next week, Stigler was our opponent. Another hard-fought game with us prevailing by a score of 14-6—both of us were ranked in the top three or four statewide in our class. Little did we know then that we would see them again before we finished the season.

The final game of the regular season was against archrival, Poteau, played on our field. They had beaten us unmercifully the previous year, so we were out for revenge. We started strong and ended strong, beating them like a drum, final score was 78-20. A couple of memories from that game worth noting...

Traditionally, in the last game of the season, the coach would let those of us linemen play in the backfield on a play or two so we could end our career without having to say we never had a chance to carry the ball or catch a pass. Since we were going into the playoffs, Coach Collins, rightfully so, decided that he didn't want to risk getting anyone hurt by playing a position that we weren't familiar with. It was a disappointment to me, but I understood.

Toward the end of the game, we ran some crazy plays with lots of laterals, basically having fun at Poteau's expense. On a punt return, Jerry Johnston fielded the punt and took off down the field. I was blocking, as was everyone else, and we had a wall of blockers that wasn't going to let anyone through—Jerry was headed for yet another touchdown. As I ran along beside him, I yelled for him to lateral the ball to me, which he did—and I took it in the last five yards and scored my first and only touchdown of my football career. Coach didn't like what we did but was good natured and didn't say anything to us—no harm, no foul. I even got my name in the paper for scoring that touchdown. Linemen seldom got our names in the newspaper.

Late in that game, Coach told me to put together a fourth team defense to go in the next time Poteau got the ball. I was one of the tri-captains, a leader, and Coach often asked me to help him out. I grabbed the young, mostly sophomore, rookies and started telling them the position they would play. There weren't enough for a full team of eleven, and I wasn't inclined to pull someone down from the third team to fill the one empty position. I decided I would play with this team. When the ball changed hands, these young guys headed out on the field, average weight of probably 140 pounds or so, thrilled to have the chance to play against Poteau. One lone big guy went out with them…me. Two plays later, Coach noticed I was on the field and sent in a substitute and gave me a good-natured chewing out when I came to the sideline.

For the second time in my three-year high school career, we had earned our way into the state playoffs. Again, as during my sophomore year, our first opponent was Idabel Washington. With several of us remembering how tough they were in 1958, we did not take them lightly—and they were a tough team to beat. Final score of that game, played on their field, was 18-14, with us winning and moving on to the quarterfinal game on Thanksgiving Day.

We were still undefeated, the only undefeated team still in the Class B playoffs, and would again be playing Stigler, this time on our field. Stigler, from a different conference, had beaten Okmulgee Dunbar to earn their way into the quarterfinals and a rematch with Heavener.

Thanksgiving morning dawned clear and warm, for November. It was a perfect day for a football game. The morning dragged by as I waited to head to the gym to get dressed out for the game. Probably earlier than I needed to, I drove my blue and white 1953 Chevy to the parking lot and went into the dressing room, eagerly anticipating what would be the most memorable game I ever played.

As we came out onto the field for warm-ups, the crowd was larger than I ever recall seeing at one of our games. All the stands on both sides were full and people were standing all around the field. The weather continued to be perfect, bright sunshine and temperature in the low 70's.

Stigler had prepared well for us. What had worked three weeks earlier, was shut down on this day. Our favorite plays were 'Tear Right' or 'Tear Left'. It was a simple play, similar to a Student Body Right or Left play. The ball was snapped to the quarterback, he tossed it to the halfback who was in motion, the entire backfield headed right (or left) and the two guards pulled and led the blocking around whichever end the play went. Coach kept calling it, and it didn't work. Time and time again, Stigler stopped the play, we ended up having to punt, stopped them when they had the ball, and then did the same thing again. There were other plays mixed in, but it seemed to Jerry Johnston and me that we were running the "Tear" plays too much. So, the two of us decided that we knew more than Coach, and changed the play one of the times he sent it in. I don't remember what we called, but it didn't work either.

Coach was furious and immediately pulled Jerry, not realizing that I, too, was a guilty party. He chewed Jerry up one side and down the other, told him to NEVER change a play that he called, and sent him back in. Jerry had a sheepish look on his face as he came back to the huddle, and we always ran the play that Coach sent in.

To net it out, the game ended in a tie—6-6. In those days before tie breakers, ties in playoff games were decided by penetrations inside the twenty-yard line, then by first downs, and finally by total yards gained. Stigler had us on penetrations, 3-2, and we were out of the playoffs while they advanced—a heartbreaker for every player and fan of HHS.

A few specific memories of that game…It was a tough fought game, played hard and fair by both teams. There was no question that we were evenly matched. One play stands out in my mind, an error made by the referee, Danny Thomas. On a fourth down attempt at a first down, the pass was completed, and the end moved past the first down marker, I was right next to him and had a straight look from where the ball was across at the first down marker. The referee, however, had a different angle than I did and placed the ball back a few feet, just missing the first down. As the captain, I could talk to the referee and gave him quite a few words showing my discontent with his call before he told me to shut up and leave him alone. Who knows what would have happened if that play had been called correctly.

Two more memories came at the very end of the game. The first one is hearing the town fire alarm go off. In small town Oklahoma, we had a volunteer fire department. They were alerted, as was the whole town, when the fire alarm siren at city hall was blown. With only minutes left in the game, those on the volunteer fire department had to leave to go take care of the fire—I never knew what it was and can only wonder how tough it was for those firefighters to leave the game in those critical last few minutes.

The final memory was when we were trying to stop the clock after our timeouts were all used up. We were on defense and knew an injury would stop the clock. Before the next play was run, I told Mickey Wynn to act like he was hurt (he was good at faking injury). He put on quite an act and the referee called timeout, Coach came out and helped Mickey off the field, and Stigler kept their heads, knowing they didn't need to rush up to the line to get a play off. They took the allotted time and time ran out. The game was over.

Thus ended my high school football career, but the memories live on. The following Monday, Coach Collins and those players who also played basketball turned to the hoops and I did whatever I did, no memories survive of how I (and the whole team and town) survived the disappointment.

My last attempt at playing football

Thanks to contacts that John Tatum, my boyhood friend had, I had a chance to play football in college the next fall. John had been recruited by Carnie Smith at Kansas State College of Pittsburg (now Pittsburg State University), when he graduated high school and decided to play for Bud Wilkinson at OU. Based on John's recommendation, Coach talked to Carnie and got me an invitation as one of seven freshmen to show up in late August 1961 to work out with the varsity.

My college football career lasted little more than a week. At 170 pounds, I was too small to play center, but that was my position. Plus, Pittsburg was destined to go undefeated that year and win the NAIA National Championship. Suffice it to say, those world class football players beat me to a pulp in the days that I went through two-a-day practices with them. I was also homesick, knowing that I would be stuck on campus in Pittsburg until football season was over in November. I vividly recall celebrating my 18th birthday with my Aunt Opal and Uncle Byron and their friends who lived in Pittsburg, a beat up, homesick young man who had serious second thoughts about my decision to play college football.

The next morning, with much dread, I walked into the coach's office and talked to Carnie Smith and Joe Thomas, his veteran line coach, and told them I was going to quit (that is the only thing I ever quit in my life). I had heard the stories about how football coaches would mercilessly brow beat quitters, but they were total gentlemen, class acts that I will fondly remember the rest of my life. Rather than berate me, their first question was, could I afford to go to college without my football scholarship? When I said I could, they offered to let me go home and come back in a couple of weeks when the rest of the freshman class turned out for football.

I gave it some thought but decided against it. Their final offer was for me to lay out that fall and come back out the following spring for spring football. I did that, but quickly decided that my talent wasn't good enough to play at the college level, so I turned in my pads and never again played football (other than touch football). Throughout my four years of college at Pittsburg, every time I saw Carnie Smith or Joe Thomas on campus, they spoke to me by name, smiled, and asked how I was doing—two true class acts.

My favorite football picture, 1960

The seniors from our 1960 undefeated football season

Final Miscellaneous Memories About My Growing Up Years

The Paying Jobs I Held

As a teenage boy growing up in the 1950's, it was common to have a job. My oldest brother Jim had worked at the Railway Express Agency, loading freight onto passenger trains as they came through town. Brother Bill had worked at several places, including Day Drug Store. It never crossed my mind that I would go through high school without paying my own way for my "wants." By then, I had had my first date with Phyllis and if I was going to take her to the movie, I needed money for that and when I got a car at 16, gasoline had to be bought, as did tires—I always ran used tires on that first car. Plus, I treated myself by paying the exorbitant price of something like $5 for a pair of Levi's, instead of $3 for an off-brand. (Jan bought a pair for me a few weeks ago and they cost about $60—shocked me.)

T&M Pharmacy — Summer Between 9th and 10th Grades

The soda fountain at the T&M Pharmacy on the main street of Heavener was the hangout place for kids in the 1950s. When whoever was working there graduated high school and left for something bigger and better, someone else always stepped up to be the local soda jerk. George and Harry Meeh, the owners, knew me and when I asked for a job, they hired me immediately.

Since I had spent so much time there, I pretty much knew the job, it was just stepping behind the soda fountain and doing it. If memory serves me right, I was to be there for two or three hours each weekday afternoon, all day Saturday, and every other Sunday from noon (after church) to closing time about 5:00 PM. Regardless of my schedule, I was to be paid $10/week.

As it turned out, I was making about 35 cents an hour when I didn't work Sunday, and more like 20 cents an hour on the weeks I worked Sunday afternoon. I forget the math, but I do recall that 20 cents an hour rate...But that was okay with me, it put some money in my pocket, and I was a happy camper. That was when I got my Social Security number, and they took less than a dollar out of each paycheck for income tax.

I rocked along all summer, happily working, and looking forward to starting football practice in August—my first year on the high school team. I told George and Harry that I wouldn't be able to work after school because of football practice. That brought a big "Whoa!" to my soda jerk job. The after-school crowd was prime selling time for them. I had to be there, or they would get someone else, and I would be out of a job. That was one of the easiest decisions I ever made—football practice or 20 cents an hour. Farewell soda jerk job...

Janitor at the State National Bank
10th Grade through Graduation

My parents and Ray and Rena Hall were great friends. The Halls had five kids, we had four, and we lined up closely in age. Ray was president/owner of the State National Bank. Each of his oldest three boys had the janitor job covered. When one graduated from high school, another one was old enough to take over — that was just the way it was.

Luckily for me, when I started high school, their daughter, a year older than me, was the only option from the Hall Family for the janitor's job. Back in those days, girls didn't do janitor type work in a business, especially working after hours, alone, in a bank building. With a comment to Ray from my Daddy about me looking for a job, I suddenly became the janitor at State National Bank. Talk about an improvement!

My hours were whatever I wanted them to be — just make sure the bank was cleaned between the time they closed in the afternoon and when they opened the next morning. And the pay was $1/hour — a tremendous increase over my 20 cents an hour work as a soda jerk. (Another beauty of growing up in a small town, it wasn't uncommon for a bank president and railroad engineer to be close friends, and for families with different levels of income to be good friends).

It was then when my first checking account was opened. They deposited my payroll direct into my bank account, I never saw a paycheck. I kept that bank account as my primary account until the State National Bank was sold many years later, well into my IBM career. They spoiled me — they covered my overdrafts, at no cost to me, if I miscalculated what I had in my account. They were truly a community bank that treated their customers like Family and friends, which we were. The experience in this small community bank became a key to one of the best jobs I ever had during my IBM career — national sales leader for the 14,000 community banks across the US. I still miss the days before the mega banks overtook most of the community banks.

If football practice ran long, I could get up early the next morning and clean the bank before school. On weekends I did the weekly work—window washing, mopping floors, etc. If I had to be out of town, I could send Joe, my brother, to do the job. I had a key to the side door of the bank, which I guarded with my life. One evening I walked into the bank, the lights were on, and the vault door was wide open. My hackles immediately went up, wondering if there was a bank robber on the premises—and how had he gotten in. I went to the phone and called Ray, who lived two blocks away, and he was there in no time. We jointly searched the bank, he confirmed that nothing was missing, and chewed out the last employee to leave that day who had forgotten to lock the vault and turn off the lights.

Babcock & Sons Hobby Shop—trophy parts manufacturer—high school and college

My brother Bill's "making a fortune in California" lasted no more than a year before he headed back to Oklahoma. He moved to Dallas, Texas and went to work for Wilson's Sporting Goods, stringing tennis rackets and other things. Somehow, he got a job with Dodge Trophy Company, who at the time was the world's largest trophy company. Among thousands of routine trophies they produced, they were the ones who made the Oscar, the Emmy, and a few other prestigious trophies.

One day, Mr. Dodge was complaining because he couldn't get all the wooden trophy parts he needed as quickly as he needed them. In those days, before everything became plastic and metal, most quality trophies were made of solid walnut wood. Bill, knowing full well that our Daddy loved to work with wood as his hobby, and walnut was his favorite wood to work with, called and asked Daddy if he could make 1,000 small trophy parts. He gave the specs, a simple 2 ½" block with a counter-sunk hole drilled in the middle. Within a week, those parts were made, Bill came up to pick them up, and Babcock & Sons Hobby Shop was born.

Mr. Dodge loved the quality of the work, the price, the consistency of delivery when he needed them, and we started getting regular orders—not only for the #75 (the 2 ½" square piece), but for lots of other sizes, to include three different sizes of a complete wooden trophy (1st, 2nd, 3rd places), ready for a metal sports figure to go on top of it (Bill named those trophies the HB1, HB2, HB3 for Hermann Babcock).

And where does Bob come into the picture? You guessed it, Daddy needed help, he taught me how to run the sander, the drill, and to spray lacquer the pieces when they were finished (he cut the pieces to size, he didn't want me using the table saw, and I didn't argue, though I later ran that a lot). He was still working on the railroad so when he was out on a run, Mother and I, with some help from Joe, kept the trophy business moving. As I did that, I had school and school activities, my bank janitor job, and my free time, but I knew that before long I would be going off to college and this would be a good source of income to help pay for that.

In a small town, everyone knows what everyone else is doing, so we started getting questions about could we fill trophy orders for the school and other organizations around town. That led to us getting into the retail trophy and plaque business. And that led to buying an engraving machine with Daddy and me both learning to engrave. You'll hear more about that later in my story of my life.

I'm sure he paid me something when I was in high school but can't remember how much, probably not as much as the bank paid. But I did get room and board and unconditional love from my parents, so I wasn't about to complain.

That wraps my jobs while growing up. Of course, like most

boys in small town America in those days, all my brothers and I had some days where we helped haul hay for one of our friends who needed help. I think I made two cents a bale for hauling hay—a hard job but every boy back in those days could tell you stories about hauling hay.

Family Friends

The beauty of living in a small town where your grandparents and parents (my Mother was born there, and my Daddy since the late 1930s) have lived virtually all their lives is a real blessing. As I thought about covering our close Family friends, I decided against it. I don't want to leave someone off the list that should be there. We had Family friends that had kids we grew up with, we had friends who were close friends of our parents and, by default, were people we considered our own friends. We had friends who were neighbors, we had friends who were businesspeople and railroad people in town. There were friends who lived "out in the country" (outside town). There were friends that we sometimes vacationed with, that we went to church with each week, and the list goes on and on.

In Heavener, Oklahoma, and I'll extend that to many, many places in small town America, we seldom saw a stranger. We might not know that person, but most likely we knew someone who was a relative of theirs and/or we had a connection of some type.

One guy in particular, Bill Dyson, every time he saw one of the Babcock boys would say, "Hello, Bob, Bill, Jim, or Joe." He knew we were brothers and didn't try to keep us straight in his mind (he didn't even call us out by our birth rank). Those who have lived in the same small town for a long time understand what I'm talking about. Those from a large city or who moved frequently are envious of those of us who have friends of the Family who are always willing to be friendly and helpful.

I learned many things from those great citizens of Heavener, Oklahoma. There is never a time that I go "home" that I don't stop by the cemetery on the north side of town. Walking through that cemetery is a melancholy time for me. As I read the headstones, I remember faces, names, incidents we shared, good times and bad. My parents and grandparents are buried there, my oldest brother is buried there, as are my first wife's parents and Family members. Freddie Sonaggera, who I grew up with and was killed in Vietnam is smiling back at me from the picture on his headstone, and the list goes on. You can bet the next time I'm in Heavener, I'll spend a half hour or more walking through the cemetery, stop at a grave, and walk away with a smile from a good memory.

And I also enjoy signing on to the "You know you're from Heavener if…" Facebook page. Many that I chat with I haven't seen for 60+ years, but I remember their name, their Family members, and we share memories like we had never drifted apart over the years.

I've been a "big city" boy all my adult life, currently living in Athens, Georgia, the smallest town I've lived in except for Heavener. I will always consider my home as Heavener—and I'll always call myself a proud Okie.

Unexpected Twins and a Baby Girl
December 1, 1960, and March 10, 1961

My brother, Bill, and his wife, Virginia, were expecting a baby in late 1960, my senior year in high school. They were living in

Wills Point, Texas, east of Dallas. The time came, they went into the small hospital in Wills Point and were awaiting the birth of the first Babcock grandchild. Bill called home and alerted us that it was about time for the baby to be born. A few hours later, he called back, extremely excited, and said, "We have twin boys!" Once William Haynes Babcock was born, the doctor told Virginia, "There's another one in there." A few minutes later, Bert Calvin Babcock joined his twin brother.

Later that day, a Thursday, Bill called us, again in an excited, almost panicked voice, "We have to take the boys home from the hospital. There is someone in the hospital with a contagious illness (long before COVID, probably mumps or something) and they want to get the twins out of here."

Mother and Daddy had planned to go down as soon as the baby (now babies) was born, and Phyllis and I were going with them if it hit around early December. The Heavener High School Quarterback Club had bought tickets for our undefeated football team to attend the Dallas Texans and Houston Oilers football game to be played in the Cotton Bowl in Dallas on Sunday, December 4. As football queen, Phyllis was also invited so it worked out great that she could go with us to Wills Point and then she and I would drive over to Dallas for the Sunday game.

We left bright and early on Friday morning, got to Wills Point by noon, Bill and Virginia and the boys had just gotten home, and chaos reigned supreme. The boys were in the single bed that had been bought. Since they were born early, most of the required "baby supplies" had yet to have been bought. Once we finished admiring the beautiful baby boys, Bill turned to Phyllis and me, handed us a Dr. Spock Baby Book, turned to the back of the book, and said, "Go buy two of everything on this list." It was Spock's recommendation for what you needed for a new baby.

My obvious first question was, "Where do we go to get it?"

Bill said, "I don't know, go downtown and figure it out." Being the smart guy that I was, I handed the book to Phyllis and effectively told her, "You're in charge, I'm your driver." And we went shopping for two baby boys, less than two days old. By the way, this was before everything was bought by credit card. Bill gave me some amount of money and we made it work.

We survived the chaos of the first day having the twins at home, things semi-settled down, and on Sunday, Phyllis and I drove my parents' car over to the Cotton Bowl and sat in the rain with our HHS football team watching the Dallas Texans beat the Houston Oilers, with George Blanda as their quarterback, known more for his field goal kicking later in his career than for being a quarterback.

While Bill and Virginia were expecting, so was my brother Jim and his wife, Sue. They lived in Heavener at the time. Phyllis and I took the train to Pittsburg, Kansas to do our initial enrollment into college, and when we got home, my oldest brother Jim was sitting there with his daughter, Tami Louise Babcock, in his arms. She had been born on March 10, 1961, four months younger than Bill and Bert. My parents had gone from zero to three grandkids in record time, and they loved them all deeply, as did the whole Family.

As I write this, it is hard to believe that Bill, Bert, and Tami are all 60 years old. Time flies...

The Howe Tornado — May 5, 1961

Friday afternoon, May 5, 1961, the annual Heavener High School Letterman's Club outing was held at Cedar Lake. Basically, it was a bunch of football players getting together for a final fling before the graduating class of 1961 moved on to the next phase of our lives. It was a typical spring Oklahoma day, humid, cloudy, warm, nothing unusual. I don't recall why, but I had to leave before most of my teammates—probably to go to my janitor's job at the bank because I didn't want to get up early Saturday morning to clean it before they opened.

As I was driving closer to Heavener, I saw an unusually dark and heavy cloud moving from west to east ahead of me. It was low to the ground, was ominous looking, and made me want to hurry up and get home and off the road. Those were the days before all the modern-day storm warning systems that now come in over your phone, your watch, the radio, etc. It was just a feeling, from experience, that the cloud meant trouble for those north of my hometown.

I got home, went inside, and honestly don't remember what was said or heard, who was there at the house, or if anyone was even there. I also don't remember when or how we heard that a tornado had hit Howe, five miles to our north.

The after-effects—I remember vividly. My grandparents and Auntie Lou were stopped behind a train crossing the highway in Howe, otherwise they might have been directly in the path of it when it swept through. Death and destruction devastated the small town.

As a result of this tornado hitting so close to us, under the leadership of Daddy, our neighbors banded together and contributed money to have Pat Gregory Construction Company dig a strong concrete storm cellar in our side yard. From then on until they died, whenever it clouded up, you were likely to see my grandmother, Mrs. Ledbetter, and Mrs. Edge sitting out in the storm cellar. For as long as I can remember, it seemed to always flood. I can't say how many pumps were bought to keep the water out of that over the years. Also, the storm cellar did a good job of screwing up a perfectly good Wiffle Ball field. With that said, 1961 was the year I left home to head for college, so it didn't upset me too much. I was happy my parents, grandparents, and neighbors had a place to go during tornado weather. I've always required a basement in every home we bought, because of my Oklahoma tornado background.

High School Graduation — 60 years ago from when I'm writing this

Late May 1961, can't remember the exact date, was a big time for my classmates and me. We went through several assemblies in the high school gymnasium as end of year awards were passed out, followed by the evening ceremony in the Westside grade school auditorium for graduation. I was pleased that I had earned the honor of being Valedictorian of the HHS class of 1961. That meant I was the one to give a speech at the ceremony. I wish I could find that speech but it, like many pieces of paper, have been lost over the years. I recall I talked about Alan Shepard, Jr. who on May 5, 1961, had piloted the first sub-orbital flight, Freedom 7, by an American and the second ever in history (Yuri Gagarin, a Russian, had orbited the earth early in April 1961 to become the first ever).

I also remember my Daddy gave me a silver dollar to use in my speech. I don't recall the purpose of that in the speech, but I still have it safely stored in a box with other small memorabilia.

Talk about a small world...as I was ready to pass the first part of my memoir over to my wife, Jan, to read and give me her honest feedback, she had been busy sorting through boxes in our basement. She handed me two pieces of paper and said, "Look at this — do you know what it is?" Lo and behold, it was the original (and only) typed copy of my valedictorian speech that I gave in May 1961—exactly 60 years to the week before I read it again. I'll spare you reading it here, but for a young boy from small town Oklahoma not experienced in speaking to large crowds, I will say it was a decent speech. (That complete text is included in the Deeper Dive section at the end of this book.)

Our class was small, normal by Heavener standards, with 56 students graduating. Many of us had started in the first grade together in late August 1949 and had traversed twelve years as a class. I still have fond memories of my 1961 class, the two before me (1959 and 1960) that I played football with, and the class of 1962 behind us.

This chapter of my life had come to an end. Next stop, Kansas State College of Pittsburg. But first, one more thing to summarize…

The Benefits of growing up in small town America

I often reflect on the advantages I had from growing up in Heavener, Oklahoma. Many today, and even back then, believe that we small town kids were disadvantaged. My perception is 180 degrees opposite that. While we didn't benefit from large school budgets, a wide breadth of class subject offerings, and teachers with exotic credentials, we had many advantages that kids in large school districts miss out on. I know from what I speak; I've lived in both environments.

Our youngest son, Mark, attended a high school with a population of 2,400 students, larger than the entire town of Heavener, OK. He had classes that weren't offered in Heavener, took a trip with his high school orchestra to Italy, and had lots of other benefits that weren't offered in a small town (including early morning Latin classes that he took before school), but I still contend that my experience growing up in Heavener was much better than his was.

Without appearing to brag, I had the privilege of many leadership and honors situations in Heavener. During my senior year, I was president of the Student Council, tri-captain of an undefeated football team, was selected as an all-conference football player, lettered in baseball, was valedictorian of my class, dated (and later married) the football queen, and throughout high school was selected to attend Oklahoma Boys State and served as a page in both the Oklahoma House of Representatives and the Oklahoma Senate, among many other good things that happened to me during my time at HHS. And, because of my booming voice and being president of the Student Council, I had a radio program on KLCO each Thursday during football season as the emcee of the weekly pep rally. All these things were great opportunities and stepping-stones for my adult life.

Speaking of my booming voice, many people believe that one of the greatest fears in life is public speaking. To me, my greatest fear is not getting to talk—I love to give speeches and talk about things I'm passionate about. My first opportunity to talk to a large crowd was when I ran for Oklahoma State FBLA (Future Business Leaders of America) president in the spring of my senior year in high school. Delegates from all over the state assembled in the huge auditorium at the University of Oklahoma where candidates for office had five minutes to make a speech. I was sweating bullets as I looked out on the audience as I sat on stage waiting for my turn to speak. There were close to 3,000 people in the audience, a thousand more than the population of my small hometown. As I stepped up to the podium, I looked out at the crowd, froze for a second, let out a loud 'whew…' breath, the audience laughed, and my brain kicked into gear, and

I gave my speech. I came in second in the voting but had a good experience in the process.

Also, while at the FBLA state meeting, I participated in the typing competition. I didn't win anything, but it was great to be one of few boys in a room full of girls from all over the state. I'm still a good typist, a requirement for my publishing business.

I was a big fish in a small pond. With that, and the support of my parents, coaches like Carl Twidwell and Bob Collins, other teachers who influenced me, and many classmates, teammates, church members, family friends, and townspeople who took the time to show an interest in me and others in our school, I grew up with great leadership experiences, many positive memories, a high level of self-confidence, and, to this day, give credit to my Heavener upbringing for what I've accomplished in my life.

Life wasn't always easy—I had a big let-down when I got to college and became a small fish in a big pond. Flunking biology my freshman year was a bigger shock than I ever expected to experience. I had never made a C in school, let alone fail a five-hour class. But, once I got over the culture shock of that change, coupled with the experiences I later gained in college and in the Army, I was able to leverage the experiences I gained in Heavener, Oklahoma to propel myself forward in life.

While I never learned a foreign language in high school or seldom took a trip any farther than Oklahoma City, I would never trade the other things that came from growing up in Heavener in the 1950's and early 1960's. Although I've lived in large cities all my adult life, I still consider myself to be a small-town Okie boy. And for the rest of our lives, we high school football teammates will get great joy as we replay our experiences on the gridiron during our glory years playing football for Carl Twidwell and Bob Collins in the years of 1958, 1959, and 1960.

My Granddaddy, Jeff Thompson, engineer on KCS Railroad

The Babcock Family in front of our home, 1962

Kansas State College of Pittsburg
Pittsburg, Kansas — 1961 to 1965

After my aborted attempt at playing college football, I went home for two weeks to lick the wounds to my pride for having quit the only thing I ever quit in my life (before or since). I recovered and mid-September 1961 was the time to start fresh into the next phase of my life — a college freshman.

It was an interesting sight, I'm sure, as two 18-year-old girls, an 18-year-old boy, and their three mothers boarded the 11:00PM departing KCS passenger train #16, along with an untold number of suitcases, boxes, and an ironing board, which Grace Coggins' mother carried on board the train, to start the new phase of their lives. For Phyllis, Grace, and me, it was the unknown adventure of college. For our mothers (and fathers left at home) it was getting started into what was fast becoming an empty nest for them. To say it was a scary and melancholy time for all of us would be a fair statement.

In all three cases, college was breaking new ground in our Families. My daddy had attended two years in the early 1930s to get an associate printing degree at the same college we were now headed for, my brother Jim had attended one semester at Oklahoma A&M in 1954, and my mother had attended a year at Oklahoma A&M in the early 1930s before the Great Depression cut short her dream. Otherwise, college was foreign to our Families.

We were met in Pittsburg the next morning by my Aunt Opal and Uncle Byron and cousin, Mike Mason. I don't remember but odds are they had to make a couple of trips to get the six travelers and all our "stuff" hauled to their home. Their home would become a haven for we three students over the next four years.

Somehow, we made it to the college on the south end of Pittsburg, checked into our dorms, Phyllis and Grace (friends since first grade) as roommates in Willard Hall and me checking in across the campus into Bowen Hall. Back in those days, all the girls' dorms were together on one side of campus and boys' dorms were on the other side.

I walked into my first-floor room and saw a young kid sound asleep on one of the beds. He didn't stir, I put my bags down and headed back to join the ladies to tour the campus. I mentioned that my roommate's little brother was asleep in our room, and I didn't know where my roommate was. A few hours later when I returned to the room for my first night, I found out that little brother was my roommate, Martin from Oelwein, Iowa. Nothing like having a roommate who looks to be all of 14-years old.

I don't know when, but probably the next day, our mothers left and there we were, Phyllis, Grace, and Bob, no friends, no connections on campus, and stranded without a car in Pittsburg, Kansas. Although it was 207 miles from our hometown by rail, it might as well have been on the moon. This was before cell phones, email, instant messenger. Effectively we were by ourselves. Classes started, we met to eat together at the Student Union, and made our decision that on Friday evening, we were headed home—enough of this foolishness. We would be driving back on Sunday in my 1953 blue/white Chevrolet or likely we were ready to blow the whole adventure of college off.

I'm guessing Mike Mason took us to the Pittsburg depot to catch #15 headed south at about 11:00 PM, to arrive about 6:00 AM the next morning in Heavener. We didn't care, we had a mission to take care of—get a car for us to use while we were in college. With virtually no pushback from my parents, they agreed that taking my car back made sense and by Sunday evening, we were back in our dorms with my car parked in the lot outside my dorm. We were no longer stranded on campus—and never were for the next four years.

ROTC (Reserve Officers Training Corps) was required for all men during their first two years. As I recall, we had one or two classes a week, had drills in uniform on Thursday, and didn't think much of it. All men in a land-grant college across the country had the same requirement. As for me, who had played Army all my young life, I was in hog heaven. I got to carry a real-life M-1 rifle, the one that won World War II. ROTC became my favorite subject and most life-changing experience in college.

I had no idea what I wanted to major in, so I started as a non-major, taking the basic classes that all students had to take. As stated earlier, I had aced out of Freshman English so started my college career with six hours of "A" on my transcript, not a bad start. Being naïve as a small-town Okie, I took whatever faculty advisor they assigned me—a dude from the Social Studies department. Lo and behold, I found myself enrolled in a bunch of social studies classes that I cared little or less about. What the hell—you play the hand that was dealt you.

One of my classes was a speech class. While I had often spoken in front of a crowd in high school and before, I had never been in a class to teach me how to give a speech. I was nervous but did okay and learned a lot. One of our assignments was to write an analysis of a speech we had heard in person. It so happened that President John F. Kennedy came to a highway dedication just south of Heavener, Oklahoma in late September 1961. I went home that weekend, went down early to get a good spot to watch and hear the speech on Sunday afternoon, and took the overnight train back to Pittsburg. The entire text of the speech was in the newspaper, so I had great crib notes to write my report from. The teacher and my classmates were impressed with what I wrote, and I made an A on the report and the class.

Our KSC football season our freshman year was fantastic. The team that had beat me into submission during early season August practices went on to have an undefeated season. They won the NAIA National Championship in the Camilla Bowl in California in early 1962. That took the sting of quitting football away some — it isn't quite as bad to quit a national championship team as to quit a run of the mill team.

I made it through the first semester okay, nothing special, and then the same advisor lined me up with my classes for second semester. Among the 16-hour class load was a five-hour class called Biology 101, taught by Professor Brandon Brantley (I will always remember his name). It was apparent that his sole purpose in teaching his class was to flunk freshmen out of college. His lectures were beyond comprehension, his tests were so hard that a 35 out of 100 earned an A grade, and it went quickly downhill from there. I stuck with the class, walked in for my three-hour final, looked at the test, signed my name to my bluebook, and five minutes later walked out. There wasn't a damned essay question I could answer. I think I got five points for turning in the bluebook and flunked the class. I did okay in the other courses, not the grades I'd made in high school, but passing. Of course, I made an A in ROTC, but that was just a two-hour class.

That summer, I went to what is now Carl Albert State College in Poteau, Oklahoma, 14 miles north of my hometown and took two classes to offset the F in biology. One was a two-hour course on office machines and the other was something I breezed through with minimal problem. Interestingly, the office machines class helped me the rest of my life. I have always been great on running adding machines and other things in the business world. When I wasn't in school that summer, I was back at work in our woodworking shop making trophy parts. That business was helping finance my education.

Somewhere along the way (sophomore year I think), Phyllis and Grace pledged Alpha Gamma Delta sorority and got involved in the sorority life. As a dorm boy with little interest in a fraternity, but a strong interest in Phyllis, I became a wimp and entered a fraternity (since I never was active in it, I won't mention the name here). I did make it through the pledge training, the hell week of harassment, and became an active member. I showed up at their weekly meetings but had zero interest in it, except that it kept me in synch with Phyllis and her strong fellowship and friends made in her sorority. I was a fraternity boy by name only.

I did play on the fraternity softball team. We made it to the finals of the intramural tournament, our fraternity playing the K-Club (Letterman's Club) — the football and other sports stars on scholarship. My pledge advisor was our fraternity's pitcher and Phil Vogrin, All-American quarterback of our 1961 National NAIA Championship football team (that I had quit) was the opposing pitcher. I was the starting catcher. In one of the best softball/baseball games I ever participated in, we beat them 1-0.

Speaking of intramural athletics, I was a referee for three years in intramural football and softball. I loved being a referee and made something like $2 per game. In fact, I was good enough and so unassociated with my fraternity that I was even allowed to referee football games they played in. I didn't care, I was a no-nonsense referee, and my fraternity brothers could go pound sand if they tried to get me to favor them.

My roommate the first year turned out to be a disaster. He was sloppy, lazy, slept a lot, and basically didn't want to be in college (I think he dropped out after that first year). But I was stuck with him. I started shopping around and found a much better roommate for my sophomore year and an even better one my junior year. Kutlu Isin was from Mersin, Turkey, a Muslim who had the Koran and the Holy Bible sitting side by side on his bookshelf. He regularly attended church at the Christian Church, was meticulously clean in himself and our room (totally different from my freshman roommate) and was a joy to share a room with (only problem was he kept the room too hot).

Sending me to out-of-state college was a financial hardship on my parents and I felt honor bound to do whatever I could to earn money to help offset the cost of college. The first year, I had to focus on my grades and getting established, but the second through fourth years, I worked at various things. I became an intramural athletics referee for touch football and softball for three years (loved doing that), and my last three years I also took it upon myself to make the name badges for each incoming class of ROTC students. Each needed a plastic name badge for his Army uniform, and I convinced the ROTC staff to buy them from me—Babcock & Sons Hobby Shop. At the start of each school year, I collected the names of the incoming freshmen, took a Friday night train ride home, and spent all day and night on Saturday and Sunday engraving about 600 ROTC name badges. I delivered them on Monday and collected my $1/badge charge—not a lot of money now, but very significant in 1962 through 1964.

Still living in the dorm through my junior year, I became a dorm proctor my sophomore year, which I think gave me free lodging, and then my junior year I became head proctor for Bowen Hall and had responsibility for the whole dorm. That gave me free lodging plus some money.

My last three years in college I started my first sales job (never knowing I'd spend the rest of my life in sales and sales management). Since my Family was in the trophy and engraving business, I made a sales call on every organization that I thought would buy trophies for anything and made a decent amount of money selling trophies, which my dad put together and engraved. I would pick them up on a weekend at home and take back to deliver. I bet there are still trophies sitting around the college that I sold back in the early 1960s.

Phyllis had gotten involved on the yearbook staff our sophomore year and talked me into helping her (easy to get me to do anything with her). I made friends on the Kanza staff and my senior year I became Business Manager of the yearbook. I forgot what I was paid, but it helped us out since Phyllis also got paid.

And the last two years in college I was in advanced ROTC, which paid the whopping amount of $30/month to each cadet in the program. That sounds like pocket change now, but our last year in college after we were married, Phyllis and I could buy a week's worth of groceries for about $10 and have enough left over to go to a movie.

On November 3, 1963, I asked Phyllis to marry me. We had been dating since ninth grade, we had gone through a few rocky times but felt we were a great match. She accepted and we started planning our marriage for August 1964, after I returned from ROTC summer camp and before we started our senior year in college.

On November 22, 1963, at 12:30 PM CST, I was laying on my bed in my dorm room, getting a little rest before heading out for my 1:00 PM class on a Friday afternoon. The radio was playing music in the background. The music was interrupted with a terse announcement, "President Kennedy has been shot in Dallas…" I bolted up from my bed, headed downstairs to the TV room and saw Walter Cronkite talking about it on the TV screen. I did not make my 1:00 PM class—I was glued, along with many others, to the TV all afternoon. Later, Phyllis and I drove out to my aunt and uncle's home where we watched TV non-stop well into the evening and all day over the weekend, including watching the live gunshot picture of Jack Ruby shooting Lee Harvey Oswald on Sunday morning. This was a shock to us and to our country that we will never forget.

Back to speaking of ROTC...for many years I've told anyone who asked what my favorite subject was and what was the best thing I did in college to prepare me for my future life. Hands down, it was taking advanced ROTC. I also tell people that I graduated from college with an Infantry officer commission in the United States Army (and a bachelor's degree in accounting—a subject I still hate but was good at and never worked in).

While I loved all four years of ROTC, the best time was when our class went to Fort Riley, Kansas for ROTC summer camp—six weeks of intensive training in how to become an Army officer. I loved all parts of it, did well, was top man in my platoon and third among the 35 or so cadets from Pittsburg who went to Fort Riley that summer. My two favorite summer camp stories are...

I was given command of the company I was in during a daylight mechanized attack on an enemy position (simulated, of course). I had my own mechanized command vehicle and looked to my left and my right and saw the M-113 Armored Personnel Carriers full of my fellow cadets ready to launch from their vehicles and destroy the enemy in front of us. It was an exhilarating experience for a young cadet from small town Oklahoma. I was graded well for my work that day, checked the duty roster on the bulletin board that evening...and saw I was assigned KP (Kitchen Police) duty the next day. There is no bigger put-down to your feeling of importance than to go from mechanized attack company commander to peeling potatoes and washing dirty pots and pans the next day. We aspiring officers needed to personally know what KP duty was.

Second favorite story, I spent six weeks at Fort Riley in an organized program that had every day planned and every action organized so no time or effort was lost. I left there as honor graduate of my platoon and showed up at home ten days before my wedding day. Talk about chaos—anyone who has ever gotten married knows a wedding and chaos go hand in hand. I had a hard time adjusting, but I did (no thanks to me—but to Phyllis and our parents who told me to get my ass in gear and do what I was told) and the wedding went off without a hitch on August 8, 1964.

Continuing with the story of our wedding, we were given two great things for our honeymoon. Dale Campbell, Phyllis' dad, loaned us his car to go on our honeymoon to Pensacola, Florida (my car was not in good shape) and my Daddy gave us his credit card to buy gasoline for the trip down there and back.

While on our honeymoon, we heard an announcement that we didn't know at the time would totally change our lives. Far away from Pensacola where we were beginning our married life, in the waters off North Vietnam, an attack was made on an American Navy ship by hostile North Vietnamese forces—called the Gulf of Tonkin incident. That became the official beginning to the escalation of the Vietnam War, where we had advisors for several years, but now was going to explode into a full-scale war that would involve both of us.

Home from our honeymoon, we moved into brand new married students housing on the far east of the Pittsburg campus, just beyond the intramural fields where I made money as a referee. It was so new, we had to sweep sawdust off the floor that was left as the workers finished it a day or so before we moved in.

Our senior year in college was a busy one. Phyllis was wrapping up all the courses for her home economics and teaching degree, including her semester of practice teaching to close out her graduation requirements. I had an internship scheduled for six weeks in Kansas City early in the final semester, working for a public accounting firm (working on the TWA airline and a lumber company audits), and wrapping up some pesky classes that I needed to graduate. I was heads down as a senior ROTC cadet with second in command responsibility for one of our battalions of freshman and sophomore cadets.

Some Random College Memories

My Oklahoma Sooners played football games at Kansas twice while I was in college at Pittsburg. It was a reasonable two-hour drive to get to Lawrence, home of KU. My best friend, John Tatum, was starting center for OU my sophomore year. It was a sell-out crowd, we were late getting there and sat on the hillside outside the stadium until the 4th quarter when we could get in and stand near the south end zone. OU won 7-0 on a touchdown by Joe Don Looney. John, my Heavener friend, earned the game ball for his defensive play. I ran out onto the field to see him as he left the field.

I reached down and pulled the chinstrap off his helmet and stuck it in my pocket. He asked me if I'd like to meet OU head coach Bud Wilkinson. Is the Pope Catholic??? Of course, I did. I went into the locker room, he introduced me to Bud, and I floated on air out of there and back to Pittsburg. The next week I got a letter from John (remember those days—before email) asking me if I'd taken his chinstrap. He said even though he had won the game ball for his play, he had to run laps because he lost his chin strap. I wrote back and confessed to my theft and kept that as a trophy for a long time.

Two years later, my senior year, we went back to KU when Gale Sayers was the star running back for Kansas. We had seats that year, Phyllis wanted me to go buy her some popcorn just before the game started, which I dutifully did. As I was heading back to our seats, a mighty roar came out of the stands, and I got to see the field just as Sayers crossed the goal line with a 98-yard touchdown run with the opening kickoff. Oklahoma scored twice and led 14-7 with less than a minute remaining in the game. KU scored on the last play, made the two-point conversion, and beat us 15-14, a big upset.

We were staying with Judy and Ron Girotto, a sorority sister of Phyllis' who were at KU where Ron was in graduate school. I was so upset by the loss that I pouted like a three-year old the rest of the day and evening. On the drive back to Pittsburg the next day, you can bet I got chewed out royally for my bad manners and attitude.

Train Trip to New York City

In early December of our senior year, after we were married, Phyllis and I took a train trip with my parents to visit my brother, Jim, in NYC. He was flying for a non-scheduled freight airline out of New York, and we spent several days there. Highlights were seeing the Rockettes at Radio City Music Hall performing their Christmas program, seeing the hustle and bustle of Times Square, shopping in the well-known NYC stores (Tiffany's, Saks Fifth Avenue, the big Macy's, and others), a carriage ride in Central Park, and overall falling in love with the hustle and bustle of the big city.

The thing that stood out with Jim, that he told on me the rest of his life, was that we went into the famous Astor Hotel and Astor Bar. Jim asked me what I wanted to drink (I was legal age) and I told him I didn't drink. He pushed and pushed, and I held my ground. For the next twenty years, until he died in 1995, every time he introduced me to one of his friends, he told the story about how Bob passed up a chance to have a drink in the world-famous Astor Bar on Times Square—which was torn down in 1967.

We successfully completed all our college requirements, Phyllis with a straight A record in her final semester and me just happy to get all the courses completed to graduate. The same day, I took the oath of office as a commissioned officer in the United States Army—a second lieutenant in the Infantry. My date of rank was 6 June 1965—21 years to the day after the 4th Infantry Division that I would be assigned to landed on D-Day in France during World War II.

Our parents were filled with pride as we walked across the graduation stage. For both Families, we were the first college graduates.

As our college graduation present to ourselves, Phyllis and I bought a brand new, maroon, 1965 Ford Mustang, our first new car. We paid $1,995 for it, buying it just above cost from one of her sorority sister's father, who had a car dealership close to Pittsburg. We loved that car from the first time we put our eyes on it. It was the most basic model, no frills of any kind—no air conditioning, no windshield washers, just plain vanilla basic car, and we loved it.

With a two-year commitment in the US Army as our next step, we headed home to Heavener where we found a small furnished apartment in a friend's home that we could rent for two months until we were scheduled to report to Fort Benning,

Georgia in early August 1965. I continued my normal summer work schedule making trophy parts for our Family trophy business and waited for my Army orders to find out where we would be assigned after our training at Fort Benning.

I remember vividly when President Lyndon Johnson came on national TV with a press conference on July 28, 1965, during my noon lunch break as I recall. He stated that "…today I have ordered the Air Mobile Division, and other units, to Vietnam…" This announcement brought our authorized troop strength in Vietnam from 75,000 to 125,000 troops. (In 1968, we peaked with troop strength of just under 550,000).

A week later, Phyllis and I were headed south in our new maroon 1965 Mustang to start the active-duty Army phase of our lives at Fort Benning, Georgia — the post where the 1st Cavalry Division (Airmobile) was based.

ROTC — CPT Frank Scott and Cadet Bob Babcock — 1964
CPT Scott talked me into choosing Infantry, a great decision

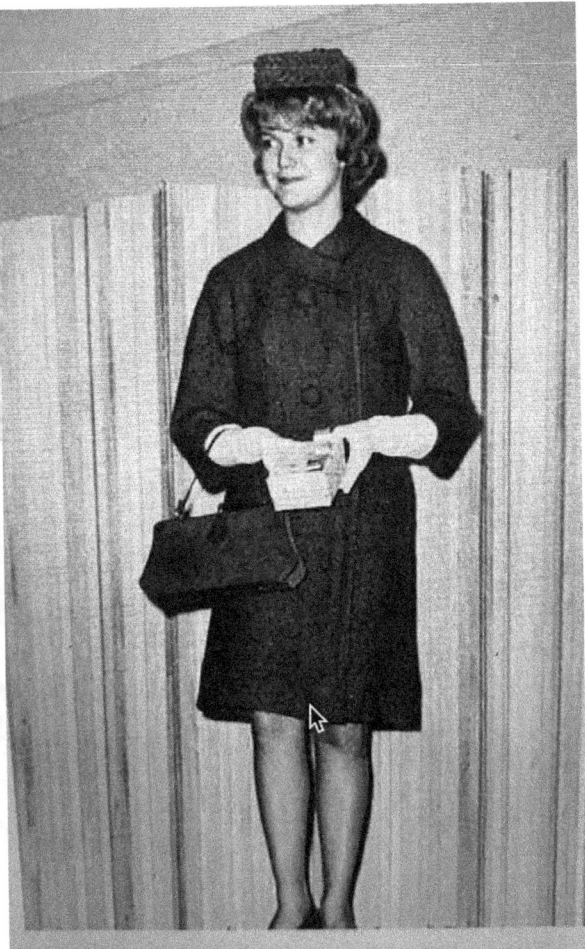

Phyllis Campbell models a new fall fashion in the A.W.S. fashion show. The A.W.S. presents this show annually for KSC's women students.

Phyllis in Fashion Show

Phyllis and Bob
Senior class pictures, 1965

Bob and Phyllis—both on Kanza yearbook staff—1964

We're in the Army now
Fort Benning and Fort Lewis
August 1965 to June 1966

8 August 1965 to 14 July 1967 is what my DD-214 Official Record of Military Service states as my time on active duty in the Army. As many veterans will attest, these are some of the most memorable days of our lives. We had many experiences, met people from all over the country, made lifelong friends, have stories burned into our brains that we will never forget (good and bad), and without hesitation would do it again if asked to. I am one of those who will go to my grave as a proud and patriotic American Veteran.

Sometime in July 1965, I received my official Army orders. I was assigned to Fort Lewis, Washington, the 4th Infantry Division, with temporary duty to Fort Benning, Georgia for training. Fort Lewis was my first stateside choice, so I was happy to get that, even though I had hoped to get Germany as my first assignment out of training. My brother Jim had served in both places, thus my choices.

Since I had turned down my Regular Army commission, which I had earned by being a Distinguished Military Graduate from ROTC, I was not expecting Germany—that was a three-year assignment, and my active-duty commitment was only two-years as a Reserve officer. Later, that proved to be a smart decision—Regular Army officers were frozen during the Vietnam War and those expecting to be in the Army three-years often had to stay five years or more before they could start another career.

The first thing Phyllis and I noticed as we pulled through the main gate of Fort Benning on that hot August day in 1965 was all the railroad flat cars sitting on the sidetracks, loaded with military equipment. We knew immediately what we had heard President Johnson say about ordering the "Air Mobile Division" to Vietnam was quickly becoming a reality.

We had arranged for an apartment just outside the main gate of Fort Benning in the Camilla Apartments, a complex where many young lieutenants and their wives started their Army careers. A one-bedroom apartment cost exactly what the housing allowance was for a new Army lieutenant. The apartment was furnished, had a black/white TV included, and a swimming pool at the front of the complex, facing Victory Drive. Floors were black to not show the scuffs of combat boots that were worn most of our waking hours, the most austere place we ever lived. It was a new adventure so we didn't complain—we would only be there for three months.

When we bought a Columbus, Georgia newspaper, the town Fort Benning is connected to, on the front page we saw a warning. It said, do NOT use the laundromats in and around Fort Benning. The 1st Cavalry Division troops were using them to dye their underwear from white to Army green as they prepared to depart for Vietnam. Those were the early days of the Vietnam War, later the Army issued olive drab underwear—but not then. I remember the notice well but have no clue how Phyllis handled that warning, I had to get my head focused on the Infantry Officers Basic Course that would occupy my time for the next eight weeks.

In-processing started with physicals, shots, haircuts, equipment issue (officers had to buy our own clothing), and filling out all kinds of paperwork and test taking. Our class was full of second lieutenants, just like me, fresh out of ROTC programs from all around the country. In typical Army style, they divided us into four platoons, alphabetically. They chose the platoon leader for each platoon from whoever was at the top of the list. Since there were no last names starting with A in our class, Babcock was at the top of the list for 1st Platoon. Our Tac Officer (Tactical Officer) called me out and said, "Lieutenant Babcock, you are first platoon leader for the next two weeks — take command." And he walked away; he expected me to know what to do.

Thus, I started my Army career with the hardest job there is. Most any 2nd Lieutenant will acknowledge that there is no group harder to lead than a bunch of other lieutenants — they all know it all and are quick to point out your mistakes. Fortunately, we all knew how to march, my loud voice, as always, served me well, and by being in charge the first two weeks, I got to know all the men in my platoon quickly.

It was a hard hitting eight weeks, working five and a half days per week, including Saturday morning. We started each day by being in formation at 0600 for PT (physical training), then doing whatever the training schedule called for. We got home whenever we got home each afternoon or evening and immediately collapsed, ready for rest and sleep so we could go do it another day. Of course, we had to spit shine our boots before the next morning and insure we had starched fatigues ready to wear. "Breaking starch" every day was standard as a new 2nd Lieutenant at Fort Benning. It cost more than we could afford, but we sent our fatigues out to be professionally cleaned and starched rather than be deemed unfit for duty. Spit shining boots was something we lieutenants did ourselves before going to bed.

Fortunately, Larry Mathis and his wife, classmates from our ROTC days in Pittsburg, were in our class so Phyllis had Betty as an immediate friend to keep her company, with lots of pool time. They met other wives and we seemed to always have another couple to do things with when we had some off-duty time on the weekend.

Highlights in a nutshell—lots of weapons' training and familiarization, classroom training, field training, night patrols, compass and map reading classes, hand to hand combat, pugil stick training, and the list goes on. Randomly they would pull someone out of the ranks to be platoon leader and squad leaders for each exercise we were going through. You had better perform well when given a leadership mission or it would be reflected on your grade for the class. As we moved from class to class and started and ended the day, the assigned platoon leaders had to get their platoons to the proper place—that rotated weekly after I had the first two weeks.

A couple of favorite memories/stories…we had an officer in our class who had been a halfback on a small but well-known black college football team. He was strong, in great shape, and had mentioned to me that when he was in college, he took ballet lessons to improve his balance and quickness on the football field, which I thought was a smart thing to do. Fast forward to training on the field in front of Building 4, the headquarters at Fort Benning, with pugil sticks. Pugil sticks are a rifle length wooden pole, padded on both ends, and used to teach hand to hand combat. We were suited up in a helmet with mask, a crotch protector, heavy gloves, and told to go at each other until one of us won. I looked forward to it but didn't want to fight this strong halfback who had taken ballet lessons, I knew he would kick my butt. As you would expect, he's the one I was lined up against. I knew I couldn't out finesse him, so I attacked like a wild man, shocked him with surprise, and beat him to a pulp. It gave me a lesson that surprise and brute force can beat finesse.

One night I came home from work about 8:00 PM after a very hard day in the field, worn out. Phyllis met me at the door with excitement in her eyes, "Bob, I saw Renny Reaves on the TV news, you've got to watch it on tonight's news!" Renny was a year ahead of us in college, a ROTC graduate and was in Vietnam with the one brigade of the 101st Airborne Division that was in country. I never stayed up as late as 11:00 PM to watch the news but did that night. Sure enough, they replayed the clip and there was our friend, his eyes full of emotion and saying something like, "…as we came in for a landing on the Huey's, all I saw were green tracers coming up at us…"

Whatever he said, long forgotten by now, was the first time someone I knew personally was talking about a current experience in Vietnam. It got my attention. Our instructors kept telling us, "You guys with a 4th Infantry Division patch on your sleeve, pay attention because you're going to be in Vietnam sooner rather than later." I started thinking, "Babcock, the odds of you going to Vietnam appear to be getting stronger all the time."

As we neared the halfway point of IOBC, lots of our class members were volunteering for AIRBORNE and Ranger Schools. I had thought about volunteering for Ranger School but couldn't imagine why anyone would want to jump out of a perfectly good airplane. With that said, the mob instinct clicked in, and I kept asking myself, "Babcock, are you afraid of jumping out of an airplane? Go ahead and volunteer, prove you aren't a coward." And I did—volunteered for both AIRBORNE and Ranger Schools. We were all quickly approved for AIRBORNE school, to start the week after we completed IOBC, but the class leader told us, "You guys with the 4th Infantry Division patch, you aren't approved for Ranger School. You are needed back at your unit."

The plot thickened. Although Vietnam was never mentioned, we quickly surmised that we likely were needed at Fort Lewis because the 4ID had a rendezvous with Vietnam in the not-too-distant future.

Graduation from IOBC was a nice ceremony, our wives were in attendance, and the pomp and circumstance of the Army made us cross the stage with pride as we were presented our graduation certificate and officially became members of the long tradition of Infantry officers...our first step in our Army career had been accomplished.

AIRBORNE School

AIRBORNE School started the next Monday morning. It consisted of three weeks—Ground Week, Tower Week, Jump Week. They were all tied together with running everywhere we went, in formation, and if moving by yourself from one place to another. Plus, dozens of pushups any time you made the slightest mistake, and often just for the hell of it because they wanted us to be in prime shape and to wash out any who weren't up to the task at hand. We had about 650 in our class—all ranks, with a Marine captain as our company commander. (He was harassed constantly by the AIRBORNE NCO instructors).

We showed up every morning at 0600 with spit shined boots, freshly starched fatigues, and started the day with PT. By 0630, our shine on our boots was gone, the starch in our fatigues was out, and our day had barely begun. Next morning, you better show up with boots equally as spit shined as they were this morning, and you never wore a uniform two days in a row. It made for expensive cleaning bills on a second lieutenant's pay of $292 per month. And each night we had to spit shine our own boots to be ready for the next morning's inspection.

We jumped from C-130 four-engine airplanes. After two weeks of training, we were convinced we were invincible. The fall leaves in Georgia were beautiful as we floated down under that beautiful parachute canopy that had opened shortly after we exited the airplane into the prop-wash of the propellers. On my last jump, I hit wrong and felt a pop in my left ankle. I got up, gathered my parachute into my arms, and limped toward the waiting trucks. They saw my limp, came to me and I was re-routed to an Army ambulance, along with about 35 others who had hurt themselves. The wind had come up and we had more injuries on that jump than normal. We were treated in Martin Army Hospital in assembly line fashion. Two medics argued over how they should set my broken ankle, the ranking one won the debate. I left there on crutches with a still drying walking cast that I was to wear for the next six weeks.

I called Phyllis (pay phone), who was processing us out of our apartment as we prepared to leave the next morning for home, en route to Fort Lewis, Washington. She thought I was kidding when I told her I had broken my leg. I had convinced her that nothing could go wrong. After I got stern and convinced her I was serious, she had no idea where the hospital was, nor did I. She finally got there, picked me up, we stayed in a local hotel, I out-processed from school the next morning, and got my orders showing I had successfully completed AIRBORNE School (I had sweated that all night).

We left Fort Benning in our rear-view mirror and headed to the next phase of our Army adventure. Oh yes, another detail, our Mustang was manual transmission. I couldn't operate the clutch with my broken ankle, so Phyllis had to drive the almost 3,000 miles we had ahead of us. (I am not a very good passenger—but she did an excellent job despite me telling her how to drive).

When we pulled into the driveway at our home in Heavener the next day, my mother came bursting out the door and started with, "Why in the world did you jump out of an airplane…" I had not told her I was in AIRBORNE School, knowing she would be upset. I had told my Daddy (didn't ask, told him I was doing it, and he agreed not to tell mother). The circumstances were—Larry Mathis, from Pittsburg, was in my jump class, he had called home and told his parents I had broken my ankle, his mother happened to run into my Aunt Opal at the grocery store and told her. Aunt Opal called my parents (long distance was only used for emergencies in those days) and asked how I was. Daddy had to fess up that he knew I was in AIRBORNE School, and she had another day to get totally worked up by the time I got home (remember no cell phones and instant communications then). It's nice to be loved by your mother...

After a couple of days at home, we proceeded on to Fort Lewis, with Phyllis at the steering wheel. All went well until we got into the Colorado Rockies and ran into snow. Signs gave warning that in certain areas, snow chains were required. We didn't have chains, so we stopped in the next town and bought them—an expense we didn't need. The roads were still dry until we headed up a pass and the signs said, "Do not proceed without snow chains installed" or words to that effect. There was a parking area to stop and do that.

I got out with my leg in my walking cast and put on snow chains for the first time in my life. You can imagine how much fun that was—reading the instructions, laying down in the snow to get them on the back tires, and making sure I was doing it right. I was finally satisfied they were okay; we drove on them for maybe five miles until we got over the pass and hit dry highway again. They were easier to get off than put on, and we never used them again.

As we were driving across Colorado, Utah, Idaho, and Washington, we kept hearing reports on the radio news about a fight going on in Vietnam between the 1st Air Cavalry Division and the North Vietnamese Army, in a place called the Ia Drang Valley. We listened with keen interest. One of my classmates at Fort Benning had not attended AIRBORNE School but had gone straight from our class to Vietnam to join the 1st Cavalry Division. We were wondering if he was in this fight. News wasn't instantaneous in those days like it is today, we were hearing things that had happened a day or two before it was reported. Vietnam more and more was moving to the forefront of our minds.

We arrived in Fort Lewis early the week of Thanksgiving 1965, checked into the Fort Lewis Inn while we were waiting to be assigned on-post quarters, and did the in-processing required of us. I reported into my company, Bravo Company, 1st Battalion, 22nd Infantry Regiment, met 1SG Bob MacDonald, 1LT Sandy Fiacco, and SSG Frank Roath. I won't go into the details of their disgust with me having a broken leg here, that is covered in my *What Now, Lieutenant?* book. Suffice it to say they needed me at full speed, not limping around with a cast on my leg. Fiacco believed we would be heading for Vietnam 'soon'.

When SSG Roath took me upstairs in the barracks to meet my platoon, there were only eight assigned out of an authorized strength of 43. We were sorely under-strength. By the end of January 1966, my leg had healed and was back at full strength. The rumor Lieutenant Fiacco had heard was true and my platoon was filled, overnight, with 48 men, most of them fresh out of basic training and ready for Advanced Individual Training (AIT). Our entire brigade was filled with troops to "train and retain." Even though it was unofficial, we all felt certain we would be in Vietnam before the summer was over.

AIT consisted of weapons training with the M60 machine gun, .45 caliber pistol, 81mm mortar, M79 grenade launcher, M90 rocket launcher, hand grenades, and other specialized weapons. We also did extensive training on small unit tactics at the fire team and squad levels.

Many other subjects, such as map and compass reading, radio procedures, first aid, land navigation, escape and evasion, artillery fire adjustment, and other skills infantrymen needed to survive and perform their mission in combat rounded out the eight weeks of AIT.

Most of the teaching load fell on the four platoon leaders. We tried to share the load as best we could. The intense lecture load was tough, but that was nothing compared to the responsibility of teaching troops how to work together under combat conditions, with live ammunition, without shooting each other. And I was still a rookie myself.

After successfully completing the eight weeks of AIT, capped off by a graduation ceremony with all the military pomp and circumstance, we took a deep breath over the weekend, and went into our platoon and company training phase. It was during that two-month period we really learned to work together as a unit. Feeling certain we would be going into combat together, the leaders made special efforts to learn everything we could about the individual men—their strengths and weaknesses, their quirks, and other important idiosyncrasies.

Every day we learned something new and valuable. During hand grenade training, we learned one man could not master the skill of throwing one. Despite repeated attempts at teaching him with dummy grenades, we had to dive for cover behind the protection of the concrete bunkers every time he threw a live grenade and it landed only a few feet in front of his position. We made sure Jesse did not carry hand grenades when we got to Vietnam.

Too many men went into combat without knowing the capabilities of the men they were depending on to do the job. By training together as a unit, we gained an advantage far too few men in Vietnam had. I have always been thankful we had the advantage of five months training together before we saw actual combat.

Some leaders are born, others must be trained. We were successful in training some outstanding small unit leaders during those long, rainy days at Fort Lewis. Each day we gave our men the opportunity to show their leadership skills. Soon we had an outstanding group of young leaders, not just in my platoon but across the entire company. Again, we had the advantage of building a team before we came under enemy fire.

Physical conditioning was an element of training Lieutenant Fiacco led by example. Before we completed our training day, he led us in daily five mile runs around the back roads of the training areas. This was in marked contrast to the other companies who sat back and poked fun at us as we ran by. Our men complained, but we knew Bravo Company was better prepared than most for what lay ahead of us.

Towards the end of company training, we got the official word. We were shipping overseas to USARPAC—United States Army, Pacific. Vietnam was not mentioned in the orders, but we all knew beyond a shadow of a doubt what our destination was to be.

*****

The first of June was the beginning of our final training before we left the States—a fourteen-day Brigade Field Training Exercise (FTX). After two days of intensive preparation, we were up long before daylight on the first day of the FTX. Our brigade was to attack a mythical southeast Asian objective, pacify the natives, and wait for further orders. Our battalion was to lead the attack, Bravo Company led the battalion, and my third platoon had the lead for our company and thus led the brigade into the FTX.

We had a spring in our step as we entered this "final exam" stage of our training. Soon after we left the line of departure, we came upon a river. A sign reading 'Bridge Blown Out' attached to a roadblock kept us from crossing the bridge. Several umpires stood by to insure we followed the rules.

Not to be slowed down, we quickly found a spot to ford. Our teeth chattered as the freezing cold water from the spring thaw raced by us on its way from the Cascade mountains to nearby Puget Sound. We had barely reached the opposite bank after wading through the chest deep water when the "aggressors" opened fire. We spread out and returned fire, forgetting how cold we were.

The radio quickly crackled to life as Lieutenant Fiacco called, "Do you want an air strike?" Without hesitation, I replied, "Affirmative!" as I tried to assess the situation in the confusion of the gunfire. He told me, "Mark your position with smoke." In less than a minute after I threw out a yellow smoke grenade, two F-4 Phantom jets came screaming out of the sky toward us. The noise was deafening as they came to the bottom of their bomb run and turned their nose back skyward and hit their afterburners to make a quick getaway.

I had frequently called for an air strike during our training. Everything was always simulated, and no real airplanes ever appeared. You can imagine the shocked look on all our faces when real airplanes responded to our call. That really brought it home to me, we were about to finish training and go on to the real thing. (The "real thing", we found out, was much more spectacular and awesome than this).

Fortunately, the planes did not drop real bombs, or they would have gotten us. We learned from that experience to respect the power of an air strike and to hug the earth and use whatever terrain features were available for protection when we called one in.

The FTX was a success but it strongly pointed out to us the confusion and chaos that can reign when so many men are involved in an operation. We saw which leaders responded well under pressure, which ones did stupid things, and the true meaning of SNAFU—Situation Normal, All Fouled Up. We were all sobered with the knowledge our next operation would be for real and mistakes would be paid for in American lives—potentially our own.

Our five months of training at Fort Lewis were very eventful. I was transformed from a green, broken legged "shave tail" to a qualified, confident infantry leader. During that time, I also gained the confidence and respect of Sergeant Roath. He was always true to his tradition of looking down his nose at second lieutenants, never failing to point out he was a "senior" NCO, and I was a "junior" officer, only slightly more intelligent than dirt. But he showed me in subtle ways he thought I was doing okay.

As we concluded the FTX, we had a couple of weeks of final preparation before we were released for leave prior to our July 21, 1966, port call to leave by ship for Vietnam—our orders still read USARPAC, destination unknown.

A series of battalion, brigade, and brigade task force parties were held for the officers and their wives, three weeks in a row. For me, dress was simple—put on my dress blue uniform and show up. For Phyllis, she wasn't about to show up each week in the same dress. Thus, each week as I was doing final preparations of our unit for deployment, she was using her great sewing skills to create a new dress for the following Friday night party. She was always the best-looking lady at every party we attended—at least in my opinion, and probably most of the others in attendance.

One particular story from our series of parties warrants including here (it is also included in my *What Now, Lieutenant?* book). It comes from our final, brigade task force party, hosted by the 4th Infantry Division commanding general.

The officers and wives of Bravo Company were a close-knit group and always stuck together at these functions. Breaking with protocol, Sandy Fiacco and his fiancé, Sandy, mingled with us rather than with the other company commanders. Bill Saling, from Headquarters Company, and his wife also joined us each week. It was this select group which added the excitement to the Brigade Task Force officers' party. With a grin on his face, Colonel Morley came up to us and said, "Come out in the hall with me, Sandy, I have a mission for you."

There were three battalions plus the associated support units at the party. Each of the infantry battalions had their own tradition and motto. We, the First Battalion of the Twenty-Second Infantry, were the "Regulars, By God!", the First Battalion of the Twelfth Infantry was the "Red Warriors", and the Second Battalion of the Eighth Infantry was the "Black Panthers."

The Commander of the "Black Panthers" had brought their mascot to the party—a three-foot long ceramic replica of a black panther. The battalion adjutant stood careful guard over it as it was displayed with pride on the Panther CO's table.

"Sandy, I want that panther," was the simple order given by Colonel Morley.

Working to stifle a smile, Sandy assembled the officers and wives out in the hall to give us each our responsibility. Our exhaustion and marginal desire to be at the party quickly disappeared. We tingled with excitement as we all committed ourselves to making sure the mission was completed successfully.

Lou Dinetz, our rotund first platoon leader, was dispatched to the kitchen to prepare for his key role in the capture.

We moved back into the banquet hall and began to mingle into the crowd. As we passed the table where the black panther was sitting, the adjutant eyed us suspiciously as if he knew we were up to something.

No one noticed the waiter, dressed in white shirt, bow tie, and apron wrapped around his dress blue uniform trousers busily cleaning off tables as he approached the prized panther. Finally, when the time was right, Bravo Company's officers, wives, and fiancé struck!

Still unnoticed by the adjutant, Lou Dinetz, the "waiter", reached across the table and grabbed the panther. In a single motion he turned, handed it to me, and I passed it on to Walt Ferguson. As Lou and I stood in front of the adjutant, Walt tucked it under his arm and sprinted for the exit door. Before the startled adjutant could react, the wives all congregated around him to block his pursuit.

An officer in the United States Army would never run over a lady, so he was helpless! Sandy, Bill Saling, and Russ Zink, our executive officer, formed a blockade across the exit door to stop the pursuit of anyone who might try to rescue their mascot.

Walt flew out the door of the officer's club. Ron Marksity, our weapons platoon leader, sat poised at the front curb in his shiny green 1965 Corvette, engine running and ready for action. Walt unceremoniously plopped the panther on the front seat and scrambled back as Ron squealed away into the night.

At reveille formation on Monday morning, Colonel Morley marched an elite sixteen-man honor guard from Bravo Company across the parade field to the spot where the "Black Panthers" were holding their morning formation. He saluted the battalion commander smartly and proudly presented the panther back to him in front of all his troops. One minor alteration had been made—a pink bra and panties had been painted on it and a yellow yolk of an egg ran down its head.

*****

One of the last things we did before taking leave was to turn in the M-14 rifles we had trained on and issue and qualify on the new M-16 rifles we would use in Vietnam. I was given lead responsibility for that training. It's difficult to teach a rifle that you've never touched until a few days before training started. Fortunately, several of the guys in our company had been in an experimental basic training unit at Fort Jackson, SC who trained with the M-16 and two other rifles that were competing for the final decision by the Army on which would become the standard Infantry weapon. They did a lot of the teaching while I stood back and learned along with the other men in the company.

We had a final parade, on the tarmac of Grey Army Airfield, and then were released for our leave. Phyllis and I headed down the coast to San Francisco and Las Vegas as we headed back to Heavener for her to decide what to do while I was deployed. Very quickly she got a Home Economics teaching job in Topeka, Kansas where she would room with a sorority sister while both of their husbands were deployed to Vietnam.

A nationwide airline strike was declared while I was on leave. I had to scramble to find a way to get back to Fort Lewis in time for my deployment. John Tatum, my best boyhood friend, had a neighbor in Oklahoma City who worked at Tinker Air Force Base and arranged for a flight on an Oklahoma Air National Guard flight to get me to McChord AFB, which adjoins Fort Lewis.

It was a sad departure, not knowing what lay ahead of me. As I walked to the plane after saying goodbye to Phyllis, my parents, her parents, and John, I had a hard time holding the tears back (in fact I still have a hard time holding back the tears typing this 55 years later). I boarded the plane, waved at them, said a prayer, and wondered if I'd ever see them again.

Thus began the biggest adventure of my life...

Army 2LT Bob Babcock, Fort Benning apartment, Aug 1965

AIRBORNE School, October–November 1965

AIRBORNE School, October–November 1965

My Vietnam Experiences
July 1966 to July 1967
(Already written in *What Now, Lieutenant?*)

While my year in Vietnam ranks at the top of the most memorable year in my life, I am not going to cover that in detail in this book. I have already written and published it many years ago (started writing it in 1986 and published it in 2007). For any reader who wants to read the day-by-day experiences I had in Vietnam, you can go to Amazon.com and find *What Now, Lieutenant?* by Robert O. Babcock.

Be careful to order the right copy—there is also a book with the same title that came out several years after my book, written by retired Marine General Richard "Butch" Neal. His is also an excellent book. He served after I did in Vietnam and rose through the ranks to retire as a four-star general, Deputy Commandant of the Marine Corps. To read about my experiences in Vietnam, my version of *What Now, Lieutenant?* by Robert O. Babcock is where to go.

Rather than totally ignore my Vietnam experiences in this book, I have extracted below the After Thoughts section of *What Now, Lieutenant?*

Vietnam After Thoughts

This was written on my 50th birthday, August 30, 1993. Less than a month after I arrived in Vietnam, I reached the ripe old age of 23. Today, I am celebrating my 50th birthday with friends and family. (And as I wrap up my memoir, I have passed my 78th birthday). Little did I realize back then that 27 years later, those twelve months in Vietnam would loom so large and important in my life's memories (and still do now 55 years after those experiences).

Lee Sherman Dreyfuss, past president of Sentry Insurance Company, former governor of Wisconsin, chancellor of the University of Wisconsin at Stevens Point, and renowned motivational speaker, described his World War II experiences far better than I could, therefore I quote: "With the Battle of Okinawa rated as a ten on my life scale, everything else I have done before or since then, is no more than a two." Vietnam had the same profound impact on my life.

As I wind down the seven-year odyssey back into my Vietnam experiences and wrap up this book, several thoughts that have not been covered still churn through my mind. I will conclude with some random thoughts that still need to be written.

Why did I go to Vietnam? Why didn't I turn against the war as it dragged on and on? Why would I do it again if I was called on? I guess the answer is very simple—patriotism and love of my country. I grew up in a protected small-town environment where I learned simple values—the American flag, motherhood, and apple pie. I was young and naive. In a way I did not understand at the time, I believed in what President John F. Kennedy had said my senior year in high school, "Ask not what your country can do for you, ask what you can do for your country."

I was also influenced by World War II, the Korean War, and the Cold War. Communism was a real threat in our world in 1966 and I was going to do my part to help stop it before it hit the shores of America. Again, it may sound idealistic, trite, or naive, but I never once considered not serving my country. In fact, I would be very upset today if I had not answered my country's call to duty. I have zero regrets about serving my country in Vietnam.

It should also be noted I was in the Vietnam War during its early troop buildup stage. Grace Coggins Kidwell, a lifelong friend who lived through two tours when her first husband flew bombing missions over North Vietnam from the aircraft carrier Kitty Hawk, explained it this way: "We are the in-between generation. Even though the Vietnam war was never popular, we were in it before it became unpopular. The public thinks of it in its later stages when it got such bad publicity and had so many protestors and dope users."

Marian Faye Novak, in her book "*Lonely Girls with Burning Eyes*," stated it a little differently. "We faced the future in those days of 1967 with what I think must be called courage. It's true that we were too inexperienced to feel fear and too unwise to be afraid of the abstract. But we knew something; I see it in the pictures of the wives. And yet we smiled and danced, and I remember laughter, too. I call that courage. And we had it."

In summary, we were a trusting, idealistic, young generation. We had not, at that time, lived through the Vietnam War, Watergate, nor experienced a press corps obsessed with sensationalism and digging up dirt on public figures. We were fresh off the assassination of JFK and still believed in Camelot. We, the young and naive, were led to war by leaders we had never had a reason to distrust. Oh, to return to such simple times.

Why was I so lucky? What made Bravo Company, 1st Battalion, 22nd Infantry Regiment, 4th Infantry Division so different from our sister units? I have thought long and hard about this one. It always comes back to the same things—good leaders, good people, common sense, people who cared about each other, courage to do what is right, luck, and God looking over us.

I had the chance (when he was still alive) to ask LTC Len "Rawhide" Morley, our battalion commander, what he thought about Bravo Company and why we were so different. His response was the same, "Good leaders at all levels and the courage to do what was right."

As I have talked to veterans of Bravo Company who served later in the war, I find their luck did not hold like ours. They, however, did not have the advantage of training together as we had, served under different leaders, used different tactics, and were in different political times.

And I frequently ask myself the question, how would I have acted if I had been in a big battle? How would it have changed my life? And the answer is—I'll never know. Would I have done a good job, would I have been a coward, would I have been killed or wounded, would it have changed the rest of my life? Like every person who has never faced the situation, I can only wonder. And I wonder frequently.

I will always hold in very high esteem those veterans of all wars who were thrown into the breach of a major battle. Over past years, I have talked to veterans of the D-Day invasion, the hedgerow fighting across France, the Hurtgen Forest, the Battle of the Bulge, Iwo Jima, Guadalcanal, and the Anzio beach landing in World War II.

I have talked to veterans of major battles of the Korean War and veterans of the battles of the Ia Drang Valley, Soui Tre, Dak To, Fire Base Burt, Ap Cho, Khe Sanh, the Tet Offensive, the Battle of Good Friday, and numerous other major clashes of the Vietnam war. As an Infantryman, I can identify with them. I can never, however, quit wondering how I would have reacted in those battles. (And since I wrote this, I've talked to hundreds who fought in Iraq and Afghanistan).

I once heard, "Any battle is a big one, if you are in it…" That statement has stuck with me. You do not think about the size of the battle when bullets and mortar fragments start flying around. You become quickly convinced each one is aimed directly at you. And I have experienced that.

What is it like to stay at home and wait while your son, or your husband, or your brother is in a war zone? That question did not really enter my mind until Operation Desert Storm and I had a son approaching draft age. I looked at it from a whole different perspective when I realized that one day, I may be the one waiting at home thinking about my son at war.

I asked my parents, my brother, and Phyllis, my first wife, to answer that question. My parents, Hermann and Dorothy Babcock, still live in the house I was born in. When I initially asked the question, my eighty-year-old mother answered it very quickly, "It's hell." I asked them both to think back twenty-seven years and write down what they remembered about having a son in a combat zone.

Mother's response, "When Bob waved before boarding the plane to leave for Vietnam, that is where my worry began. Already the news in the papers was not good. You wonder why I read the news—I think it is something a mother cannot help doing. Many a night I lay awake wondering how he was faring—was he being fed right, did he have a good place to sleep, I knew he wasn't safe.

"I wrote to him every day, not knowing if or when he was getting the letters. We heard from him as often as he could get a letter off. I cannot think of words to describe how I felt. I always had the feeling maybe he would not make it home again. When he did come home was one of the happiest days of my life." (My mother, Dorothy Babcock, died on February 25, 2004).

I think I understand better now why she blocked the war out of her life when I came home. It is a normal human response to try to block out and forget painful experiences.

My Dad's response, "Being the father of four young adult boys, one could naturally expect I have had many very good experiences and joys. Also, one would expect there have been a few 'dark' days. The darkest day of my life was when we saw the air transport plane take-off with Bob on board, knowing full well he was going to Vietnam for full scale combat duty in a war that should never have happened.

"On the bright side, I knew Bob had a strong faith in God, and never did I allow a day to pass that I did not pray for Bob's safety in Vietnam and a safe return home. I kept in as close contact as possible with his whereabouts via radio, TV, and the newspapers. But in those days the coverage was nothing to compare with what we have today. We received a lot of letters from Bob, and it was always a great lift to his mother and me when those letters arrived. Another thing on the plus side was the fact I knew Bob had always been a winner and he did not go to Vietnam expecting to change that image." (My father, Hermann Babcock, died on July 21, 1995. It was exactly 29 years to the day after I left for Vietnam).

My older brother, Jim, summed it up this way, "Bob is seven years my junior. I knew little of him as we grew up. He was a quiet, accommodating, non-assertive boy. I left home to join the Army while he was still in elementary school. When Bob was in Airborne School, he visited me in Atlanta one weekend, and I will never forget my thoughts. 'How was this frail (to me) young man going to survive in the real Army?' I was extremely proud of

Bob for choosing the Army as I had. I was not ready for him to go 'in harm's way'.

"It was easier for me to put it out of my thoughts while he was in Vietnam. To this day, I do not recall writing him. Fortunately, the year went by rapidly for me and soon Bob was on his way back. What a weight off my mind to hear he had landed in Oakland. We have since become very close friends and rarely do more than two weeks go by without some contact." (Jim was my editor and valued critic as I wrote my *What Now, Lieutenant?* book. (On February 22, 1995, Jim died after almost 26 years as a quadriplegic).

Finally, my ex-wife, Phyllis, had this poignant memory when I asked her what it was like to be the one who stayed home and waited, "You mean, what was it like to wonder, every time I saw an Air Force officer walk up to the school where I was teaching, whether he was coming to pick up his children or to tell me you had been killed." (Forbes Air Force Base is in Topeka, Kansas and many Air Force children were in her classes).

Marian Faye Novak summed it up eloquently in her book. "When the man you love is at war, life becomes a minefield, and you are forever—even in your dreams—walking point."

Why is the Vietnam experience such a powerful force in my life? That question has gnawed at me for years, and I think I understand it much better today than I did (many) years ago when I started writing this book. And the answer is complex, not simple.

Probably the most important factors are the intense individual experiences and friendships I developed. I had experiences, almost daily, which stand out above most others in my life. No other bond measures up to those forged when operating at the most basic of levels. Mutual trust and support of the men you worked with became primary considerations over everything. All else became secondary in importance.

Again, a quote from Marian Faye Novak (I really enjoyed her book), "I watched Bob (another Bob, not me) and Dave together, and I began to see the love that men can have for one another that has nothing to do with sex or romance. It is a kind of love that has to do with caring, and loyalty, and even the special sharing of knowledge about certain things." Never have I developed a bond and respect like I did with the men I served with in Vietnam.

At the age of twenty-three, I had to make more important decisions than any I have ever made in my life, before or since. Much of what we did was potentially a life-or-death situation. It is an awesome responsibility to be in charge of the lives of so many young American men. It is a great source of pride that I did my job; and did it well. That is not unique to Vietnam; it is true of all wars and all veterans. I am proud to say that all the men in my platoon came home alive, a few wounded, but all made it.

It makes a lasting impression on you—and puts other decisions in your life in a different perspective. When making tough decisions even today, the question often comes to mind, "What are they going to do, send me to Vietnam?" That helps to put things into proper perspective.

There is a great deal of pride in answering the call as a Soldier and living to talk about it. I have always liked the comment George C. Scott, in the title role of the movie "Patton", made as he was talking to his men prior to their going into battle. "When your grandson sits on your knee and asks, 'What did you do in the great World War II, Granddad,' you won't have to say, 'Well, I shoveled sh*t in Louisiana.'"

We Vietnam vets will not have to tell our grandsons that we

fled to Canada or sat the war out on a draft deferment or missed it for some other reason. We can point with pride at our service to our country. I'm sure there are other factors I have not yet found. I recognize the impact Vietnam has had on me, even if I cannot eloquently explain why.

How about those who did not serve? What do you think about them? I have never had a big problem with people who did not serve in the Vietnam War. Our national leaders did not mobilize the country and I cannot expect everyone to have the same streak of patriotism I have. The Vietnam period was a time in America where we lacked strong leadership and national purpose. I cannot fault others of my generation for doing what their conscience dictated.

Those who flocked to the national guard and reserves took a legal and logical, for them, approach to service. I served in an Army reserve unit for several years after my return from Vietnam and worked with some outstanding individuals.

I never did agree with some of their philosophies. Neither did I ever get overly worked up with those who protested the war. What they did was detrimental to our fighting men but part of what we were fighting for was to preserve that very right to dissent. Even Jane Fonda did what she thought was right, and the Constitution I was fighting for gives every living American that right. (I am not a Jane Fonda fan.)

However, I have no respect for those who overtly and openly avoided service to their country. Those who went to Canada to avoid the draft and those who did other less than honorable things to avoid service, in my opinion, let themselves and their country down. But I can overlook that by attributing it to their youth and inexperience (or their cowardice) at the time.

They are the ones who must live with their decisions, not me.

Again, a quote from Marian Faye Novak's book sums up my feelings. "I see the lines of people when we go to the Wall; some are veterans or the friends and relatives of veterans, some are too young to remember the war. But many are not, and I wonder at all these others. Where were you, I think, when these men needed you? When we all needed you? How can you look so long and lovingly on the silent names of these dead when you were so quick to turn your backs on their living faces?"

I think many people may be silently living with the ghosts of decisions made so long ago in their late teens or early twenties.

Have I accomplished my objective of letting my children know about my Vietnam experience? I am very pleased with how my kids have reacted to this book. When I started writing, my oldest daughter was seventeen and my youngest son was two. At that time, none of my four children had any interest in my efforts. Over the course of the seven years I have been working on this book, they have all learned how important my Vietnam experience is to me (and, by association, to them).

Both Kristen and Rob have read various drafts of the book and regularly question me, with great interest, about my experiences. They cannot wait to read the final draft. Mark, now nine years old, frequently asks me to read him a chapter or two. Stephanie has not yet shown much interest, but I think, in time, she will.

Two very recent events show me the kids are in tune with what I am doing. On a family vacation to Florida a few weeks ago, we were riding on a rubber, banana shaped raft being pulled by a motorboat. When we hit an extra-large wave, the raft turned over. We all found ourselves bobbing around in our life jackets waiting for the boat to circle around to load us back up. In unison, the group asked me, with big smiles on their faces, "What you gonna do now, Lieutenant?" Their comment made me beam.

Today (27 years ago), for my fiftieth birthday present, the kids gave me the best present I could ever get. They had a draft copy of this *(What Now, Lieutenant?)* book bound in a hardback green cover with the title and my name printed on the cover in gold print. Along with the book, Kristen had needle pointed a plaque which will always hang in a place of prominence in our home. The 4th Infantry Division patch, my Combat Infantryman's Badge, my AIRBORNE Wings, my Lieutenant bar, and my Crossed Rifles of an Infantryman are prominently displayed. The plaque reads:

For you Daddy,
Because We thank God each
day for the Freedom you Fought
to give to us. We Love You, and
are Proud that you're our Father.
Krissie, Rob, and Mark

My kids know the answer to the question, "What did you do in the Vietnam War, Dad?" Do yours? So now you have heard my story. There are three million more Vietnam stories to be told. Who is going to tell the next one?

As most veterans of any war will always say, my year in Vietnam in 1966-1967 was a defining point in my life. Some of my best friends are those who fought alongside me in the jungles of the central highlands of Vietnam. I am proud of my service to my country, glad I had the opportunity to do what my country asked me to do, and if needed, I would do it again.

In December 2021, Gary Swanson, my IBM boss, and mentor,

who is an early reader of this book, suggested I add at least one story about my experiences in Vietnam. Always listening to my friend and mentor (you will be introduced to Gary Swanson throughout the IBM portion of my life), I've thought on his suggestion and decided to include a specific story from my *What Now, Lieutenant?* book. It struck me that the best experience to include here is the first one I wrote on the evening of November 20, 1986—the 20th anniversary of the day that we lived this sad experience. It is titled simply, *November 20, 1966*, and is a day that I remember vividly every year...

19 Nov 66

...A few of our people are starting to get sick. We have sent in eight or ten men within the last week with fever. LT Lou Dinetz went in yesterday morning with 103 temp. I am still feeling just fine...

(Letter to my folks)—No, Mother, that is not me in the picture you cut out of the newspaper. As Dale said, the face is too full. I have no idea where the picture was taken or who it is. I told you I am okay, why don't you believe me? Also, just because his pants leg is torn, that is no sign he is injured. There are a million thorn bushes over here that just love to tear GI's pants. They have already torn one pair off me during this operation and I am starting to get rips in the new ones I got just a week ago.

His facial expression is not of pain, either. It gets tiresome running around these hills. He is probably just plain bone tired and has sore feet or something. Besides, that guy is too sloppy for me. He has his helmet chin strap hanging loose and I never do that, I keep it tied up on my helmet...

...Think positive and don't worry about me. Quit letting your imagination run away with you, Mother. I am safe, just tired and dirty.

21 Nov 66

Your past 24 hours have to have been more pleasant than mine. We had a tragic thing happen yesterday afternoon. (See story on "November 20, 1966").

November 20, 1966

The jungle air was thick with tension as we trudged along under its thick, triple canopy. All morning we had been monitoring radio reports of first one and then another of our sister units as they made contact with the NVA. Muffled explosions could be heard as artillery and air strikes pounded the jungle.

For seventeen days, our luck had held. We had moved along unscathed as units to our right and left took casualties regularly. Since we did not have to stop, regroup, and lick our wounds like Alpha and Charlie Companies, we were far in front of them in our movement northward through the Nam Sathay River valley. Two days earlier, we had run out of our supporting artillery battery's range.

Rather than halt our progress, we had been attached temporarily to a battalion of the Third Brigade of the 25th Infantry Division. They were to provide artillery support for us while we were under their operational control.

Just as we stopped for noon chow, Sandy Fiacco received a radio call from the battalion commander. "Oscar 6, this is Cactus 6. We have a unit in heavy contact with a large NVA unit to your right flank. I want you to move over and provide a blocking position to cut the bad guys off if they try to withdraw toward Cambodia. Over."

Sandy and I studied his map as he replied, "This is Oscar 6. Roger. We will be moving in five minutes. Out." We continued studying the map coordinates to determine the best blocking position for straddling their most likely avenue of retreat.

The troops grumbled as they gulped down the C-rations they had hoped to enjoy while relaxing. The tension continued to mount as we made a right turn and headed toward the ridge line where we would set up our position. It was mid-afternoon when we reached our objective. Security outposts moved forward as we started to build our normal triangular defensive position. The muffled sounds of artillery and air strikes continued to vibrate through the thick jungle. The radio traffic indicated the unit was still slugging it out with the NVA as we started to dig in.

None of us needed encouragement to dig deep and cut down large trees for overhead protection on our bunkers. We knew that something bad was happening to the unit we were setting up to help. Now we were between the NVA and their sanctuary in Cambodia.

Suddenly, the artillery and mortar rounds started hitting closer to us. Our artillery forward observer grabbed his radio, called the fire base, and told them to, "Cease fire! You are getting dangerously close to our position." The response from the fire base was quick, "Get off this frequency! We are on a fire mission!" Before a warning could be shouted to our troops, the next round landed with a deafening roar in the trees directly above where the second platoon was digging in.

Shrapnel clattered through the trees as we all dived for cover and tried to get as much protection as possible in the holes we were digging, behind big trees, or just flat on the ground. As the ricocheting shrapnel fell to the ground, we heard the cry, "Medic, medic!" I had dived into a hole beside our platoon medic. I told him, "Get up and go help out." He lay there with two big wide eyes looking up at me. He was not about to get out of that hole.

As I started crawling out, I grabbed him and his aid bag. "Come on, let's go see who is hurt." As I pulled on him, he took his aid bag and followed me to the second platoon. As we ran the interminably long forty yards from my position to where the round had hit, Sergeant Roath started checking our platoon position for dead or wounded and to make sure they were maintaining tight security.

We did not know whether we would get hit with another round or not. We could hear our artillery forward observer screaming into his radio, "Cease fire! Cease fire! Cease fire! You are dropping rounds right on top of us! Cease fire, Dammit!"

As I ran into the second platoon area, many of the troops were still in their holes feeling the shock of what had happened. The smell of explosives hung heavy in the air. Green leaves littered the ground. Walking with a severe limp, Walt Ferguson, the platoon leader, was up checking his people. Blood from a piece of shrapnel oozed from his knee. Walt and I got to David Mendez, his radio operator, at about the same time.

Walt said, "Get up, Mendez, and tell Captain Fiacco to call in a Dust-off." There was no response from Mendez. I reached down and turned him over. Blood oozed from a small hole where shrapnel had gone into his heart. He never knew what hit him.

We kept looking around to find out who else had been wounded. Stanley Cameron, my radio operator, ran over to report, "None of our men were hit." "Good, tell Sergeant Roath to keep them alert and I will stay here and help Walt's platoon."

We heard a call for, "Medic!" come from the headquarters area. Sergeant Reynolds, our communications sergeant, had been hit in the chest by a large piece of shrapnel. Air whooshed from the sucking chest wound. The medics responded rapidly. They covered the hole with a piece of foil and wrapped it tightly with combat dressings. That stopped the bleeding and cut out the air escaping through his chest.

As we took inventory of the injured, we found that ten men had been wounded and Mendez had been killed. We directed the troops to keep digging and to maintain security. While monitoring the radio, we heard the NVA had broken contact with the unit to our east. We expected them to be withdrawing through our area at any time.

Sandy Fiacco called for a Dust-off. We had one major problem. We were still in triple canopy jungle and there was no place for a helicopter to land. We knew we had to get Sergeant Reynolds evacuated immediately. Three or four others needed to get out as quickly as possible.

Finally, a Chinook helicopter hovered above the jungle canopy and lowered a line with a stretcher down through the trees. In no time, we had Sergeant Reynolds sandwiched between the two pieces of the stretcher and strapped in securely. He was pale from fright and loss of blood as the chopper crew started winching him up through the trees.

It was getting dark and the chopper pilot, understandably, did not like hovering up there like a sitting duck with all the NVA around. We still had not seen any of them, but we knew they were close at hand. "Do you have any more that are critical? If not, I am going to take this guy and get the hell out of here." The rest could wait a little longer, so we released him. Quiet returned as the Chinook headed for the 18th Surgical Hospital. Within minutes, Sergeant Reynolds would be on the operating table. (He survived but never returned to the unit).

We knew we had to have an LZ. Sandy had been on the radio

trying to get help in creating one. A helicopter flew over, hovered momentarily, and dropped two chain saws, some C4 plastic explosive, and rope charges. The fall through the trees broke the chain saws. Despite our efforts, we never could get them to work.

The C4 and rope charges were quickly put to use knocking down big trees. It was totally dark and took several hours, but we blew down trees until it looked like we could get a helicopter in. We called again for a Dust-off.

Within twenty minutes, we heard a chopper approaching. Harry Troutman fired a flare through the hole in the jungle canopy to mark our position. "Oscar 6, this is Mercy 2. I see your flare. Is your LZ hot or is it secure? Over."

So far, we had not seen or heard from any of the NVA, but we knew they could not be too far away. "This is Oscar 6 Echo; at this time, it is secure. We cannot promise you how long it will stay that way. Over."

The pilot responded, "I'm coming in with my lights on," as he circled trying to find the widest part of the LZ. The bright lights formed strange shadows which danced across the LZ as he started his descent. The main rotor blades chopped leaves and branches off the trees that seemed to try to reach out and snatch him from the air. He continued his descent, "How tall are those stumps sticking up down there?"

"They are four or five feet tall, watch me and I will let you know when you are down as far as you can go," responded Captain Fiacco. He had personally taken responsibility for guiding the chopper down. He stood in the LZ, bathed in the light from the chopper, a perfect target for a NVA sniper.

As Sandy guided the chopper down, several of us moved under it with the most seriously wounded man. The down-thrust from the chopper rotors at full power blew dirt, leaves, and twigs into our faces as we waited for it to ease down. I was one of the tallest men and had to extend my arms as high as I could to reach the floor of the chopper.

With the help of the crew inside, we got the stretcher and the wounded man loaded. The pilot circled up out of the hole and radioed, "I will take him to the 18th Surg and then be right back to get another one."

In less than an hour, he was back and repeated his feat. His rotor blades again clipped branches and leaves as he brought his bird down into the clearing with his lights on. The enemy still had not shown his face. We knew we were pushing our luck. They would hit us when he came in again for sure.

He made a total of three trips to take out the most seriously wounded and offered to come back for more! We told him, "The others are not as serious. They can wait until daylight. Thanks for the help, we owe you a drink." Words cannot describe the admiration we had for that courageous pilot.

After midnight, we finally settled down. All afternoon and evening we had not even stopped long enough to eat. It was a tired, sad, and tense bunch of GIs that settled in for the night, waiting for an attack, or waiting to see daylight.

David Mendez, our KIA, had been wrapped in a poncho and placed across the top of my bunker. It was a strange feeling to be lying in a bunker with a dead man laying across the sandbags that made up our roof. What we had learned in training was now crystal clear—the order of evacuation is most wounded to least wounded. When all of those are out, you worry about evacuating the dead.

Daylight had barely broken when we heard a chopper approaching. "Oscar 6, this is Mercy 2. Do you have any more folks that need a ride out of there?" The same pilot was coming back in to get the rest of our wounded.

In daylight and with walking wounded, he could take two

men out at a time. In three trips, the wounded were all out. The sun was starting to bathe the LZ as he picked up LT Walt Ferguson and David Mendez' body on his final trip.

Later that morning, a small observation helicopter circled over our position. "Oscar 6, this is Rawhide. I want to come down and see you, but my pilot says your LZ is too small. Knock down some more trees so I can come in."

You can imagine our disgust. This pilot had a bird about half the size of the Dust-off chopper, it was broad daylight, and we had to enlarge the LZ for him. We finally got the LZ enlarged, and Rawhide landed.

His first words as he got out of his chopper, wearing his freshly starched fatigues, were, "Damn, you guys sure do stink." It had been a week or more since we had stopped for a bath. He did not win any friends with us that day.

After he had talked to Sandy for a while, he took me aside and said, "Bob, you have got to get Sandy to calm down, he gets too excited." Rawhide did not realize how personally Sandy cared for each of his men and how upset he was to lose Mendez and the wounded. Sandy had done a fantastic job in insuring we got help when we needed it. My hat was off to him for the leadership he had shown throughout the ordeal.

Disgusted with the way he had handled that very traumatic event, we were all glad to see Rawhide finally get back in his chopper and leave.

In retrospect, Rawhide was probably correct in his actions. As a professional soldier, he knew in order to get our company back on track, there had to be a diversion. His order to enlarge the LZ and his taunts did that. Now, we had someone to be angry at, instead of dwelling in our own misery and sorrow. Rawhide was an outstanding Battalion Commander—by far the best of the three we had that year.

David Mendez' name is engraved on panel 12E, line 96 on the Vietnam Memorial Wall in Washington, D. C.

21 Nov 66 (cont'd)

…The only officers left now are Captain Fiacco and me. Lou is still sick with fever and is in the hospital, I think. Do not write Sandra about Walt getting hit. I do not know whether he will tell her about it or not.

Today we are staying in position and not moving. We really need it, too. We have been constantly on the go since the end of October. Everyone is getting physically pooped. That accident yesterday took a lot out of the men emotionally. It is bad to be here four months without serious injury and then lose eleven men because a friendly unit made a stupid mistake. It makes you wonder if it is all worth it. Fortunately, none of the men in my platoon were hurt.

It is difficult not to feel a sense of depression after our "friendly fire" incident. Tomorrow will be much better. I will sure be glad when they get us out of this damn jungle for a few days. If they would just give us two days off so we could relax, we would be ready to go another twenty days. Well, maybe they will before too much longer.

… Your letters mean an awful lot to me. The letter I got from you today helped perk up my spirits.

I'll close and fix a C-ration meal. Don't worry. I'm just trying to talk to you in this letter since we cannot talk in person…

Gary Swanson also asked me to summarize my thoughts on Vietnam. I have done a fair amount in what I wrote above, but I'll add a few more things that come to mind…

I am extremely proud to have been able to serve with the men of Bravo Company, 1st Battalion, 22nd Infantry Regiment, 2nd Brigade of the 4th Infantry Division. In January 1966, roughly 150 men came into our company, fresh out of Basic Training, bringing us up to a strength of about 180 men. We trained and retained them and went to war with them. We had men (average age of 19 or 20) from all walks of life, from all parts of our great country, who became a team. From this group, we selected our leaders (we were sorely lacking in experienced NCOs) and they immediately rose to the job we had given them.

I am also proud of the leadership we had from our two company commanders—Captain Sandy Fiacco and later Captain Buck Ator. I was the only officer who stayed in our company the whole first year in Vietnam, so I had the privilege of serving under both. Though very different personalities, they had the same strong leadership skills and always did what was right. When required to do so, they were ready to verbally fight the leaders above us as well as the real enemy in the jungle. In July 1966 to July 1967, we had two men killed, both by "friendly" fire, and one man died of malaria when he left the hospital while still very sick. We had several wounded, but few in comparison to our sister units in our battalion.

Many years later, I asked Colonel Len "Rawhide" Morley, our first of three battalion commanders, why he thought Bravo Company was so much more fortunate than the rest of the battalion. He thought a minute and said, "You had excellent leadership, at all levels—who did what was right." As part of that leadership team, I am proud to have been a factor in getting our men home alive and selecting our best Soldiers to be leaders at the squad and fire team level. I will always thank God that we, unlike most in the Vietnam war, got to train and retain our Soldiers at Fort Lewis rather than to be thrown together in a combat zone.

Enough Vietnam (for now). I pretty much put Vietnam behind me for the next 15 years of my life, then I started becoming active with Vietnam and other veterans. That has been a key part of my life since then. But now, it's time for Bob to find a job in the civilian world…

Christmas Day 1966—the day my platoon was awarded our Combat Infantryman Badges

With my parents soon after my return from Vietnam—July 1967

Post-Vietnam, Pre-IBM
First civilian job — Phillips Petroleum — Kansas City and Chicago, July 1967 to September 1968

Coming Home (from *What Now, Lieutenant?*)

A huge roar engulfed the Air Force C-141 airplane as its wheels touched down at Travis Air Force Base outside of San Francisco. We had made it! The fear that came across me as we sailed past Seattle almost a year earlier was over. I had made it home alive!

Busses took us from Travis to the Oakland Army Terminal as the sun dropped down in the western sky. All that stood between the last leg of my trip and me was to get an Army physical, get paid, and finish my out-processing. Then, I would be on the way to my wife who would be waiting for me at the Kansas City airport.

Oakland Army Terminal was a bustle of activity as our busses pulled up and unloaded. By now, it had become the primary processing center for returning vets and operated around the clock—with one minor exception. Officers still on active duty just had to sign the register and were on their way. Enlisted men processing out of the Army or to other posts got into the appropriate line and were processed in sequence as they arrived. But officers who were processing out of the Army were handled only between the hours of 8:00AM and 5:00PM. I fell into the last category. It was now 8:00PM—another twelve hour wait before I could continue my journey toward home.

After paying for a room in the holding facility (another sign I was back in the States—for the past year I had slept free, at government expense. Of course, often it was on the jungle floor). I found the nearest pay phone and placed the long-awaited call home. Phyllis was already in Kansas City. We had agreed I would let my parents, in Oklahoma, know when I would arrive. She would stay in touch with them to find out when to be at the airport (this was long before cell phones and the internet). Naturally, my parents were ecstatic to hear from me. Their prayers had been answered—I was home, safe and sound. It would be several days before they saw me, but their worries were now behind them.

Finally, my processing was completed. I was a civilian again (still wearing my Army uniform while I traveled—it was later in the war when troops were told not to wear their uniform while flying home) and boarded a cab to take me to the San Francisco airport. I drank in the sights as we crossed the Bay Bridge. I appreciated them much more than I had a year earlier.

My first dealings with civilians were at the San Francisco airport and on the plane flying to Kansas City. I was not spit on, heckled, called a baby killer or dope addict, or ridiculed. All of that came later in the war. Instead, I was ignored.

Although I proudly wore my Army uniform, Combat Infantryman's Badge, and appropriate ribbons, no one acknowledged me any more than they did a businessman traveling in his normal business day. I expected more than that and had a hollow feeling until we came into our final approach for Kansas City and my excitement overtook me. (On an IBM business trip, when I was flying from Denver to Kansas City soon after our Army's excursion into Panama in 1990, I saw a young man no more than nineteen years old with a 7th Infantry Division patch and a Combat Infantryman's Badge preparing to board the plane. Knowing that he had just returned from Panama, I talked to the pilot of the Continental plane and convinced him to move him from the rear of the plane to sit next to me in first class—I wasn't going to ignore another American veteran like we Vietnam vets had been ignored. When we arrived in Kansas City, I made a detour to drop him off at his home rather than have him catch a taxi. The look on his mother's face as she looked out the kitchen window and saw him get out of my car is something I'll never forget.)

My greeting in Kansas City was much better—Phyllis was standing by the gate anxiously awaiting the moment she and I thought would never come. Everything was as I expected it would be as we ran to greet each other. We were in our own world as the other passengers deplaned and moved past us—either ignoring us or allowing us our moment together.

Three final things stand out in my mind about my coming home experience.

First, after four days together in Kansas City in the July heat, I decided it was too hot to drive to Oklahoma in our Ford Mustang with no air conditioning. The fact the Mustang was the soon to be classic 1965 model, that it only had 36,000 miles on it, and that it was almost paid for, did not cross my mind. All I thought about was I had just spent twelve months in the heat of Vietnam, and I was not going to put up with it anymore.

So, we went to a local Chevrolet dealer, picked out the top-of-the-line model sitting on the showroom floor, called Ray Hall, the president of the bank where I had worked as a janitor all through high school (a close family friend), got his approval for a loan, paid for the car, and drove it off the lot. There went the money we had saved over the past twelve months and began my life of having to work to make payments. I have often said there should be a law that did not allow Soldiers to make major purchases until they had been home at least sixty days to get acclimated to reality again.

Second, as we listened to the radio while driving home from Kansas City, we heard stories of a major battle going on in the Central Highlands involving the 4th Infantry Division. Knowing my mother would be glued to the TV and getting all the details, my first question of her after our initial greetings was, "What is going on with the 4th Infantry Division?"

Her answer still bothers me today. "I don't know. I quit paying attention after you got back to San Francisco." To her, I was all that was important in Vietnam. To me, my friends were still fighting in a war I believed in. And, like most Americans, she went on with her life now that she did not have a direct involvement in the war.

The last thing that stands out in my mind is the reception I got in my hometown. Having lived in the same small town of Heavener, Oklahoma all my life, I knew most of the people. As I walked down the streets and saw someone I knew, it was not uncommon for a conversation to go something like this—"I haven't seen you in a long time, Bob. Where have you been?" When I responded I had just come back from Vietnam, I got an "Oh…", there was an awkward pause, and the subject was changed and they said something like, "…Oh, it sure is hot today, isn't it…?" To say the least, that hurt. My welcome was much different from the patriotic welcome I remembered the town giving "Patch" Patton upon his return from Korea.

This is not to say everyone was that way. There were people who welcomed me, asked about my experiences, and made me feel good. Many of those people were veterans of World War II, my family, and my good friend, John Tatum, who had put me on the airplane in Oklahoma City a year earlier to start my experience. Dale Franklin, a WWII vet and family friend came to see me and said, "Give me two dollars, Bob." I asked why, and he told me, "You are going to join the American Legion." He was president of the local chapter. I've been a member of American Legion ever since. Those receptions were nice and expected. The other ones still hurt.

*****

As I became acclimated to being home, I knew it was time to start looking for a job. Even though I had been paid for 35 days of earned leave that I had not taken in Vietnam, it did not seem right that I was effectively unemployed.

I started sending in applications. It seemed that everywhere I applied, their first question was, "What is your draft status?" When I responded that I had just returned from Vietnam and had completed my military obligation, every place I talked to offered me a job. I have often said that in those days if you could walk and chew gum, and had your military requirement behind you, getting a job was a piece of cake.

One of the most promising offers came from Hallmark Cards in Kansas City for an accounting job, which was my major in college. The pay offer was a little better than average for that time, but I had this empty feeling when I thought about taking the job. I pondered what my problem was and then it hit me…I couldn't bridge the gap of coming from a job leading Infantrymen in combat in the jungles of Vietnam to accounting for greeting cards. That was too big a gap for me to absorb.

Thus, I passed that job up and accepted another job in Kansas City, with Phillips Petroleum. This was also an accounting type job, being trained in Kansas City for three months and then going to Chicago to work as a credit guy for Phillips in the Illinois, Wisconsin, Michigan territory. The oil industry seemed more to my liking and my experiences as an Infantryman than greeting cards.

Phyllis and I packed our new car with all we could get into it, rented a short-term apartment, and started our new adventure in early September 1967—roughly two months after I had returned home from Vietnam.

While going through my training in Kansas City, I started waking up with night sweats. They kept getting worse and I finally left work early one Friday afternoon to go to a doctor. After he talked to me and examined me, he had no idea what my problem was. When I told the doctor I had just returned from Vietnam, he recommended I go to the VA Hospital in Kansas City as soon as possible. Since it was late afternoon on Friday, I had to wait until Monday morning to go to the hospital. It was one of the longest weekends of my life—my brain was playing tricks on me as I envisioned I had picked up some exotic tropical disease and would likely die soon.

Monday morning, I was processed into the VA Hospital and within a couple of hours, a doctor from Bangkok, Thailand, working in the US, diagnosed me as having Vivax and Falciparum malaria. You can't imagine the relief I felt—many of our Soldiers had gotten malaria in Vietnam and I knew that could be treated.

After a few days in the hospital, watching part of the 1967 World Series on TV, I was released and went back to work to finish my training. Around Thanksgiving, Phyllis and I flew to Chicago and were met by Bob Glass, the Phillips Petroleum credit manager I would be working for, and his wife. We found an apartment and drove from KC to Chicago the first week of December 1967 to continue our new adventure.

After having missed the past two Christmases at home, our parents paid for our flights to fly us from Chicago to Oklahoma.

With no vacation, we flew out on Friday, December 22, spent the weekend and Christmas Day at home, and I caught a flight back to Chicago Christmas night so I could be at work the next morning. Welcome to the civilian work force. To add insult to injury, it was 10 degrees when I landed in Chicago. It had snowed and all cars looked the same—piled high with white snow. I walked around the top parking deck for a half hour before I found my car. Phyllis flew in a few days later and we became determined to enjoy Chicago—which we did.

In late March 1968, I had a relapse of malaria and was admitted to Hines VA Hospital in Chicago. I told them I had been diagnosed with malaria in Kansas City but, of course, they wouldn't take my word for it. Their original diagnosis was hepatitis or something that required me to be put into an isolation room. This, of course, was before online medical records and they wanted to do a biopsy on my liver. I told them to forget it until they had my records from Kansas City, then if they still thought that was necessary, I'd consider it.

While I was in isolation, Martin Luther King, Jr. was assassinated. Anyone alive that day remembers the riots that broke out all over the country. From my hospital room I could look out the window and see the southside of Chicago burning. When Phyllis came to visit me, she told me about how each overpass on the interstate highway was guarded by National Guard troops. It was a very tense and scary time.

My records from Kansas City finally arrived and the doctor came in and told me, "Mr. Babcock, you have a relapse of malaria..." Duh...I told him that ten days ago. He released me from the hospital and filed a VA claim for me. The only good thing about that is I received a monthly VA benefit check for a year or two before it ended. The financial shot in the arm was one I needed and appreciated (Phyllis wasn't working—those were the days before it was common for women to work outside the home).

In June 1968, the Army contacted me and sent me orders to report to two weeks Summer Camp with the Louisiana National Guard at Fort Chaffee, Arkansas (that was the closest post to my home of record in Oklahoma—I hadn't told the Army I lived in Chicago). Phillips had to give me the two weeks off, so Phyllis and I took another road trip. The good news during my two weeks back In the Army was, she stayed in Heavener with our parents, which was less than an hour drive from Fort Chaffee. It was a good vacation for her, and I spent a weekend there before we headed back to Chicago.

My training with the National Guard was interesting. The first week was classic WWII infantry assault training (why they were still training like that instead of Vietnam jungle training, I'll never understand) and the second week was riot control training, which was becoming a very big need as our country was breaking out in more and more riots. I decided then and there that I never wanted to be sent to quell a riot. It was hard to tell which was the most out of control group, the Army troops, or the rioters. To add to the confusion, Bobby Kennedy was assassinated while I was at Fort Chaffee—the continuation of a very volatile 1968.

By July, I had mastered my job at Phillips Petroleum, my customers with credit problems were well understood, I had them on a program to get current and stay current, and I was bored out of my mind. I looked at my boss, his boss, and the Treasurer of Phillips Petroleum in Bartlesville, Oklahoma and decided I didn't want any of their jobs—I was in the wrong line of work.

Over the 4th of July weekend, Phyllis' cousin, Gwyn, came from Oklahoma to spend a long weekend with us. During the intermission of watching *Gone with the Wind* at a local theater, she said to me, "Bob, you should get into the computer business."

My response was, "I wouldn't know what to do with a computer if one came and tapped me on the shoulder." She said, "They'll teach you. But don't go with IBM, they are too big."

By Monday morning, I had written letters and sent resumes to about ten computer companies, including IBM, and had also written a letter to the Army asking if I would come back in as a Captain and if they would send me to Vietnam since I had had malaria.

In two days, I got a call from IBM wanting me to drive to Rockford, Illinois for a job interview. The branch manager, Greg Williams, that I interviewed with and offered me the job was putting a hard sell on how great Rockford was. Phyllis and I went back to Rockford on the weekend and Greg had one of his employees show us around and look for places to live.

The following week, I drove over to Rockford to talk to Greg about his offer, having made up my mind...I didn't like Rockford but did like IBM. My first question after he made me a nice offer was, "Can you send me to Kansas City instead of staying here in Rockford?" Shocking to me, since I had IBM pictured as prim and proper, his reply was, "You son of a bitch...I knew you were going to ask that." He had recently moved from Kansas City so he told me to step outside his office and he would call Dave Hodges, the KC branch manager. Long story short—he did, Dave invited me to KC, offered a job, and I started my 34-year career at IBM on 16 September 1968. It was a decision I would never regret.

I wrapped up my Phillips job, took my two weeks' vacation that I had earned, and we visited my brother Jim in Miami. Highlight of that vacation was going fishing from an air boat in the Florida Everglades. We caught lots of fish and had a fun time in the Everglades and on the beaches.

Phyllis and I packed our car again on a Friday, drove to KC

Saturday, checked into a motel, and I started work at IBM on Monday. I was one of a class of about 30 from the district who started our careers that day. I have no idea how many of that class retired from IBM, but I did. I am very proud of my IBM career—that's the next part of my story—a 34-year career building memories during my IBM days.

After I had been with IBM a couple of months, the Army sent me a form letter on how to apply for a direct commission. As you can guess, I just shook my head and threw the letter away.

BEST BASIC SYSTEMS UNIT
IN THE WORLD
KANSAS CITY   1971

Early IBM Days — Trainee and New Business Salesman
September 1968 to December 1974

On my first day at IBM, September 16, 1968, I walked into the branch office at 1400 Baltimore Avenue in downtown Kansas City, Missouri, sharply dressed in one of my two good suits with a white shirt and tie, ready to take on this new world of opportunity. Don't forget what I had told Phyllis' cousin, Gwyn, when she first told me about going to work on computers back in July in Chicago...I still had no idea what to do with a computer, even if one came up and tapped me on the shoulder.

All the managers I had talked to in Rockford and Kansas City assured me IBM had the world's best training program, and they would teach me all I needed to know. I believed them. As I talked to some of the other new hires, I picked up that some of them had worked with computers in their previous job, had studied them in college, and I started to get a little knot in my stomach, wondering if I had made the right decision.

Dave Hodges, the branch manager and Russ Mueller, the administration manager responsible for in-processing us, getting all our paperwork taken care of, and teaching us the basics that we needed to know that first week, took us to lunch at the Kansas City Club, about a block's walk from the branch office. For a small-town Okie, I was impressed. This was much nicer than any other place I had ever eaten lunch before.

As I looked around the branch office that afternoon and met the experienced people I would be working with, I noticed that all of them wore dark suits, white shirts, and a tie. Not one of them wore sport-coat and slacks, nor a colored shirt. The next day I wore my other suit with my other white shirt. After looking around at the attire the next day, I quickly realized that my wardrobe had been cut in half. The two sport-coats that I wore working at Phillips Petroleum in Chicago were obviously not acceptable attire for the IBM sales force, nor were colored shirts.

That first weekend, Phyllis and I went out and picked out another suit and a couple white shirts, an expense I hadn't planned on this early in my new job. Fortunately, we had gotten a Sears credit card while in Chicago, and I paid for the suit on the installment plan.

The training period I was in was slated to last for 15 months, taking me from being a raw rookie to a qualified IBM salesman ready to take my own territory on January 1, 1970. The first class was ten weeks long, held in Kansas City (thank goodness) and was called CST (Computer Systems Training). They started with the basics—input, process, output—and went deeper from there. The more they told me, the more confused I became. Having always prided myself in being smart, I was starting to panic as I saw I was having a hard time grasping all that was being fed me with what appeared to be a fire hydrant.

I went back to our apartment in Overland Park and studied. Phyllis, having been home by herself all day, was anxious to spend some time together but I had to try to get my arms around all the new things IBM was force-feeding me. After stumbling on the first test, I kept digging into my study material and suddenly a light went on—I got it! From then on, I was challenged but I understood what they were throwing at me and loving to learn it. I was determined to be one of the best Systems Engineers that IBM had.

My manager, Bob Arrington, had other plans for me. "Bob,"

he said, "we (the management team) think you will be a good IBM marketing representative (salesman in non-IBM terms)." In my mind, salesman equated to used car salesman, huckster, or anything but what I pictured myself as being. I liked the quality of all the people I was working with. The rookies and I were bonding together and the experienced people in the office were always reaching out to help us and make us feel a part of the team. I decided to go with the flow and see how things developed. I was confident that if I chose to be a technical Systems Engineer, I could switch to that.

I loved the classes and working on computers. This was in the early days of the System/360, the family of computers IBM announced in 1964 that made the company take off like a rocket ship and separate themselves from their competitors. I learned to program in Assembler language and lost track of time as I took on the challenge of not letting that computer get the best of me. During one of our lab sessions, I started working on an assignment about mid-morning and after what seemed like a couple of hours, I looked at my watch and it was 10:00 PM at night! It took a little explaining when I called Phyllis and told her time had gotten away from me.

Classes continued with a few weeks break interspersed to go out to real customers with qualified IBM personnel to apply what we had learned. Then back to more classes. Some were in Kansas City and others were in the regional office in Chicago. By then, Phyllis had gotten a job working as a home economist for Kansas City Power & Light and had something she enjoyed, keeping her busy while I was away and entrenched with IBM. Plus, between the two of us, we were making enough money to no longer be stretched like we had been ever since we had graduated from college.

Unlike my year at Phillips Petroleum, IBM encouraged me

to take days off to go home to Oklahoma for Christmas. Instead of an expensive turn-around airline flight, we rode the KCS train from Kansas City to Heavener (we still had access to our free railroad passes). It was a relaxing Christmas at home and turned out to be the last time we saw my grandfather, Jeff Thompson. He died on January 22, 1969, at age 82, just under a month after we had been there for Christmas. IBM had a policy of time off for funerals, so we went back to our hometown for the funeral.

During January, Phyllis had not been feeling well, couldn't wait to go to sleep when she got home from her KCP&L job, and we wondered what was wrong. She went to her doctor and, sure enough, we found out we were going to be parents for the first time — due date late September 1969. We had been thinking about buying our first home; having a new baby meant our apartment wasn't going to be big enough.

With the advantage of the GI Bill, we started looking for our first home and located the perfect home at 3506 West 78th Street in Prairie Village, Kansas. It was a three-bedroom, one bath brick home with a full basement and fenced back yard, at the end of a cul-de-sac, built in the 1950s. We had one minor problem, we needed both of our incomes to qualify for the GI Loan and Phyllis was starting to "show" from her pregnancy. When we went to apply for the loan, she cinched up her stomach and we made no mention of her condition. We got the loan, closed on it, and moved in during the early summer. Our biggest challenge was the house didn't have a refrigerator and we had to come up with money to buy one (did I say we were over the hump financially — not really). We got it (think it cost less than $300) and all was well.

Our long-time friend, Grace, who had gone to college with us in Pittsburg was now married and heading out to California and on to the Philippines with her Navy pilot husband who was deploying to Yankee Station off the coast of Vietnam. They had a dog they couldn't take with them, so she gave us our first dog of our own—a schnauzer named Ralph. We were quickly becoming the classic domesticated American Family—two working parents, a dog, and a baby on the way.

Sometime in late 1968 or early 1969, I decided to join an Army Reserve unit in Kansas City, Kansas. The Vietnam War had reached its peak, the country was turning against it, and I still felt the tinge of regret that I had gotten out of the Army after only two years on active duty. Thus, becoming a "weekend warrior" seemed like a good fit for me. Plus, it would help our Family income with Phyllis becoming a stay-at-home Mom.

The 89th Training Division had the mission, if ever called to active duty, to take over training troops in AIT (Advanced Individual Training), next class after Basic Training. The organization I joined was made up of instructors who would teach supply, clerical, and other non-combat jobs to Soldiers. We also had a Drill Sergeant Academy to teach young sergeants how to train new troops. That is where I ended up. I had been promoted to captain and was the only person in the unit who wore the Combat Infantryman Badge that was earned by an Infantryman in a combat zone. I stood out as being different from most of the other leaders who had never been to Vietnam and who, like most of the troops in the unit, had joined the reserves to stay out of Vietnam and full-time active duty.

I enjoyed the monthly weekend drills and the summer camps. When I showed up at an active-duty post for summer camp (Fort Leonard Wood, MO; Fort Polk, LA; Fort Ord, CA; Fort Benning, GA), I was treated better than the other reservists who were looked down on as draft dodgers by the regular Army cadre we worked with. My CIB (Combat Infantryman Badge) and 4th Infantry Division combat patch showed that I had been a real Soldier, not a weekend warrior. The monthly checks earned in the Reserves helped with our monthly expenses, a nice perk in addition to me getting to stay around the military. (Starting in the early 1990's, Reserve and National Guard units have been regularly called up to serve in combat zones during Operation Desert Storm and in Iraq, Afghanistan, and other hot spots around the world. They have proved their value wherever they go).

In January 1969, during the last days of the Lyndon Johnson administration, the US Government filed an anti-trust case against IBM. The case would go on for 13 years and be dismissed as being without merit in 1982 (the first days of the Reagan administration). However, that caused some significant changes in the way IBM did business.

On June 23, 1969, IBM made a major announcement—they unbundled. What does that mean? It means that after years of "sending the man with the machine" there was a lot of pressure from small competitors that IBM was being unfair. Thus, IBM decided to "unbundle" and start charging for support services provided by IBM systems engineers. The impact on me, a trainee who had been working at H.D. Lee Clothing Company (Lee jeans) was to pull me out of the customer office where I was getting great experience and bring me back into the branch office, wondering what to do. A lot of gnashing of teeth went on, both by IBM and by our customers who were used to IBM "sending the man with the machine" to them.

About this time, a new manager came into our IBM office, which had moved from 1400 Baltimore in downtown Kansas City to 301 East Armor in mid-town Kansas City. His name was Gary Swanson. I found out quickly that he had been a salesman in Kansas City, had been promoted to Detroit as a branch manager with the IBM Service Bureau Corporation, and was now coming back into the mainstream IBM as we were disengaging from the Service Bureau business. Unlike my current manager, Bob Arrington, a rather easy going and laid-back manager, Gary seemed to be full of fire and brimstone—"Go Sell Something!" we quickly learned was his favorite comment. I was moved to his new unit and told, "Babcock, you're going to be a new business salesman." What in the hell did that mean to me, I wondered? I would find out early in 1970.

July 20, 1969, my brother, Jim, a Delta pilot, flew to Kansas City and sat with us all that day and night as we watched the moon landing. The next day he flew back to his home in Miami. We had no idea at that time that it would be the last time we would see him walk.

July 30, 1969, IBM scheduled a major customer announcement event for small customers from the Kansas City area. Almost all our trainees, especially those of us who were going to be marketing reps, were thrown into the preparation for this major announcement. We were quickly trained on this funny looking new system that IBM was going to announce—the System/3. It was a miniature size of the larger IBM System/360, didn't require the special air conditioning and raised floor for cabling of that system, and had a funny looking new punched card—with 96 characters in a card about a third the size of the long-time traditional 80 column IBM punched card.

The IBMers who handled our large customers, Hallmark Cards, H.D. Lee, the big banks, manufacturers, and many others, looked at this new system and smirked. We who were to introduce it thought it was cool. We scheduled a full week of several times a day customer events, with we trainees being the designated demonstrators. I had the duty of demonstrating the card sorter—with the little 96-column card. It was fun to become a showman. You could wad up that little card, smooth it out, and run it through the sorter and it worked—that wasn't the case with the older and industry standard 80-column card sorter, it would jam.

Our customers loved it; our new business salesmen who were already on quota made a killing selling the new systems—they sold like popcorn. We trainees suddenly thought it was really going to be cool selling this system when we went on quota as an official IBM Marketing Representative on January 1, 1970.

In the meantime, life was going to get memorable, both bad and good, for the Babcock Family. On September 23, 1969, my Delta airline pilot brother Jim, had a motorcycle wreck while taking a fellow pilot fishing in the Florida Everglades. Jim severed his spinal cord and was left in the Everglades, unable to move, while his fellow pilot went for help. After several hours of Jim laying there helpless, knowing alligators might show up at any time, a rescue helicopter came in to pick him up and take him to the hospital. My parents received the call late that night, called his brothers immediately, and we started to worry and wait. Would he survive, would he recover, would he die? It was one of the toughest times of my life. My brother Bill was the first one to get down to see him (Jim had gotten a divorce a few months before his accident and was alone), my mother flew down a day or two later.

Bob (me) was sitting in despair in the IBM office, unable to focus on anything. I couldn't go to see Jim because Phyllis was within days, if not hours, of giving birth to our first child. My priority was to be there for that.

Early in the morning of September 25, Phyllis woke me (I hadn't slept much the night before) and told me she was in labor. I didn't respond, was too worn out. She finally got my attention and I bolted up. By 8:00 AM we had gotten in touch with the doctor, he told us to come to the hospital and at 2:17 PM on

September 25, 1969, the most beautiful baby girl I have ever seen in my life was born—Kristen DeAnn Babcock. Those were the days when fathers were not allowed into the delivery room. I stood there with my nose up against the door but was not allowed to go any further.

We had called Phyllis' parents (Dale and Pauline) before we headed to the hospital, and they were on the road from Oklahoma to Kansas City to see their new granddaughter. I don't recall when they arrived, but it wasn't too long after Kristen was born (she will always be Kristen to me—to herself and most of her friends over the years, she is Krissie).

A few days later, don't remember how long it was, Phyllis and Kristen were released from the hospital, and I drove them home—never drove so carefully with this new bundle of joy in the back seat. I settled them in for the night, showed Pauline and Dale where everything was, and the next day I boarded a Delta flight from Kansas City to Miami to see Jim. In those days, with the Vietnam War in full swing, military personnel in uniform could fly for 50% off full fare. I was in the Army Reserves by then and stopped by my Army Reserve Center and got them to cut emergency orders for me to fly to Miami.

As I boarded the Delta flight, the flight attendant at the door saw my name tag with BABCOCK on it. She asked, "Are you any relation to Jim Babcock, a Delta pilot?" I confirmed I was, that he was my brother, and I was on my way to go see him. Information about his accident had quickly spread through the Delta family (back then they were as employee focused as IBM was). Once she knew my connection, my seat in the coach section was no longer good enough for me and she seated me in the first-class section.

On the flight to Miami, don't recall if we stopped in Atlanta or went nonstop to Miami, they kept the free drinks coming my way. I was drinking the small bottles of Scotch. As the plane was about to land, the flight attendant (we called them stewardesses back then) brought me a "burp bag" full of those small Scotch bottles. I was feeling no pain as I got off the plane.

My dad had gotten down there by that time, taking time off from his railroad job, and picked me up at the airport. We went straight to Baptist Memorial Hospital to see Jim. I had no idea what I was walking in to, but he was my brother; I was ready for it.

Jim was on a circular bed, in traction. Periodically they moved the bed from flat with him looking up at the ceiling to partially tilted to over with him facing the floor, strapped into the bed so he wouldn't move. It was a tough thing for me to see but I held my emotions. The rule was that someone could stay with him ten minutes out of every hour. Jim, being as much a salesman as I have become over the years, never let the truth get in the way of him getting what he wanted. He told the medical staff, "This is my brother Bob, he is going to ship out to Vietnam early next week, so I want him to stay with me as long as you will let him." They went for his story—hook, line, and sinker—and I had free run of the intensive care unit day and night while I was there, even though I didn't wear my uniform again until my flight home.

Long story short for now—Jim improved, never walked again, maintained a positive attitude until the day he died, spent a year or so in the Memphis VA Hospital (which had a specialty in working with quadriplegics), and then moved back to Miami where he lived with live-in help until he died on February 22, 1995. I will talk more about Jim as I move through my memoirs, but this summarizes it for now—he was an inspiration to me and everyone who met him. Never negative, always positive, the person to call if you're feeling down.

One short Jim story for now. He always took pride in his mental ability, which was outstanding. Ben Bruton, one of the IBM marketing managers in Kansas City, had a sign in his office which had EGBAR on it. In a sales meeting one morning, he brought his sign in, gave a very positive talk, and explained that EGBAR means Everything's Going to Be All Right. I engraved that on a piece of plastic, sent it to Jim and told him to guess what it meant. After a week of him calling me with a wrong guess, I finally told him. From that day until he died, he always had an EGBAR sign on the wheelchair he rode on for the last 25 years of his life.

After about a week in Miami, I headed back to Kansas City and Phyllis, Kristen, and IBM work. I continued to work as a trainee helping to demonstrate and sell the System/3.

In early December, I flew out to San Jose, California to my final class—Sales School. I believe it lasted two weeks where we had to give tough practice sales calls every day, pass them, and learn the final things IBM wanted to teach us. As Christmas and the New Year ended the busy and emotional year of 1969, I was prepared to start the next phase of my life—an IBM New Business Marketing Representative (salesman). No longer was I earning my full salary. I was paid 50% of what I had been making and the other 50%, and more, came from my ability to sell. Phyllis did not go back to KCP&L after Kristen was born (we had agreed to that a long time before) so I was the sole bread winner as we went into 1970. Phyllis was a full-time mother.

IBM New Account Salesman—1970 to 1974

January 1, 1970—Oh my God…I am a salesman being paid half my salary—the rest had to be earned on commission. If memory serves me right, we had a three-month recoverable draw where we continued to receive our full salary, but once we got beyond that, the draw would be deducted from our earnings, and we had to sell to make money.

As you would expect, IBM managers don't give the best territories to a rookie salesman, those go to the veteran salesmen (back then, they were virtually all salesmen, not women). I was assigned zip code 64050, Independence, Missouri. The best thing in that territory was former President Harry Truman, who I frequently saw on his daily walk, accompanied by his Secret Service agent. Also in my territory was the Truman Presidential Library. Neither former President Truman nor his Library were much of a candidate to buy an IBM computer. Beyond that, it was a lot of nothing in the way of businesses, with a few business parks that had some potential.

I also had Lees' Summit, Raytown, Blue Springs, and a sprinkling of other zip codes surrounding the eastern edge of metro Kansas City. Not any of my first territory was the cream of the crop of the metropolitan Kansas City territory. It was mine and I had to make a living selling there, so it was time to get to work.

January is cold in Kansas City and going door to door calling on businesses is cold and hard work. Gary Swanson, my boss, told each of us New Business Marketing Reps (salesmen) that we had to make 25 prospect calls a week—no excuses. To say I was uncomfortable doing that was an understatement. The situation was, I was a 26-year-old rookie salesman calling on self-made business executives, trying to convince them to get into the computer age and buy a computer from me (really from IBM). I had the confidence of a gnat.

After spinning my wheels with dismal prospect calls during most of January, I finally admitted to Gary that I was lost and needed his help. We scheduled a day to make prospect calls. I marveled at how comfortable and confident he was as we called on a half dozen or more customer presidents that first day working my territory. Among the calls we made was on the president of Summit Lumber Company in Lees Summit, Missouri. I forget the president's name, but he quickly bought into the ideas we (Gary) brought to him. As we left his office and walked back to my car, Gary said, "Okay, Babcock, now sell that—he is ready to buy."

Sure enough, Summit Lumber Company became my first new account as an IBM salesman. I came into the office with the signed contract, a big smile on my face, gave it to Gary and he came out of his office and rang the bell (in those days, most IBM new business managers had a bell hanging outside their office door which they rang every time somebody brought in a new account). More importantly, the administration manager immediately wrote a $300 new account bonus check and gave it to me. The pressure eased—$190 of that went to my house payment and the rest of it could pay other expenses.

A vivid memory from that first year as a new business salesman…On a cold February day in 1970, I was in Blue Springs, Missouri in a business park that my prospect list said had potential, but I'd never been to before. It was a typical small business park with a single road going into it with businesses lining both sides of the street, up to a dead-end where you had to turn around and head back out. I decided I would work the left side of the street first, get to the end and come back down the other side of the street, making prospect calls on each business.

I was dressed in my pinstriped IBM business suit, white shirt, and tie, and went into each of the businesses, talked to the receptionist and asked to talk to the president of the company. Sometimes she would send me back to talk to him, I'd make my sales pitch, he most likely would listen and then dismiss me with,

"We're too small, we can't afford a computer." Seldom were they dressed in a suit.

On other occasions, there would be truck drivers and other workers lounging in the lobby as I walked in. They looked at me with a smirk on their face, made a few wisecracks, and the receptionist might send me back in to see the president, but most likely blew me off with "he isn't in" or "he's busy" or "we already have a computer." After doing this from 9:00 AM to 11:30 AM, I was beat down and ready to call it quits and go to lunch. There was one company on the street I hadn't called on. My thought was, "I'll go ahead and call on this place and then I'll never have to set foot in this god-forsaken business park again." So, I walked in to Fike Metal Products.

I asked to talk to the president, told the receptionist that I wanted to talk to him about how he could be more profitable, and she sent me in to see Les Fike, Junior. I gave him my standard introductory sales pitch, he brightened up, and two hours later I walked out of there with a smile on my face and a lot of work to do following up on what we had talked about.

Long story short, I sold him a $600 services contract to prove a concept, and before the year was out, he had installed his first System/3 computer. When I left Kansas City at the end of 1974, they were still a very happy customer and likely still are today. Les, Junior was son of Les, Senior, the founder of the business. He had to argue with his father about what we were talking about, but I helped him prevail in the fight with his father, we helped them grow, and Fike Metal Products is a successful company still today.

My rookie year as a salesman was not stellar, but I made the Hundred Percent Club, which is what every IBM salesman is expected to do (if he wants to stay around). I made decent money, took care of my Family, and in March of 1971 Phyllis joined me for a ski trip in Aspen, CO after I had attended my first Hundred Percent Club, in Denver. I can proudly say that was the first of a string of never missing making the Hundred Percent Club during my IBM career of 34 years.

The next year, 1971, I was getting smarter and more confident. Gary Swanson continued to push all of us to sell more and more ("Babcock, nobody's going to buy anything in the IBM office, go out and sell something.") When we salesmen met to go out to lunch together, Gary was the first to say, "None of you are going to buy anything—take a customer to lunch, not each other." As I continue to write, you will see why I still today call Gary Swanson my mentor and friend. I learned more about selling from Gary than anyone else I ever worked with or for. I also earned my second Hundred Percent Club pin in 1971.

In 1972, all the good things seemed to fall into place. By June, I had attained my annual quota, made a lot of money, and was sitting on top of the world, and getting very confident. At one of the new accounts where I had sold a System/3 Model 6, the Systems Engineer assigned to install it left IBM and left the customer and me high and dry. Since I was already in the Hundred Percent Club for 1972, I decided to handle the installation myself (remember from early in my IBM trainee days, I was a decent technical guy). Dumb move...when you are working all day and night making a customer's system work, you aren't generating more new prospects and selling more current year business.

I also took my eye off my IBM target when a fellow salesman, John Rockeman, and I started a side business—Bo-Rock Trophies and Engraving. As I have written earlier, my Family had been in the trophy and engraving business since I was in high school so John and I decided to become partners, buy an engraving machine, and make some extra money selling trophies and engraving. It was a fun business, which I did most of the work in since I had been engraving since I was in college and John was a novice. It was a fun side business but did nothing to keep me focused on my primary responsibility—selling computers and solutions to IBM customers. Plus, I was still a Captain in the Army Reserves, enjoying that one weekend a month staying current on my love of the Army.

(On a personal side note, John Rockeman died on December 30, 2021. I was unaware he had been fighting COPD for two plus years. My note to you readers, if you have a best friend you haven't seen or talked to in a long time, give him/her a call or go see him/her before it is too late. I am sick that John and I went so long without seeing each other—now it is too late.)

At the same time this was going on, Phyllis and I had decided to buy a new house to replace our starter home. My confidence was strong. It hadn't hit me yet that I was headed for a crash in 1973. I ended the year with my third consecutive Hundred Percent Club, attended the Hundred Percent Club in Los Angeles where our Kansas City IBM branch office was named top new account unit of the year. All that was great—but I wasn't ready for the almost tragic year that lay ahead of me in 1973.

A salesman is a man who sells. That is what Gary Swanson always impressed on those who worked for him. In the last half of 1972, I rested on my excellent success in the first half of 1972, wasted my time doing the job of a systems engineer and starting my Bo-Rock business, and entered 1973 with an empty backlog, not only of customer orders but also of hot prospects. I was starting the year in no better position than when I was a raw rookie in 1970.

To say 1973 was a dismal year for me would be an understatement. I struggled, lost confidence, and was on the road to failure. In May, we found out Phyllis was pregnant with our second child and the pressure continued to build on me. By mid-August, I had made my mind up that I wasn't going to make my quota in 1973, would write the year off, and start building for a strong 1974. I left for two weeks of Army summer camp at Fort Ord, California, got my mind off IBM, and accepted that 1973 was not my year.

When I got back after summer camp, Gary gave me a "Blue Bird"—an order that came in unexpectedly, made me some money, and started to bring me out of my failure mind set. Gary also brought in one of IBM's legendary successful sales managers, now working in headquarters, to spend a couple of days helping me try to generate new potential. He spent two days making prospect calls with me. Grant Cornwell even went home with me for dinner between the two days to meet Phyllis and Kristen and told me to give him some time alone with Phyllis. He told her ways to help build my confidence back up and showed me that I had people who believed in me more than I believed in myself. He also pointed out that we should say a prayer before we had dinner—we needed to teach Kristen at her young age the importance of prayer (a smart man—not many like him these days).

On December 31, 1973, I got a new account order from a company in Independence, Missouri which allowed me to fall over the Hundred Percent Club line and not break my string of successful quota years. I went out for more than a few drinks with my fellow sales reps. When I made it safely home, although not entirely sober, I walked into a room where Phyllis' mother and daddy and her teetotaler Southern Baptist aunt and uncle were sitting, visiting us after Christmas.

I had called her before I went out for drinks, told her I had made the Hundred Percent Club, so she wasn't surprised or upset when I came in late and less than sober. She motioned me to go on upstairs, which I did. The next morning, I heard nothing from anyone about my condition the previous evening. Phyllis had explained it and they understood. My toughest IBM year thus far had ended without being a total failure.

As I entered 1974, my confidence was intact again, my backlog was strong, my territory had improved with some more lucrative zip codes. Also, on January 1, 1974, IBM announced the creation of the General Systems Division, a new sales division that focused only on small and medium businesses. In the past, IBM only had one sales organization that handled the largest to the smallest customers. As you would expect, often the smaller customers didn't get as much focus as the large ones did.

The new president of the General Systems Division (GSD) was Jack Rodgers. He was told by IBM corporate executives in New York to find a place outside the northeastern United States and establish a headquarters operation. GSD was to be a combined manufacturing, research, and sales division, unusual in those days of IBM when those functions were normally in separate divisions under different leadership.

Kansas City GSD was designated as Branch Office #G66, Gary Swanson was promoted to become our branch manager. Don Reynolds came in under Gary to become my immediate boss (but I basically ignored Don and continued to work closely with Gary when I needed management help). Lew Gray, a rising star in IBM was Gary's boss, Regional Manager of the Southwest Marketing Region, located in Dallas, Texas. All of we salesmen who were ready for moving forward in our careers were happy to see Dallas as a promotions path, rather than Chicago as it had been under the old organization when we were part of Data Processing Division (DPD). Jack Rodgers had selected Atlanta as the national headquarters for GSD and was bringing IBMers in from all over the country to build his team in Atlanta.

With this new focus on the smaller customer set that I had

always worked with and with my promotion path appearing to be to Dallas or Atlanta, I was ready to have a great year and use that as a springboard to move forward in my IBM career. The year started great, on February 4, 1974, Phyllis and I were blessed with the birth of Robert Owen Babcock II, our second child. 1974 was the year for me to sell a lot, leave the sales territory, and go into a staff position so I could then become an IBM manager.

One day over lunch as Gary and I were discussing my future, he told me, "Bob, I don't think you are tough enough to be an IBM marketing (sales) manager. You are too nice, and you never make a customer mad. I've never had a customer complaint about you in all the years you've worked for me." I was shocked but couldn't really argue with him. We agreed that maybe instead of going to the regional staff in Dallas where the next step was always to a sales manager's job somewhere in the region, I probably should consider going to Atlanta to the General Systems Division headquarters where I could be exposed to opportunities other than as a territory sales manager.

I had a solid sales year from start to finish and while I was at my Army Reserve summer camp at Fort Benning, Georgia, Gary set me up to drive to Atlanta to meet with the industry marketing manager of the new General Systems Division (GSD). (As a side note, that was the only time in all my time associated with the Army that I went AWOL (Absent Without Leave). And sure enough, I was called on by name in the class I was supposed to have been in that day at Fort Benning. A fellow officer covered for me; said I was sick).

I must have made a good impression at that Atlanta IBM interview because as 1974 ended, I was leaving my territory salesman job and headed to the bigger picture of GSD headquarters in Atlanta. I had my fifth consecutive Hundred Percent Club pin securely pinned on the lapel of my suit.

IBM Industry Marketing Staff Job
Atlanta, 1975 to 1976

I flew to Atlanta for my final interview in early December 1974, was offered the job to be effective as of January 1, 1975. Exactly what job I would have on the Industry Marketing team had not been determined yet, but I was ready for it. For five years I had sold to virtually all industries in my geographic territory. I knew manufacturing, distribution, motor freight, hospitals, lumber companies, associations, and the list went on and on. The only two industries I had not sold to were banking and government.

Yep, you guessed it. On my first day at work, my manager, Wes Guebert, said, "Bob, I'm assigning you to work with Hammond Satterfield as the second man on the GSD banking team." My heart sank—the only thing I knew about banking was how to write a check. I sat down with Hammond, explained my lack of experience, and he quickly assured me he would help me learn it.

As I was announced in a nationwide support document as being part of the GSD banking team, along with my phone number for field salesmen to call for help, I started receiving calls. My stomach churned each time the phone rang. I would sit and listen to their question, take copious notes, and tell the caller I'd get back to him (many more men than women salesmen in those days). As soon as Hammond was off the phone on the almost continuous calls he was on, I would walk across the hall to his office, explain to the best of my ability the question I barely understood, and he'd give me an answer, and try to teach me the meaning of the answer.

On one of my first calls, the rep wanted to know where he could get some good DDA software for his customer. I was so unaware of the terminology, my first question to Hammond was, "What in the hell does DDA stand for?" He looked at me in shock and realized how little I knew about banking. "Bob, DDA is Demand Deposit Accounting—check processing—the most basic job a bank does."

Somewhere along the way, I had met an IBM salesman in Topeka, Kansas who sold to banks and we had become friends. I called him and asked if I could visit his bank customer and learn what banking was all about. He arranged it, I flew to Kansas City, drove to Topeka, and worked for a week in the Topeka bank. I sorted checks on the night shift, sat with a teller handling her daily activities, sat with a loan officer, and met with the president of the bank to get his perspective. It was probably the most beneficial and smartest thing I did, which taught me to not be afraid to ask for help.

The next week, I answered the phone with much more confidence and had fewer questions I had to ask Hammond. I did get a question I thought I knew the answer for but wanted his confirmation. I walked across the hall to his office, told him the situation, and he gave me an answer. The answer didn't agree with what I had experienced in Topeka the week before, so I told him I thought he was wrong. He stopped cold, stared at me with a big smile on his face, and said, "Son of a gun, the boy has grown up and can carry his own weight." From that day forward, my confidence continued to build, and community banks became my favorite segment of my entire IBM career, to include getting a significant promotion where I got back into leading IBM's community banking efforts fifteen years later.

One of the jobs assigned to me was to lead the project for making the IBM 1255 check reader/sorter work with the newly announced IBM System/34. As I said above, check processing was the biggest job of a bank back then and the System/34 was not viable in that segment without check reading and sorting capability. The 1255 was built in our Endicott, New York plant and the System/34 was built in Rochester, Minnesota. My job was to work with both IBM development and manufacturing teams and not take "no" for an answer.

I burned the phone lines up talking to people in both plants and was making little progress. One day Wes Guebert came into my office and said, "Bob, I want you to go to Rochester for a week." My obvious response was, "Okay, but why?" He said, "Just roam around and get to know the people." Having never worked at the corporate level of getting things done, I thought that was a total waste of money, but I did as I was told and flew to Rochester.

It turned out to be a great lesson that I would use the rest of my life. Once you sit and talk with someone, see the pictures and trinkets in their office, have lunch with them and a beer after work, he or she becomes a person and not just an unknown voice at the end of a phone line. You learn about his or her Family, their hobbies, their personality…invaluable insight that serves you well as long as you work with them. The expense of a plane ticket and hotel room was nothing in comparison to the value of getting the check reader problem solved in months rather than years. (In my future IBM manager jobs, I often used this same technique that I learned from Wes with the people who worked for me).

The first month we lived in the northern suburbs of Atlanta, it seemed to rain every day. I came home from work one day and five-year-old Kristen said, "Daddy, doesn't anyone live in Atlanta, Georgia but us?" It broke my heart. We had pulled her away from the weekly play group she was in with friends in Kansas City, and she was stuck in the house all day with her mother and one-year-old brother. A few days later, the weather broke, it became an unusually warm February and the three girls who lived next door to us, Katie, Amy, Beth, came outside to play. Kristen's life changed. She became inseparable from those three girls and loved living in Atlanta.

A quick side story on that warm February in 1975. Hammond and I scheduled a trip to go to Endicott, New York to meet with the check reader/sorter developers. It had been about 75 degrees for a couple of weeks in Atlanta and Hammond forgot to take a warm coat with him on the trip—just his normal IBM business suit. Fortunately for me, I took a heavy coat. We got off the plane in New York and it was in the 20s. Hammond, always a southern boy, complained the whole time we were in New York about how cold he was.

My staff job in GSD was a great learning time. It showed me how smart Gary Swanson was in sending me to a job where I broadened my outlook of IBM career opportunities rather than going to Dallas to a regional sales support job and not learning the development side of IBM's business.

After working hard in 1975 with the developers in Endicott and Rochester and getting some high-level IBM executives involved to help knock down internal barriers, we announced the connection of the IBM System/34 with our 1255 check reader/sorter at the American Bankers Association convention in Washington, DC in 1976. I was project manager and dealt with everything from photo shoots to making promotional materials to sitting in a smoke-filled room with product people who badgered me with questions that I couldn't answer; but took as my job to find the answers and get back to them.

While doing the check project, I also visited with lots of bankers around the country, became a comfortable expert on answering questions about community banks and our solutions, and handled a good number of speaking opportunities to groups of bankers. I also learned how to be the only guy in one of the smoke-filled rooms with IBM development people who would rather do anything than work on the project I was representing, standing my ground against strong internal opposition, and making sure they did it anyway.

As the end of my second year on the banking support team came to an end, I knew I wanted to get back into the field sales force as a marketing (sales) manager. As always, you need sponsorship to make that happen. Both Wes Guebert, my immediate boss, and Val Perry, my second-line manager, were strong supporters. Since Gary Swanson, the boss I had worked for the longest had earned the national branch of the year recognition in Kansas City in 1975, his endorsement was also very important. Virtually everyone in GSD knew Gary Swanson. His seal of approval was more valuable than what anyone else said about me.

I called Gary and asked if he'd support me for a marketing manager's job. There was a long silence, then he said, "Babcock, do you remember that conversation we had over lunch your last year in Kansas City?" I acknowledged I did and immediately went into sell mode and outlined for him the battles I had won against internal naysayers the past two years, how I had stayed current in calling on customers, and helping IBM salesmen. After listening a few minutes, he came back with what I wanted to hear, "Yes, put me on your list of managers who endorse you."

Opportunities started to come my way. One was in Los Angeles. I looked at the cost of living in California, how far away it was from my home in middle America, and immediately said

I wasn't interested. I was hoping to line up a sales manager's job in Texas, Oklahoma, or other parts of the Southwest Region. I knew going back to Kansas City to my old branch was not an option, but anywhere in the general vicinity was my first choice, as it was for Phyllis.

Val Perry continued to heap praise on me and in an executive interview told me I was the best guy he had on his team, and I had a strong future ahead of me. Then one day he told me that the branch manager from Louisville was going to be in Atlanta on Friday and he wanted me to talk to him. Being naïve to the IBM power structure and egos, I simply went into the interview with Bob Coates as an informational meeting. He told me about his branch covering three locations, Louisville, Lexington, and Evansville, and that the Evansville marketing manager job was coming open the first of the year. I had no idea where Evansville was, thought he meant Evanston, north side of Chicago. After the meeting, I went back to my office and resumed my work. A little later, I came out of my office and passed Val in the hall — smiled with my normal "Hello, Val" and he glared at me and grunted, "Hello" and kept walking. I was shocked, but my naivete still blinded me to what his problem was.

My parents were at our home that night as they took their annual trip to Miami to spend the winter with my brother Jim. As we were eating supper, the phone rang. It was Wes Guebert. He said, "Babcock, you are in trouble. Val said Bob Coates told him you weren't interested in the opportunity that had been presented to you. As far as Val is concerned, you are in the penalty box and hell will freeze over before you get promoted." I explained to Wes that he knew I had another interview, in Texas, to be set up the following week, and I'd rather go there than to Evansville. He came back with, "Bob, you don't understand. You do what Val wants or you are dead in the water. There is nothing

I can do to change that. I suggest you rethink it, get in touch with Bob Coates, and sell him on why you want that job."

I hung up the phone, went back to the dinner table and absolutely exploded with my rage, frustration, and disappointment. Phyllis and my parents listened and simply said, "What are you going to do?" I replied, "Guess I need to figure out how to sell myself to Bob Coates."

With that, I called Jack Flynn, the Lexington marketing manager who had worked on our industry marketing team until he was promoted the year before. He agreed to call Coates and help smooth things over. It was a long and highly frustrating weekend as I sweated whether I had shot myself in the foot or not. On Monday, I called Bob Coates and he agreed to talk to me again and told me to fly to Evansville where we would meet. I also would talk to Jerry Barton, the manager who would be leaving for another job at the first of the year.

Net is—Bob Coates offered me the job, I accepted, Jerry Barton and I talked about the territory, the customers, the opportunity, the people on my new team, and I called Phyllis and said, "We're moving to Evansville." I stayed over another day and went around town with a realtor showing me the various places we might buy for homes. I was underwhelmed with what I saw. But, like it or not, the next phase of our lives was about to begin.

**Miscellaneous Other Memories
from my first Atlanta years**

1975 and 1976 were the bicentennial years for the US Army (1975) and our country (1976). On June 14, 1975, the Army's 200th birthday, Phyllis and I drove with Kristen and Rob to Fort Benning, Georgia, our first home during our Army years.

A big ceremony was planned, President Ford would be there, and we would be in attendance for the primary celebration of the Army's 200th birthday. There were all kinds of static displays and demonstrations. At one point, we were along the rope line outside Building 4, the headquarters of Fort Benning, watching the troops pass in review for President Ford. When that was finished, President Ford headed our way and started working the rope line. Before I knew it, he was right in front of us, and Phyllis and I both shook his hand. I will never forget the sweat dripping down his face on that hot June day.

Now I could say that I had seen two American presidents in person — Harry Truman regularly when I had Independence, Missouri as my sales territory and now Gerald Ford. A year earlier, on 8 August 1974, Phyllis and I had been celebrating our 10th anniversary on the Plaza in Kansas City when Richard Nixon's resignation was announced, and Gerald Ford became our President. Unknown to me until last year, Ed DeVos, one of my Deeds Publishing authors who has become a great friend, was the commander of one of the companies of Infantry Soldiers who passed in review for President Ford that day at Fort Benning. Small world.

The following year, on July 4, 1976, Phyllis and I spent most of the morning into early afternoon with my brother Joe and his wife, Mona, at the hospital in Fort Smith, Arkansas, where she gave birth to Michael Babcock, a true bi-centennial baby.

*****

Getting promoted in most companies means you make more money. Such was not the case when you went from an IBM commissioned sales position to a stepping-stone headquarters staff job. Since I was a successful salesman (or I wouldn't have been promoted), I was making well over what I would have made on a straight salary. In 1974 dollars, I made about $36,000 my last year on quota, plus my car expenses brought me in some more pocket money each week. I was also making another $200 or so each month as a Captain in the Army Reserves by attending meetings one weekend a month. Add my income from Bo-Rock Trophies and Engraving and we were comfortable. (Young people reading this—that was excellent money back then.)

Fast forward to 1975 in Atlanta, I was on a straight salary of $24,000 a year, no commission, no car expense (but did get actual travel expenses when I flew somewhere). I was no longer drawing Army Reserve money, Bo-Rock Engraving had moved away from our customers in Kansas City, and our house payment and other expenses were higher in Atlanta than Kansas City. Plus, we were still in agreement that Phyllis would be a stay-at-home mom.

Everyone else moving from IBM sales to first staff job went through this so I knew not to complain, suck it up, and my opportunity to increase my income would come as soon as I could successfully navigate my first staff job and move up the ladder.

In my exit interview with Wes Guebert, he appraised me a "1", heaped praise on me for the work I had done for him and told him I had a great future in IBM. He said, "Bob, you will breeze through Evansville, get a divorce, and then move on up in the business." I was shocked with that comment—more than shocked. There was no way I would ever divorce Phyllis; we had been together since junior high school and made it through Vietnam together. He was crazy as hell, and I told him that. Three years later, Phyllis and I were divorced. That takes me to the next phase of my life's experiences.

First IBM Manager Job
Evansville, 1977 to 1981

I don't remember precisely when I first met my new IBM team in Evansville. It could have been at a branch office kickoff meeting to start the year in Louisville, or it could have been later in January 1977 when Jerry Barton had already left, and I was the new guy on the block. I do remember the first team meeting I held.

Including salesmen, systems engineers, and administrators, we had 15 employees working for me in Evansville. I'm sure I told them about my background and expectations and how happy I was to be there, blah, blah, blah...What I really remember is when I threw the meeting open to the group and asked them what was on their mind and what their complaints were. By far their number one complaint was—they couldn't get office supplies.

The Evansville IBM office had four distinct entities working from the building. The largest group and the landlord for the building was the Office Products Division (OPD) branch office, with Russ Rose as the newly arrived branch manager. His administration manager was George Hanna. George was the keeper of the budget for supplies and was a tightwad.

The other three tenants were the General Systems Division (GSD) marketing unit that I now led, with my immediate boss, Bob Coates, residing in Louisville, two hours' drive, and a time zone away. The Data Processing Division (DPD) was slightly smaller in number of personnel and was led by Chuck Bauer who reported into the Nashville DPD branch office. (As was universally the case in IBM, DPD thought they were big shots and the rest of us were nothing in comparison. That was understandable since they had the largest IBM customers and GSD now focused on small and medium sized computer customers. OPD sold typewriters, copiers, and other office products across all customers). The fourth entity in the building was the Field Engineering Division (FED) which were the people who maintained the computers at the sites of the customers.

As I listened to a laundry list of the types of office supplies that George wouldn't give to our people, I decided that was the first way I was going to make a mark on my team. After the meeting, I put together a list of office supplies—everything from a stapler to paper clips to pencils, pens, the whole list of anything needed in any office. I had Betty Fellows, my secretary, type the list up, put a copy in each person's mailbox, and gave them 24 hours to return it to me with what they needed, along with their name on the paper. Naturally, everyone responded on time to the first thing their new boss asked them.

I compiled all the requests into one summary list and walked into George's office, formally introduced myself (we had seen each other in the office but never were officially introduced before then) and told him these were the office supplies we needed. He immediately said, "No way—I can't afford that." My calm response was, "George, you either buy these things through IBM supply channels where we get a better price, or I'll go to a local office supply place, pay full price, and have them bill it to IBM—you."

After leaving George's office, knowing his next stop would be to tell his boss, Russ Rose, what I was requesting, I stopped in Russ's office and explained the situation. Russ, like me, was first a salesman and knew it was little things like this that could show the team if their new manager was a good guy or not. With Russ also being relatively new, he understood. Thus, when George brought the list to Russ, George was told to buy the stuff—probably a total of $250 or less at 1977 prices for everything we needed.

A week or so later, all the supplies had arrived, I separated them into packages by individual, called a team meeting, and handed them their supplies. Previously, there had been one stapler shared by the whole team. Now, each person had his/her own stapler. I told them, "In your IBM career, you are authorized one stapler—never a second one. Thus, I recommend you put your name on your stapler so it doesn't get away from you." (That wasn't an IBM rule, it was a Bob Babcock rule. I used it again later in Kansas City when I got similar complaints after taking on a second line manager job there. Today in my office, I have a stapler with Bruce Matter's name scratched on it. He was promoted from KC and didn't take his stapler with him, so I claimed it as my own).

From that first little thing I did, I could tell the team thought I was an alright kind of guy.

The Evansville IBM GSD location was responsible for southwestern Indiana, southeastern Illinois, and the western third of Kentucky. Not a lot of our competitors could afford to put many people into this basically remote territory, so our competition was relatively light compared to big metropolitan areas. We had a mixture of strong experienced sales reps along with some new hires who had finished training and were becoming first year IBM sales reps.

IBM seemed to always begin each year with a fast start contest. Whatever it was that year, we hit our stride and were firing on all cylinders. IBM was also big at posting scoreboards, by manager name, for all to see. 1977 scoreboards had this new guy's name—Bob Babcock, Evansville—either at the top or one or two places below first place from January through the end of the year. Financially, coming off a salary job in my Atlanta staff job and going to a lucrative quota job, I was making more money than I'd ever made in my life. For the first time, by about May or June, Phyllis and I had bought everything we wanted and still had money left over—a totally new experience, which we liked.

Nationally, we were also ranked on a scoreboard from top to bottom; they put out a report of how each sales unit was doing compared to their annual quota. Again, Evansville was at or near the top. Our biggest competitor was a unit in Los Angeles who beat us, attaining their annual quota in August of that year—we were less than a week behind them making our annual quota.

One of my favorite first year manager's story...Doug Witham, a rookie salesman, was uncomfortable making cold customer calls, just as I had been back in 1970 as a rookie. Gary Swanson had made calls with me, so I volunteered to go with Doug making cold calls. We spent a full day making these calls, Doug learned a lot, and later became a real leader on our team and moved on to bigger and better things (I've lost track of Doug, would love to find him again). But the cold call that I'm writing about was with a contractor who needed a computer to keep track of his business. We were making progress in convincing him to come in and see a demo. He asked what it would cost for a System/34. We gave him the rental price, so much per month. He said, "Wait a minute, I don't rent anything. What does it cost to buy it up front?" Since IBM was focused on the rental business, not purchase then (we changed a year or two later), we gave him the standard spiel on why it was better to rent than buy a computer.

The prospect looked at both of us, then said, "What side does your dick lay on?" Doug and I looked at him and each other, stifling a laugh, looked down at our crotch, and each of us gave him an answer. He then said, "Move it to the other side." And he waited for us to do it. Then he said, "Now, it doesn't feel comfortable, does it?" He said, "That's why I don't want to rent a computer." We agreed with him, told him if he really wanted to purchase the system, we would sell it to him, and walked out the door.

As soon as we got out the door, we both burst out in laughter. Today I can't remember if he ever bought a computer from us or not (I think he did), but there was no question that was the funniest prospect call I ever made in my IBM career—and for Doug. Doug and I told that story many times over a beer with other IBMers.

During the spring and summer of 1979, Phyllis and I had an interesting American experience. Gary Swanson, my mentor, and boss in Kansas City, called in March or April and said, "Babcock, let's go to the Kentucky Derby this year." I told him, "Getting tickets this late will be impossible." His response, "We don't need tickets, we'll go into the general admissions section in the infield." And we did. It was a memorable day for Gary, Phyllis, and me. Spectacular Bid won the Derby, the infield and paddy experience were great, and none of us will ever forget that day.

Later in May, Phyllis and I drove to Indianapolis to watch the Indy 500. Our seats were in the north end of the track and the cars were just a blur as they whizzed by, but again I got to experience in person an American event that I had listened to on the radio during my growing up years. To round out the trifecta, we drove to Nashville in late summer and watched the Grand Old Opry—another American icon. Minnie Pearl was in her prime then. I don't remember what country singers performed that night, but it didn't matter. In three months, we had experienced three of America's annual iconic events, and all were within a two-hour drive of where we lived.

* * * * *

Business was good in Evansville. We were always solidly near the top of the performance charts, my boss left me alone to run my operation, and I was having more personal enjoyment than I'd ever had working. Our customers were happy, my finances were solid...but Evansville was not a place that welcomed Phyllis and me with open arms.

For many years, IBM managers had passed through and in about two years they moved on and the next IBM family came in. Thus, most people we ran into would basically say, "Welcome to Evansville, when are you leaving?" This was the beginning of the end for Phyllis and me as a married couple.

I was a workaholic, and our fundamental differences became more apparent under the stress of climbing the corporate ladder. Being a workaholic and providing well for your family was the expectation of our generation and I excelled at it. It wasn't unusual for me to tell Phyllia I would be home in an hour and as I was about to walk out the door, one of my people would say, "Hey boss, you have a minute?" And the next thing I knew, I was an hour or two late from when I said I'd be home and she and the kids had already eaten, they were getting ready for bed, and I would pull out more work to do on the dining room table. My priorities were screwed up, but I didn't see it then.

IBM seemed to always be in reorganization mode and my years in Evansville were no different. After very successful sales years in 1977 and 1978, I was looking for 1979 to be the year I would be moving on to my next job. Lynn Lynch, our regional manager, liked the work I was doing and wanted me to move to Detroit as a manager on the regional staff. That was typically a job you passed through in a year or a little more, and then went to a branch manager's job. As I looked at where the branches were in our region, every town left me cold—and I mean cold more ways than one. Remember, I'm an Okie (now transplanted to Georgia), enjoy early springs and warm weather, plus I have always loved the south much better than anything up north. Kansas City and Evansville were about as far north as I ever wanted to live.

When I turned down being considered for the job Lynch had in mind for me, I immediately became persona non grata to him (remember Val Perry's reaction when I showed no interest in the Evansville job). That didn't bother me too much. Val was once again a fan of mine and he said he would help me find a job back in Atlanta, which he did. The problem was…IBM put on a moving freeze in mid 1979 that lasted through 1981. Unknown to me and others, behind the scenes big organizational changes were being planned, thus the freeze on moving people.

As I sat frustrated in a job that I had mastered and could almost do in my sleep, things on the home front were not getting any better. Phyllis and I remained committed to Kristen and Rob and had good Family time with them. We shared many great memories of growing up in Heavener. I respect her as the mother of my two oldest children and am forever grateful for her support as a military spouse. It was many years later, after working closely with wives of Soldiers who were serving in combat in Iraq and Afghanistan that I realized the constant strain that Phyllis lived under, yet always supported me, when I was in Vietnam.

I continued to work long hours, she (rightfully) continued to be unhappy about the lives we were living, and I was getting more and more unhappy when I was home.

To net it out—as I've analyzed the situation, our biggest problems revolved around my constant focus on work while she stayed at home; she had become a liberal thinker with liberal values while I was more and more conservative; and we had our own worlds that we lived in. My work at IBM did give me positive feedback, and good financial return which we both benefitted from. I was working in a job I loved, and she was not where she wanted to be. Thankfully, she was a great mother, then and always, for Kristen and Rob. In the summer of 1980, I told her I wanted a divorce and moved into a small furnished apartment between where we lived and the IBM office.

This, of course, impacted both of us. Phyllis saw a need to do something to get prepared for going back to work, so she started working on her master's degree at the University of Evansville, which I was happy to pay for. She remained a very good mother to Kristen and Rob, and I made a point to have them spend at least one night in my apartment with me (what we now call the "roach ranch" as we look back at it—it was the worst place I'd ever lived).

I was so unhappy and spent so much time trying to figure out how to get out of Evansville that I simply went through the motions as an IBM manager. When the employee opinion survey results came out in mid-summer of 1980, what had always been an extremely positive opinion survey about me hit me between the eyes when one of the comments from one of my employees (don't know who) said, "Bob used to be a great manager, lately he isn't worth a damn (or words to that effect)." That hit me like a baseball bat. A bad employee opinion survey was typically a kiss of death for a manager wanting to move up in the business. Plus, we were having our first marginal sales year since I had arrived.

It was time for Bob Babcock to kick himself in the rear end and get back on track. I don't recall when our divorce was final, but I knew I needed to start planning a new life for myself and my career.

The last four months of each year are the best-selling season for IBM (at least it was back then, don't know how it is today). I called a fall kickoff meeting for my entire team on the Tuesday after Labor Day, 1980. I worked all weekend on making a splash and setting a new and positive course. My brain was 100% fixed on not missing my first ever Hundred Percent Club. I was in very early, sequestered myself in the meeting room with the door shut, and waited there until my team was all assembled out in the hall, wondering why the windows were covered, the door was locked, and I hadn't been seen in the office.

At the appointed time, I opened the door and told them to come in. I was dressed, not in my normal IBM pinstripe suit but in my full combat uniform from my Army days—jungle fatigues, boots, helmet, web gear. And I was in my role as an Army leader—pushing them verbally to get into the room, take a seat, and stay quiet. The looks on their faces was priceless.

I had maps on the wall, an operations order that I had projected on the screen from the overhead projector, and I started telling them about the new campaign we were starting—the attack on the HPC ridgeline. HPC, they all knew, stood for Hundred Percent Club. On the map and ridge line were smaller hills—called SRP, IRP, NA, AGU—IBM terminology for Sales Record Performance, Install Record Performance, New Accounts, Account Growth Units—all were part of the success formula for attaining the real objective—making the Hundred Percent Club.

I set objectives for everyone on how things would be changing, how we were going to monitor progress with a meeting early every Monday morning until we had made our annual objective. I told them we were not taking prisoners and nobody on the team would be allowed to under-perform. After about an hour of me being completely in my role as an Army leader, I dismissed them and walked out the door and went into my office.

I could see and hear the buzz of excitement I had put into my team. This was a different Bob than the one who had been moping around, not his normal self, for the past several months. After a half hour or so, I pulled a Gary Swanson (by then I had changed from my Army uniform to my IBM suit), came out of my office and announced in my booming voice, "Nobody's going to buy anything in here! Get out of the office and go sell something!" And I went back into my office while they packed up their briefcases and headed out the door.

I had on a flip chart the prospects they had given to me that were likely to close over the coming weeks and months. On the following Monday, I methodically went through the names of prospects and asked the salesmen to tell me precisely what he had done that week to get the order closed. If they hadn't called on anyone, I asked them why. I was tough—I didn't want excuses, just results.

That continued each Monday and orders started to flow in. I filled in my progress chart on the map, showing how close we were getting to each of our sub-objectives on the way to our overall objective. When a salesman made a big sale, I heaped praise on him (we had no female sales reps in our office at that time). If a prospect on the flip chart hadn't closed after a few weeks, I ceremoniously scratched it out and told the salesman I was tired of hearing about somebody that obviously wasn't going to buy anything—or that the salesman wasn't working to close. Everyone quickly understood that I was taking no prisoners and that I was as serious about making the Hundred Percent Club as a heart attack.

We progressed through September, October, and early November. I was out of the office frequently, going with salesmen to call on their customers and prospects. Things were looking better every week. Salesmen started making their own individual

Hundred Percent Club objective for the year and the team was moving toward the team objective. At a meeting in mid-November, I asked every member of the team—sales, systems engineer, administration—if they believed we could make our HPC objective by early December. To a person, they agreed we could do it.

Thus, I declared December 7, 1980, as VE Day—Victory in Evansville. For history buffs, they knew that December 7, 1941, thirty-nine years earlier was when the Japanese attacked Pearl Harbor, Hawaii and pulled the US into World War II. I wrote a letter to Sam Palmisano, our regional manager who had taken over from Lynn Lynch earlier in the year. I invited him to our sales meeting on December 7 to celebrate with us. I had talked to him on the phone and explained the importance of him being there. He quickly accepted the invitation.

Net is—Bob Babcock got back on track, and I brought my team with me. We finished 1980 strong. I still wanted to get out of Evansville but that still wasn't going to happen—not for another year.

*****

By now, I had a romantic relationship started with a lady in the IBM branch office. Knowing that was not acceptable, we kept it secret. One Saturday night early in 1981, we had gone to dinner at the Petroleum Club, which I was a member of, on the top floor of the Citizens National Bank building. Who walked in but Doug and Janie Witham, a salesman and systems engineer who worked for me. (They weren't married yet but were soon after that). I'm not sure who was the most shocked, them or us. Oh crap, I thought—the cat is out of the bag.

Sure enough, Doug went straight to Jay Lautzenheiser, the

systems engineering manager who worked for me, on Monday and told him what he had seen. Jay came to me at the end of the day and absolutely read me the riot act about how stupid I was. When I told him to bug off, it was none of his business, he picked up the phone and called Dan Black, our branch manager at the time, at his home in Louisville. I succeeded in telling Dan, with Jay listening, that it was neither one of their businesses and hung up and headed to my apartment. You can imagine how I was sweating bullets. As with most corporations, then and now, a manager dating an employee is frowned upon.

This is another time to net it out...Jan and I became engaged (I proposed to her at the Red Geranium restaurant in New Harmony, Indiana, thus you now know why we always have red geraniums growing in our yard) and were married on July 18, 1981. We had a reception in the back yard of Jan's parents' home on that hot July afternoon. My parents and Kristen and Rob were there, as was Jan's daughter, Stephanie, and Jan's parents and two brothers. Most, if not all, of our IBM GSD team were also there. The next phase of our life had started.

Jan had become a systems engineer trainee, was now working for Jay Lautzenheiser, and spent weeks at a time attending IBM classes in Atlanta while I was still managing the Evansville GSD location. Then, when she had completed her training, she became a key player in the announcement and selling of IBM's first venture into what later became the personal computer business, the IBM System/23 Datamaster.

With the eight plus years age difference between us, lots of people didn't think our marriage would last. We have proved them wrong. I'm proud to report that we celebrated our 40th wedding anniversary on July 18, 2021—with a week at the beach in Seaside, FL. Jan is my best friend, my sweetheart, my soulmate, the one I can count on 100% of the time, and the one who puts a smile on my face hundreds of times a day. Jan always has my back—and I always have hers, and we always will.

From this point forward in my memoir, Jan, without being mentioned very much, will be more than a main character—she's the person who has kept me going every day for 40+ years.

Second Kansas City IBM job
Regional Marketing Manager, Customer Center
1982 to 1984

Two years plus of waiting and wondering when I would leave Evansville and where I would go when I finally left came to a positive conclusion in January 1982. The major IBM reorganization was announced and implemented. DPD, GSD, OPD were reorganized into the National Accounts Division (NAD) with about 100 of IBM's biggest customers in that division. All our other customers were in the National Marketing Division (NMD). Both divisions had access to sell all of IBM's products—hardware, software, services. Lew Gray was promoted to president of NMD, with headquarters in Atlanta. Kansas City was the headquarters for the Missouri Valley Region—that was to become my home again and Jan's first time to live in Kansas City, or outside of Indiana.

Emotionally, from a Family point of view, it was going to be a tough move. I was leaving Kristen and Rob in Evansville and Jan was leaving her parents and lifelong friends and Family. Stephanie, Jan's daughter, was moving to Kansas City with us, taking her away from her Daddy. Phyllis had completed her Masters' Degree, was teaching in an Evansville high school, and was trying to decide what she wanted to do in her new life. By now I was committed to finish my career and retire from IBM sometime in the future, so I pushed these concerns to the back of my mind and looked forward to this new adventure. I did not know how high I would ultimately go in IBM, but at this point

I was still being given encouragement to keep working hard and climbing the IBM ladder.

I met Bill Falkenburg, the Director of Marketing for the Missouri Valley Region who would be my immediate boss. We hit it off well. He had heard my reputation in advance and our meeting was positive, so he basically told me to figure out what needed to be done and do it. He had Mike Welbaum as the regional leader of the technical side of the field force; Tom Wall, running the Office Systems support team; and Bob Babcock as the Marketing Support manager for computer systems. He had already hired three guys to work for me—Craig Minnich for large systems, Donn Atkins for small systems, and another one or two whose names escape me. Our job was to build the support team from scratch and help the branch offices be successful.

Jan got a job in the New Business branch office as a systems engineer with the plan to move over to a sales job as she gained more experience.

Having both gone through our divorces and effectively given up most of what we had built up financially over the years, we found ourselves looking for a new home in areas around the regional office that were less expensive than my manager counterparts who had come in from similar jobs to what I had in Evansville. That was fine, we found a new house we could afford, almost completed, less than a mile from the regional office. Jan picked the inside room colors, and we were set to start this new phase of our lives—glad to be back in our own home and not in a rental townhouse like we'd lived in in Evansville.

Soon after we moved into our new home and Stephanie started her new school, she asked if she could bring a friend home one afternoon. "Please, you'll love Jennifer—and she lives just a couple of blocks down the street from us." With us both working, that was not possible, we picked her up from after school care every day on our way home from work. We told her to ask her for the next Saturday, which worked out. Jennifer Brace's mother, Diane, walked her down to our house and Jan and Diane hit it off—in fact, now almost 40 years later, Jan and Di are best friends. They talk on the phone several times a week (we both talked to her tonight as I write this on Thanksgiving eve in 2021), and we've spent many visits with them at their home, our home, and a few times at the beach.

My job required a fair amount of travel. We supported branch offices in Missouri, Kansas, Oklahoma, and Arkansas. With the whole organization being in startup mode, we in the Region had to wear many hats to help the branch offices. There was no roadmap, we built it as we lived it.

During our first summer in Kansas City, Kristen and Rob spent most of the summer with us and Stephanie spent a good part of it back in Evansville with her dad. Phyllis was working on what she was going to do since we were no longer together. I was good with that and happy to have the kids with us.

I could look out our eighth-floor window in the high-rise in Corporate Woods and see Kristen and Rob playing in our backyard. Kristen was old enough to watch Rob while we worked, and I always found a way to get home around the lunch hour to touch base when I wasn't traveling. Jan took great care of them if I was out of town—we were quickly becoming a team.

After a successful year helping build the Missouri Valley Region marketing support team, I was chomping at the bit to get back into the branch office and into a commissioned manager's job again. As luck would have it, and IBM never leaving organizations the same for very long, the two Kansas City branch offices were consolidated at the beginning of 1983. Gary Swanson was the surviving branch manager. A new second line manager job was introduced to the branch—Branch Manager of Sales

Programs and Support. The branch manager whose job had gone away did not want the job, so Gary quickly selected me for the job, knowing I was ready to get back into a branch office.

My responsibility was to manage the New Business unit, all the Systems Engineering managers in the branch, and the Customer Center—a great job for me.

Before I could move into my new branch office job, I had one final responsibility to complete in my regional job. Donn Atkins and I had decided that we should have a New Business College in January to kick off 1983. All the sales reps from our region with new business responsibility would be flying to Atlanta, staying in the sales training apartments that IBM permanently leased, and we would run a week-long class.

The first couple of days went well and on Tuesday night, one of Atlanta's weather disasters that hit about twice a decade decided to pay us a visit. For people who had flown in from places that were used to snow in the winter, it was not a problem. But for the Atlanta IBM headquarters, it was a time to close the doors and stay home. That announcement was sent out via email (a fairly new thing then—IBM called our first internal email system PROFS), voicemail, and on the local Atlanta radio and TV stations (along with a long list of other business closings).

As Wednesday morning dawned, no snow or ice had fallen. It was cold but no problem, the sun was even peeking out a bit. I went in early and talked to the manager of the building where our classes were held and he animatedly said, "No way—this building is closed today! No exception!"

Never one to be deterred by a naysayer, I did what IBM had taught me throughout my career—call on the top man in the business. Thus, I called Lew Gray, the president of the National Marketing Division (and a guy I knew well), got through to him after talking to his secretary, and pleaded my case. I basically said, "Over 100 people from our region are sitting here ready to learn better ways to sell, and none of them are rookies in driving in the snow and ice (like so many Atlanta natives are)." Liking my aggressiveness, he said, "Okay, Bob, you can hold your classes—just promise me one thing. If a single flake of snow starts to fall, stop the class, and send everybody back to the IBM apartments. Do you understand?"

"Yes, Sir!" And I got the word back to the students standing by at the apartments and told them to come on to class. Classes started, the weather forecast kept sounding ominous, and I initiated Plan B (my Army experience taught me to always have an alternate plan). I called Donn Atkins and the other regional staff who were helping run the class into my temporary office and told them to head to grocery stores and buy food for 100 people that could be eaten without cooking—and to get enough for at least three meals. And to also bring in plenty of beer—I don't recall if they added liquor or wine to their list or not. They headed out in several directions, IBM credit cards in hand, and I stayed with the students and instructors.

Sure enough, just before lunchtime (the cafeteria was closed so we had no food options on IBM premises), the snow started to fall. Being true to my promise to Lew Gray, I told them to head back to the apartments, do not go anywhere else, and stop by whatever apartment number Donn had told me where the food had been set up to get lunch. I also told them we were going to improvise and rather than lose the afternoon sitting around watching it snow, we would move the classes to the apartment complex. Education would continue.

All liked our plan. We didn't miss a single class, although the seating was often on the floor or listening from multiple rooms of an apartment as the instructors improvised. This snowstorm made the Atlanta history book. Here is what you can find today online: In 1983, between Jan. 20 and 21, 1.9 inches of snow blanketed the metro area. Remembering what had happened a year earlier, panicked workers fled the city.

IBM was in a transition period about our drinking policy at that time. Previously, the rule was simple—alcohol and IBM business do not mix. If you have a drink with a customer, your workday is over. Never go to another customer with alcohol on your breath. That policy was being relaxed so I made a potential 'you bet your job' decision. I told the students that as they were moving between classes that afternoon, they could stop by the room with the beer and pick up one (no more) beer to drink in the next class. The students loved it (I made a lot of brownie points that day).

With snow continuing to fall, I knew I had to keep everyone off the roads, so we announced a "Happy Hour" time in one of the apartments, starting an hour after the last class was over. Those were the days when smoking was still common, so the apartment quickly became a smoke-filled room with lots of mixing and mingling among our sales personnel from all around the region (and lots of beer being consumed). It turned out to be a great learning and socializing experience for everyone.

One of the guys I had heard of by reputation, Hal Reynolds, was a top salesman in Oklahoma City. As we talked, with several other reps listening, one of us mentioned something about our time in Vietnam. We did a double-take and did what all veterans do when they find out they have a fellow veteran they are talking to—we asked when and where were you there.

As it turns out, Hal and I served in the same division, the 4th Infantry Division, but at different times. We quickly got another beer and started telling war stories (not sales war stories but real war stories). We had an even larger cluster of salespeople listening to us. As they tired of our non-stop talking, they wandered off to talk with others while Hal and I stayed together the rest of the evening. That snowy night in Atlanta with Hal Reynolds changed my life.

Hal told me about an organization I knew nothing about—the National 4th Infantry Division Association. He gave me information on how to join it (I have now been a member for 38 years, including president for eight years, re-elected for my 9th and 10th years in August 2021, and historian for 23 years). He also told me that on Veterans Day of this same year, he was going to the newly installed (in 1982) Vietnam Memorial Wall in Washington, DC to participate in the dedication of a Three-Man Statue that President Reagan was going to dedicate. I told him I'd go with him, which Jan and I did on November 10-11, 1983. The story of that experience is the first chapter in my *What Now, Lieutenant?* book, my memoir about my Vietnam experiences.

As you read deeper into this memoir, you'll see how my life from this point on has taken a sharp slant toward my passion of dealing with veterans, active Army personnel, their Family members, and military history.

* * * * * *

With the New Business College class behind us, which several other regions copied after our excellent success, I was ready to head off to my new job as a second line manager in the Kansas City branch office.

But not so fast, Bob—nothing comes without a price. As mentioned above, Jan was slated to become a new business salesman as we started the new year. But IBM policy didn't allow for spouses to fall in the chain of command of their spouse. Thus, rather than taking the new business sales job she had wanted for so long, Jan moved to the National Accounts Division branch office as an Office Systems system engineer. Not what she wanted to do, but in looking back, it turned out to be a good thing.

This was my first second-line manager job and I tackled it with a flourish. I had the new business manager, three systems engineer managers, and the customer center manager working for me, along with the office systems specialists in the branch—the copier specialist and the lady who ran the newly formed typewriter center. Talk about diverse responsibility. I knew nothing about copiers or typewriters, other than how to use them.

Don Gibbs, one of my systems engineer managers had been a manager in the branch when I was a rookie in 1968, now I was his boss. He was a real pro, did his job, and I left him alone and told him to let me know if he needed anything from me. Stan Jablonski, our copier specialist, was always the top copier salesman in the country, so I stayed out of his way and let him run the copier business (H&R Block was one of his customers, during their heyday). I kept telling Stan that he should get out of the copier sales business and learn how to sell computers. And both years he worked for me, he brought his W-2 in when he got it and said, "Boss, see what I made last year—how does this compare to what your computer salesmen and you made?" He made a lot more than any of us focused on the computer business. I smiled, congratulated him, and told him to "get out of my office" and keep up the great work.

When IBM sold our copier business to Kodak, Stan went with the business and continued as a star at Kodak.

Early in the year, I promoted the new business manager and replaced him with David Glenn, one of the best friends and best IBM managers I've ever known. I'll talk more about David later.

During this time, IBM was moving strongly into creating Customer Centers—places where customers could come at any time to see the current IBM offerings and attend classes. Each IBM sales location had some level of Customer Center. The 25 largest cities had the best of the best that IBM could offer with our focus on customer service. Kansas City was one of the top 25 Customer Centers, and that became one of the best parts of my new job.

IBM was located on the 17th to 23rd floors of the 2345 Grand Avenue building in Kansas City. We had Union Station and the Liberty Memorial to our west, Hallmark Cards and the Crown Center shopping center to our south, nothing of note to our east, and to our north we had a great view of downtown Kansas City. I was soon to become the "owner" of the 17th and 18th floors—the Customer Briefing Center on the 17th floor and the Customer Center on the 18th floor where all our computer systems were located. My office was on the northwest corner of the 19th floor with a beautiful view of downtown Kansas City and Union Station and Liberty Memorial (a great view for a guy who grew up in a railroad town and is an Army veteran).

My job, working through one of my systems engineer managers, was to finish building the customer briefing center on the 17th floor, a key part of the 25 largest Customer Center focus. The contractors were working great to make the deadline to complete the project and I was reporting to IBM Customer Center headquarters in Atlanta that we were on track. Then things started to slow down. It appeared my manager responsible for the job was never satisfied with the work and never signed off on anything. As we missed deadline after deadline, I called him in and asked him what the problem was.

He said, "It's not up to my standard." He had what he considered to be the gold standard and wouldn't accept anything less. I quickly told him that 100% quality next year is not acceptable, I'll accept 97% within the next month—get the Customer Center finished and open for customers! He refused to budge, and I took him off the project. Naturally he was upset with me but Gary Swanson, my boss, the national Customer Center team in Atlanta, and I were ready to "get the show on the road."

A lady I had worked with the previous year in the regional headquarters, Kathy Schulte, had been promoted to an administrative manager job in our branch office. She was very marketing oriented and was always asking me what she could do to help with our marketing and sales efforts. I asked her, "How would you like to own the Customer Center and Briefing Center?" She jumped on it, did a fantastic job, and on the new schedule we jointly set, we had a weeklong launch of the IBM Kansas City Customer Center. Customers flocked into the place, loved what we had to offer, our IBM sales team loved it, and the Kansas City NMD branch was near the top of the charts of all IBM branch offices. When I left Kansas City at the end of 1984, we were consistently ranked in the top five of the 25 largest Customer Centers, and the HQ team in Atlanta constantly came to see our innovative approaches to this new capability.

Jan and I took a beach vacation to Florida in June, our first vacation since our honeymoon to Williamsburg in 1981, both trips were a great time. We got home and during the week of the 4th of July, we got a call from her parents with devastating news—her dad had cancer.

Soon after that, Jan found out she was pregnant. Thus started a tough last half of 1983.

Mary Ann Barr, Jan's branch manager, saved the day for us. Not only did she tell Jan that she could take off all the time she needed to be with her dad; she also had good contacts at M.D. Anderson Cancer Hospital in Houston, one of her IBM accounts before she was promoted to the Kansas City NAD branch manager job. She pulled some strings to get Jan's dad into the hospital to determine the extent of his cancer, and Jan was there with her mother and dad the entire time. I flew down and back one day.

Things got worse, the cancer moved quickly, and on Halloween afternoon, Jan flew to Evansville to be with her dad for the last time. I took Stephanie trick or treating that evening, the saddest 'happy' event I can remember. On 5 November 1983, Raymond Donald Savage died, leaving a big hole in all of us.

My responsibilities at IBM continued. Gary Swanson had moved to Dallas to tackle another opportunity and I was now working for Phil Long who had become our branch manager. His was a totally different style from Gary's and took some adjusting, but I adapted. We worked well together. We finished a good IBM year. Jan and I drove to Evansville to spend Christmas with her mother and brothers. Jan was getting bigger and bigger as our baby was growing inside her.

That was a very cold Christmas week. It was hard to keep the car warm as we drove to and from Evansville. When we got home after dark on a Sunday night, we knew when we opened the garage door that we had a problem. There was frozen water on the garage floor. As we walked into the house, we could hear water running in the basement. I went downstairs to find water over my ankles—pipes had broken. I shutoff the water at the valve, we checked the rest of the house, no problem other than cold, and headed to a hotel to spend the night.

We got our home repaired, the new IBM business year kicked off in January, and on 9 February 1984, we checked into the hospital in Overland Park, Kansas to prepare for a Caesarean section birth the next morning. By then we knew we were having a boy. After checking in and getting all the preliminary examinations done, they told us we could go out to eat if we wanted to—just be back at a reasonable time. We went to a cafeteria (seldom in our marriage have we gone to a cafeteria but that sounded good to Jan that night) and headed back to the hospital. It was another cold and icy night in Kansas City. As we were getting out of the car to walk into the hospital, Jan slipped and did the splits, like a gymnast. It scared the crap out of me. She started laughing and couldn't stop.

I was terrified that something bad would be the result as I helped her up, with her still laughing, and took her into the hospital. The nurses assured us Jan was okay (I wasn't) and we went to bed, awaiting the birth of our son. Early the next morning, 10 February 1984, we went into the delivery room, and I watched my first and only Caesarean section birth. After Mark Ryan Babcock was born and they were sewing Jan up, she couldn't believe it when I asked the doctor, "Is that her uterus?" Heck, I'd never seen anything like that before—I might as well get my questions answered while he was working.

Mark was (and continues to be) a joy to both of us and our whole Family. Jan had six weeks maternity leave and stayed home with Mark until she had to go back to work on April 1, 1984.

Once again, Jan started a new opportunity at IBM. IBM had announced the IBM Personal Computer in 1981 and it was growing like crazy. Among the sales outlets IBM was using was a new organization called the IBM Product Center. In late 1983, David Glenn was recruited to become the Kansas City IBM Product Center manager. As much as I hated to lose him as my New Business manager, I knew it was a good opportunity for him and let him take the job. By then David and Nancy (his wife) and Jan and I had become good friends. As David started recruiting IBMers to fill his new organization, Jan was the first one he came for. Thus, Jan was no longer an Office Systems system engineer. When she came back from maternity leave, she would enter the entirely different retail sales environment of selling IBM Personal Computers in a retail store in downtown Kansas City.

The IBM Product Center, being a retail outlet, was open on Saturday. Nuts...that meant Bob would be babysitter for Mark, at six-weeks old, while Jan was working. One of the errors IBM made in selecting the location for the Product Center was overlooking the reality that few people go to downtown Kansas City on weekends. We had agreed that I would bring Mark down to the Product Center about 11:00AM on Saturday morning, after they had opened at 9:00AM. As I walked in with our precious baby boy, I noted on the counter on the door that I was the third person to enter the place that day—David and Jan were #1 and #2. Within a month, David convinced his boss that opening on Saturday in downtown Kansas City was a mistake, so Jan's Saturday IBM workdays ended.

Sometime in early summer, Jan and I took a week's cruise vacation in the Caribbean. We both needed a break but were uncomfortable leaving Mark with a babysitter. Kathy Schulte, my Customer Center manager, volunteered to stay at our home and take care of Mark in our absence. (He had a regular babysitter during weekdays, Kathy had him at night and on the weekend). When we got home after an enjoyable week's cruise, Kathy was worn out and couldn't wait to be relieved—but she had done a great job.

As 1984 ended, we started getting itchy feet again and began thinking where our next IBM destination could be. We agreed that Jan and I both needed good opportunities without me interfering with her career path. Going back northeast to "IBM Mecca" in Armonk, White Plains, and other corporate headquarters locations in New York was not what we wanted to do. A return trip to Atlanta for me and a first time for Jan seemed like our best move. We started putting out feelers and seeing what we could find. We were ready for another move...

Last Savage Family picture: Don, Greg, Don Jr., Jan, Peggy in front.
Sadly, Jan's dad died in 1983

Kristen, Rob, and Stephanie in Evansville

Return to Atlanta
Software Marketing and Operations
1985 to 1988

As 1984 came to an end and I'd proven myself in Kansas City again, I was ready for my next IBM adventure. Phil Long approached me and told me that Val Perry, my second-line manager who had promoted me to Evansville back in 1977, wanted to talk to me about an opportunity he had for a manager in software in Atlanta NMD headquarters. Val had progressed in his career and was a Division Director taking on a new area of IBM, software marketing and several other things. He was now one level below Vice President, not a bad place for me to be going.

Selling me on going back to Atlanta was easy, Jan also liked what she had seen of Atlanta during her IBM training days there, so I hopped a plane to talk to Val about the opportunity he had for me.

As I walked into Val's office with a big smile on my face, we chatted about what had transpired in both our lives since we had last seen each other and then he got down to business. "Babcock, I've changed my mind. I'm not going to put you into the Software Marketing manager's job, I want you to become the aide to the Director of Software Marketing." I looked at him like he had lost his mind. The director he was talking about me working for had one of the worst reputations of anyone I knew in IBM. He had been fired from his previous IBM job, escalated it to the top of the business and had been reinstated. My response to Val was, "You are out of your friggin' mind—no way am I going to work for that guy."

He came back with something like, "Look, Bob, if you'll keep him out of trouble for a year, I'll look out for you and make sure you are taken care of. I need somebody I can depend on to keep me up to date on what he's doing and who will effectively make sure his job gets done. You will have total access to talk direct to me whenever you want to."

I still wasn't happy or convinced. I headed back to Kansas City with his last words ringing in my ears as I walked out the door, "Babcock, one of us is going to change his mind...and it isn't going to be me."

I called Jan from the airport, told her how the day had gone, how upset I was, and knew that I had a very important career decision to make. Jan and I talked it over, knew we were both ready to move on with our careers, hated to leave Kansas City, and there was no place we'd rather go than Atlanta. The next day, I called Val and told him, "Val, you SOB, I don't like it, but I'll take the job." He laughed and told me it was a good decision and he'd look out for me. I reported into the new job in January 1985. Jan got a promotion to Insurance Industry Marketing, so it was a step-up for Jan and a lateral, for the first year at least, move for me. I had placed my trust in Val Perry to look out for me.

I showed up, met with Val who told me the problem he was trying to fix with me as his eyes and ears, and called the guy I was going to work for and told him I was coming over to talk to him. The guy (let's call him Sam rather than his real name) got into his pompous mode like he was giving a lot of thought to whether he wanted to hire me or not, and I played along with him. I knew Val had told him I was going to be his aide because I was sitting in Val's office when he made the call. Thus began a long two years in the IBM life of Bob Babcock...

The first meeting I went to, which was in Val's smoke-filled conference room of the half dozen or so directors working for him, along with each one's key staff person, was a review of each department's plans for the coming year. Sam gave me a quick briefing of the charts somebody had prepared for the meeting and told me he wanted me to present them. I barely understood enough to answer the simplest questions, let alone anything that required in depth knowledge.

When it came Sam's time to present, he introduced his new "assistant" he had just hired and told me to get up and give the status of the Software Marketing department. I started talking and Val started asking question, knowing full well that I had been on the job two days at most and had no clue what I was talking about. Most of my answers were, "I'm not sure" or "I don't know, I'll have to get back to you" or something equally as lame. I stood up there, the first time I'd met most of the 15 to 20 people in the room and was getting my ass handed to me. Finally, Val asked, "Well what do you know, Babcock?" I was fuming but kept my cool and calmly said, "Val, as you know, I've only been in this job for two days, I've still got a lot to learn." He said, "Okay, sit down—Sam, get up here and present the charts."

Sam's answers weren't any better than mine, but he said them with a lot more BS and acting like he knew what he was talking about. We were dismissed and told to come back the next day when we could answer his questions. As we walked out of the room, I was so mad I was ready to kill Val. The look on my face showed him that—and he winked and smiled at me as I exited the room.

The next morning on the way into work (our offices were in a different building from Val's), I stopped unannounced in Val's office, told his secretary I had to see him "Now!" and she escorted me into his office. I told him how upset I was with his treatment of me. He replied, "Bob, that wasn't directed at you, it was directed at Sam and everyone in the room knew it. Don't take it personally."

Thus began a long year of covering for an incompetent who had no more business sitting in an IBM director's office than the village idiot did—wait, maybe it was the village idiot I was working for.

On Valentine's Day 1986, the annual Spring Plan Review was conducted across all the directorates of the National Marketing Division. With Lew Gray sitting in the room as the President, it was a command performance for every Vice President, Division Director, and Director. Each Director had a set time of ten minutes to present his/her plans for the coming year, and five minutes were allocated for questions after each presentation.

This was the first step in the funding cycle to determine where the allocated money of our division would be spent. For the better part of four to six weeks before the event, it was an all-hands on deck project to get exactly the right presentation put together, rehearsed, and timed, approved by one or two levels above each director, and be ready to present when you were called on. For Sam, that responsibility fell on my shoulders—and I accompanied him into the meeting. We had exactly what we wanted to say, Val was happy with it, and we felt good.

Not so quick...we forgot who was making the presentation. In his inimitable way, Sam got up in front of the group, fumbled through the charts, forgot the points he was to make, and reverted to his pompous BS style. To say that Val and everyone above him were upset with the presentation would be an understatement. Val got up, headed for the door, and motioned for Sam and me to follow him. We walked in silence to Val's conference room, closed the door, and he asked me what went wrong.

He knew the answer and so did I. Being a good trooper, I

accepted that maybe we had not briefed Sam well enough. With just the three of us in the room, he said, "Babcock, get up here and give the presentation."

I started talking and Val, pissed-off more than I'd ever seen him, started badgering me. I took it for as long as I could before my blood boiled. I stopped, looked him in the eye, and said, "F**k you, Val—I quit." I walked to the back of the room, turned my back to him, and fought as hard as I ever had not to burst out in tears. It was hard to tell who was more shocked—Val or Sam (or me). Val took a moment and then said, "Sam, get up here and present the charts." Sam visibly paled, went to the front of the room and the projector, and started, once again, fumbling through the presentation.

As Val hit Sam with question after question, which he couldn't answer, I saw how this was something I had to step up to and bail Sam out (again). From the back of the room, I started answering the questions. After I answered a couple of questions, Val turned to me and said, "Babcock, I thought you had quit." My response was, "Val, you know I can't afford to quit." He said, "Okay, get your ass back up here and join the meeting."

The three of us got back on track trying to repair the damage and get Sam ready to do a "re-do" the next day. Promptly at 4:00 PM, I got up and said, "Val, Happy Birthday—I've got a date with my wife for Valentine's Day. See you tomorrow." And I walked out the door without looking back and headed home. (Val's birthday truly is on Valentine's Day—thus his name). Staff guys seldom walk out of a meeting with director level people in it until they are dismissed. I didn't care, I was not going to let Jan down. She was much more important to me than they were.

Lots of stories I'll refrain from telling, but I did learn a lot. As the year ended, IBM went through another major reorganization and consolidated a bunch of branch offices around the country, leaving a lot of IBM branch managers without a job. Much to my surprise, Val was good with his promise and while higher level guys than me were scrambling to find a job, I got a promotion to the higher level and became the operations manager for Peter Dance, the IBM Software Vice President out of New York (without having to move from Atlanta).

I believe soon after I took over that new job, Sam, my incompetent boss, stepped on himself again as far as breaking IBM rules and this time could not talk his way back into the business. I never tried to locate or talk to the guy again—was happy to see him off our payroll.

In all my IBM career to date as of 1986, the hardware divisions were the king of IBM. Most of our revenue and profit came from selling hardware. Software and services had either been given away or were a rounding error in importance compared to the revenue and profit that hardware produced. But, over the years, technology had continued to drive the cost of hardware down, competition had gotten fierce, and IBM saw the writing on the wall and was in the process of moving from a hardware focused company to a software and services company (which it remains today—along with other new innovations like Watson, the Cloud, and other technologies that I have long since quit trying to keep up with).

As Operations Manager for the Software VP, I had a team in Atlanta and Donn Atkins, who had worked for and with me in Kansas City, had moved up to become Peter Dance's executive assistant. That was a match made in heaven. Donn and I had mutual respect, had worked together for three years in Kansas City, and we understood each other. (Donn later moved up to be a high-level executive in IBM before he retired, and we are still friends, hopefully I will publish his memoir in the future).

The next two years were effectively spent on the road. I'd leave Atlanta early in the week, fly to LaGuardia Airport in New York, drive up to whichever IBM location I would be working in in Westchester County, NY and would head home Friday afternoon—and repeat the process the next week. I became a true road warrior. My Delta Frequent Flyer status skyrocketed, I became a Hertz Gold member, I even joined the Delta Crown Room because many, if not most, Friday's trying to get out of New York to Atlanta had delays at one or both airports. My justification for the Crown Room membership was the free drinks there offset what I would pay for expensive drinks in the public airport bars (that's my story and I'm sticking to it).

One unexpected benefit of the constant travel…In the fall of 1986, Delta had a program for Frequent Flyers where if you flew a certain number of segments on Delta between September and November, you earned two free first-class Delta tickets to Hawaii. On weeks when I wasn't scheduled to be in New York, Jan would ask me, "What are you doing here, can't you find a reason to go to New York?" Suffice it to say, we had a fantastic vacation to Hawaii that winter, flight compliments of Delta, food, lodging, and entertainment at our expense.

Back to the software job…it was truly an education for me of how large corporations work internally. We were constantly in high level, VP, Division President, and above, meetings. It was at the beginning of smoking bans in conference rooms. Someone was always sitting in each door of a conference room blowing his smoke out into the hallway, and I got to observe egos and power plays work in the big leagues.

It was like we software advocates were trying to steal the holy grail from the hardware organizations. As stated above, they had always been the primary revenue and profit producer in IBM. They did not want to give up that position. It was the marketplace and technology that was driving the change, but the hardware people were going to fight it to their last breath.

For many weeks, we put together presentations (this was before Power-Point had been invented), created plastic overhead charts to show on a "foil machine." After each presentation at a high level in the hallowed halls of IBM New York headquarters, we'd come out with marching orders from the top-level executive we had presented to. Peter Dance did the presentations, Donn Atkins and I were the ones taking notes and getting ready to make changes before making our next presentation later that day to another top-level executive.

My team in Atlanta was standing by the phone waiting for Donn or my call to tell them what charts to change or add and when we needed them, sometimes in less than an hour. They and the interns from University of Georgia and Georgia Tech that we always had a team of, quickly created the new or corrected charts and using the IBM Scanmaster (long since obsoleted with better technology) sent the charts to us, sometimes just in time for us to walk into the next executive's office.

It was exciting, frustrating, educational, and I learned how the highest levels of one of America's premier corporations worked. (Not surprisingly, that experience helped me significantly as I started working with Army generals and their commanders and staff after my IBM career was over.)

One of many examples…IBM always used the Sales Plan for the sales force to tell the sales managers and salespeople (note I'm not calling them salesmen anymore—by now, women were common in sales and sales management jobs) where we wanted them to spend their time and effort. There was a heated discussion going on about what did and did not belong in the next year's sales plan, and how much emphasis should be on everything.

The sales plan manager, Ruben Ray, was totally frustrated as he stood in front of the group, taking notes on a flipchart (before the days of electronic note taking). He couldn't regain control of the meeting as different factions (VP and Division President level egos) talked over each other. He stuck the black Magic Marker he was taking notes with into his white shirt pocket—and hadn't put the top on it. Everyone saw the massive black spot developing on his shirt, knowing that was now a ruined shirt. Someone got his attention, he looked down at it and the look on his face will never be forgotten. Such was one of the memories of how high-level corporate executives, behind closed doors, will fight to their last breath to beat their fellow executives in the fight for resources (money and people) going into the next year.

I'll net it out again—we were successful and got a big chunk of IBM focus and resources shifted from hardware to software. We created software specific sales and marketing organizations, to include an Area Software Manager in each of IBM's geographic areas and got the largest amount of focus ever in the next year's sales plan.

I had a conversation with Peter Dance, telling him I wanted to be an IBM branch manager. He looked me in the eye and simply said, "Bob, you're too old—that's not going to happen. Those jobs go to people younger than you." While I wasn't surprised, it was like a slap across the face. Peter was the same age as me (45 at the time) and telling me I'm too old. Also working against me was the focus on putting minorities and females in key jobs during that phase of American business. By the time I got home from New York at the end of that week, I had calmed down and told Jan that my climb up the IBM ladder had gone as far as it was going to go. It was time to rethink my career aspirations.

As I thought through my options, I knew nobody was better

qualified for an Area Software Manager's job than I was—and Peter agreed. My four-year tour in Atlanta had broadened me and opened doors that I never knew would give me a new lease on my IBM career, and Jan got her first chance to become an IBM manager.

In January 1989, I was named the Kansas City Area Software Manager and Jan was named the Customer Center Manager in Topeka, Kansas. It was a promotion to a higher level for both of us; and included decent raises.

The Babcock moving wagon started to pack up and move again...

Third Kansas City/Topeka/Lawrence
Area Software Manager
1989 to 1990

What started out looking like a great career and personal opportunity for Jan and me turned out to be an unmitigated disaster for us and our entire Family. The bright spots that we thought we were going to have were that I was to become one of seven Area Level Software Managers in IBM at a time when IBM was transitioning from being a hardware driven to a software and services driven business. At the same time, Jan was getting a promotion to her first IBM manager's job—Customer Center Manager in Topeka.

The "slight" disadvantage was because our jobs were in Kansas City and Topeka, we would have to live "half-way" between the two, in Lawrence, home of the University of Kansas. I had said for a long time that I would love to live in a college town, close to a big city. This seemed to be exactly what I had wished for.

The "half-way" between the two places where we worked turned out to be an hour drive each way for me, facing into the sun both going to and coming home from work each day. Regardless the time of day or even on weekends, the drive was a minimum of an hour each way—and that was without traffic delays. For Jan, it was an easy half-hour drive to Topeka, with the sun at her back going and coming. No problem, I could handle it.

Another disadvantage was Mark was in day-care, which we set him up in not far from our new home. If anything went wrong, he was in Lawrence with the closest parent a half hour away (and remember, this was before everyone owned a cell phone). Rob and Stephanie enrolled in middle school, Rob (who had come to live with us a couple years earlier) was in 9th grade and Stephanie in 7th grade. When we told them about the move, Stephanie immediately fell on the floor crying. She had made the cheerleading team in her middle school in Georgia, and we were taking that away from her. Rob was his normal stoic self, never expressing much emotion either way.

Thinking that might be our long-term and permanent home, Jan and I decided to build our dream home. We found a lot on the 7th fairway of Alvamar Country Club golf course, hired a builder, moved into a rental duplex while the house was being built, and eagerly watched progress begin. Despite the minor drawbacks, this was going to be a great phase of our lives. Wrong!

Job wise, Jan and I both were doing fine. I had worked in software at the IBM corporate headquarters level during the time we were fighting to get IBM hardware executives to understand a basic fact of life. Technology was driving down the cost of their products while software and services were exploding in the changing world of information technology. Although not in a quota job, I had been around long enough that my salary with an annual bonus made me not worry about having plenty of money. And I knew more about software than the executives I worked for, so they listened to me and came to me for advice.

Jan was loving her first manager's job, worked on a commission plan that paid well, and she became a key part of the IBM management team in Topeka.

Family wise…that was a different story. Stephanie and Rob had come from an environment they were comfortable in, knew lots of people they had spent several years with, and lived in a community that was basically all in the same general socio-economic category. Lawrence, Kansas was not that way. Once you got away from KU and the university environment (which we had no connection to), Lawrence was a lower socio-economic community than we were used to. Suddenly, Stephanie and Rob were "rich kids" and didn't fit in. Plus, since Jan and I worked in different towns and were seldom in Lawrence to make friends, we didn't fit into having a social life in Kansas City, Topeka, or Lawrence.

Long story short—soon after we had finished construction and moved into our new home on the golf course, Stephanie left for Arizona to live with her dad and Rob headed for Colorado, and then Nevada, to live with his mother. There had been much turmoil that led to those decisions. Jan and I were devastated, and it took a toll on Mark who was now the only child living with us. Our idyllic life we had hoped for had turned to sh*t.

To make bad matters worse, the winter of 1989-1990 was the coldest we had ever experienced. Starting before Christmas, temperatures dropped to 26 below zero and stayed in that general range for a long time. Even when it warmed up, it was barely above zero. I remember buying our Christmas tree, getting out of the car, running to pick the first one I saw, paying for it, tying it on top of the car, and out of there in less than ten minutes. No family went with me, too cold.

As 1990 started, we got the news that IBM was re-organizing (again) and the Kansas City Area was being consolidated with the one in Minneapolis. They had a (female) Software Executive, and I was odd man out, as were most of the managers in Kansas City. Fortunately, Rick Marcuson, a friend from the days he started as a rookie salesman in Kansas City, with me as his mentor, was now working out of Kansas City in a national job for IBM and was moving on to a new job. Rick asked me, "Bob, I remember you worked with community banks during your first staff job, how would you like to take over as the National manager for Community Banks?" Bingo! I had loved that job, could do it from anywhere in the country, and immediately jumped on it. I was interviewed and offered and accepted the job on the spot.

Professionally, Jan and I still had a problem. Kansas City IBM was shrinking with the loss of the Area headquarters, and two married IBM managers were going to have a hard time finding jobs that were based in Kansas City. Plus, we lived in Lawrence, and I was already tired of the hour drive each way every day. Thus, I played a card I had learned as I grew in my career. If you're a good employee, those in power above you will probably take good care of you.

I called David Richard, the Area VP in Minneapolis, who I had met many years ago when I was in Evansville. He and I had hit it off (he was a former Air Force officer and liked it that I was an Army Infantry officer who had served in Vietnam) and I had made a good impression on him. I simply laid out the facts as above, two IBM managers in a shrinking IBM population, living an hour drive from KC, having a family that had fallen apart because of living in Lawrence, and asked if he would give us a Moving and Living ticket to move back to Atlanta at IBM's expense. Immediately he said, "You got it. I hate to lose you, but I understand." And he gave me the phone number of his finance manager who would confirm the details. My respect for IBM and our Basic Beliefs spiked to a new high.

My new IBM Community Banking job could be done from anywhere in the country since I had national responsibility. My boss was in Charlotte, NC, so living in Atlanta was putting me closer to him.

Now we had to find a job for Jan. She flew to Atlanta to interview with a manager she had worked for before who was now the executive running IBM's sales education center in Atlanta. Again, first interview, Jan was offered a job as a manager in IBM's sales education organization in Atlanta. Bingo again!

We had one minor consideration. We had lived in our dream house on the golf course for less than seven months and now had to sell it. Interestingly, I had never played a single round of golf on that course, and Jan had only played it once, when the Topeka managers had an outing there. (No big loss on golf—back then and still now, neither Jan nor I are golfers). We put our house on the market and within a week we had a full-price offer. A decent investment—we cleared a $20K profit on a home we lived in for less than a year.

Things appeared to be turning around for the Babcock Family. When we told Stephanie we were moving back to Atlanta, she immediately wanted to know—"How soon and when can I come back to live with you." Rob wasn't quite as anxious, but before long, he also was back with us after we had moved and settled in.

As we saw Lawrence disappear in our rear-view mirror, Jan and I committed that we were not leaving Atlanta, that Mark would graduate with the class he would be starting school with in the Fall of 1990. And he did—Mark graduated from Walton High School in May 2002. Unlike his brother and two sisters, he didn't bounce around following us and our IBM careers during his school days. We had become what IBMers call people who won't leave Atlanta—Tree Huggers.

Being the gluttons for punishment that we are, and truly knowing that we weren't going to leave Atlanta, Jan and I once again tackled the fun job of building our dream house, which we lived in for 25 fantastic years.

Tree Hugger
Third and Last IBM trip to Atlanta
1990 to 2002

Atlanta was comfortable to move back to. My first IBM job there was 1975 through 1976, we were back again in 1985 to 1988, and we knew the area we wanted to live in. The school district, familiarity with shopping and other services, friends from before, and a church we wanted to join (Mt. Bethel United Methodist) were all factors in heading back to East Cobb County, a northern suburb of Atlanta. Our first job was to pick a lot to buy, a builder to work with to build another dream home, and a place to rent that didn't require a year's lease.

Keith Manning, an IBMer Jan had worked closely with the last time we were in Atlanta, introduced us to the neighborhood and builder (a former IBM salesman) who built his house and we quickly loved both the neighborhood and the homes the builder built. That contract was signed, and the six-month building project began. We moved in over Thanksgiving weekend of 1990.

I waded into my IBM Community Banking Manager's job, it came back to me like riding a bicycle, and I was very much enjoying the expanded scope of what I was doing. Jan loved her job managing instructors in IBM sales training, Stephanie adjusted well coming back to the school where she already had friends, Mark started first grade with the same group of kids he would graduate from high school with in 2002, and life was good.

In the fourteen years I had been away from Community

Banking, with the check reader/sorter capability added to the System/34 and its successor products, IBM had become a significant factor in the Community Bank industry. A strong group of Community Banking Business Partners had developed in my absence. Sorting the good from the bad of those companies was one of the challenges I was given.

I was committed to making Community Banking one of our strongest industries, so I went to my boss and told him I wanted to continue to run the annual week-long banking class that previous IBM leaders had run. I didn't care where or when I did it, I just wanted to bring the team together in the first weeks of 1991 to introduce myself and my plans and to get us all off to a fast start.

I was hit with an emphatic "No way!" Disappointed, I did a little more research and found that for the past several years, the class was held annually in Denver, Colorado, in late February, and it was more a skiing boondoggle than a valid educational opportunity for sales reps. (For readers unfamiliar with one of my favorite words—boondoggle is defined as work or activity that is wasteful or pointless but gives the appearance of having value).

I huddled with two strong managers, Mike Welbaum and Moe Cougher, from the disbanded Kansas City area that I had hired for my team, and we put together a plan to sell to my boss. It was so non-boondoggle like that getting permission was immediate. I had proposed that we hold the class in a hotel at O'Hare Airport in Chicago the last week of January. No boondoggle was ever conducted there—only crazy people risked the weather and other factors to be faced that time of year in Chicago.

The class was announced, banking reps from all over the country signed up, and I invited all our business partners, at their own expense, to host a hospitality suite in the hotel during one or two nights of the class. That would keep our people in the hotel, continuing to learn from our partners, and keep them off the snowy, icy streets of Chicago. That also gave me an opportunity to start getting to know which partners I wanted to keep and which we wanted to move away from.

One added attraction...I let our business partners decide how extravagant or simple they wanted their hospitality suite to be, and how much and what kind of food and beverages they provided for our sales team (alcohol was no longer prohibited). The smart ones put on great spreads of food and drink and were flooded by IBM reps; those who didn't understand how to attract a crowd had basically empty suites. Over the two evenings, I visited all our Business Partners and started getting to know them.

The final thing I wanted to do was to recognize the top community banking sales' people from 1990 with cash awards on the final day of the event. Once again, I was told times were tight and I had zero money to give out as awards. Not to be held down, I devised an awards program that became my trademark for the remainder of my time in IBM—the "Can Do Can Opener" award.

During my year in Vietnam, I had eaten unknown numbers of C-ration meals as we patrolled through the jungle. We opened those cans with a simple can opener that I could buy for 50 cents each at a local Army Surplus store across from Dobbins Air Force Base in metro Atlanta. At my own expense, I bought $10 worth of P-38s—what we Soldiers called the can opener (why we do that, I have no idea, but we still do).

Thus, during our last combined class session on Friday morning, before everyone departed to fly home, I pulled out a standard grocery store can of vegetables (don't recall what I had brought with me), showed the P-38 to the class and asked them if they knew what it was. The vast majority had no clue. A few had been in the Army, told the class what it was, and I demonstrated it by quickly opening the vegetable can. Everyone looked at me like I had lost my mind.

I then proceeded to call out the names of our top sales' people from across the country, talked about what they had accomplished, and brought them to the front of the room to give them a "Can Do Can Opener" for them showing a "can do" attitude the previous year. As they went back to their seats, those sitting around them wanted to look at it and examine it. I told those who had earned it that I expected them to always carry it in their pocket or purse as a reminder of what we expected of them. I also told the class we'd do it again next year and hopefully we would have some repeat winners and some new ones, and maybe some money to give away.

As I traveled around the country the rest of the year, I'd frequently be asked by a Community Banking rep what he or she had to do to earn a can opener. That $10 out of my own pocket to buy surplus can openers was probably one of the best decisions I ever made in my IBM career. I bought many more over the next five years I was in that job, always got a smile from the people I gave one to, and even had some IBM executives ask me about this thing I was handing out to make reps so happy. Of course, I always had several in my pocket and would give the executive a sample — never hurts to keep your "brand" in front of decision makers, even in your own company.

As I type this, I have two P-38s in my pocket, as I have always had since my days in the jungles of Vietnam in 1966-1967. In 1995, when I was promoted to lead the entire Industry Marketing teams for all segments of what then had been renamed as Small and Medium Business (SMB), David Glenn, my good friend and successor taking over the Community Banking team, gave me a P-38 mounted on a plaque as my promotion gift. It hangs in my home office today.

Dealing with Business Partners was one of the key parts of my job in Community Banking. As IBM took more and more internal IBMers out of the Small and Medium Business segments of all industries, the void was filled by IBM Certified Business Partners. With over a dozen Business Partners on the list that was given me on my first day in the job, I quickly knew that was too many. Rather than having a bunch of weak partners, we needed just a very few bigger and stronger partners to work with. My boss told me it was my job to get to know them, figure out which were the best that we wanted to keep, and start disengaging from the others.

He finished with naming a specific Business Partner that he said I should have at the top of my list. I listened but kept an open mind. I had heard in the short time I'd been in the job that his choice wasn't necessarily the one the people who worked within the Community Banking segment thought was best.

Over the next few months, after the successful Chicago kick-off class, I traveled all over the country working with sales reps and having day-long meetings with the owners of the Business Partner firms I had to pare down to a smaller number. (You will notice I capitalize Business Partners. At this stage in IBM's evolving growth, that's how important they were to us in the SMB marketplace. I believe in capitalizing that which is the most important—I also do that with Family and Soldier).

In my one-on-one meetings with Business Partner executives, it became obvious which were the best and which were simply in the way. The company my boss preferred turned out to "look good in a suit" but were loyal only to themselves and had virtually no loyalty to IBM. Another company, Jack Henry &

Associates in Monet, Missouri, who I had met in their formative years as a company during my first stint in Community Banking back in 1975-1976, was strong, loyal, and run by two men who over the years became good personal friends—Jerry Hall and Jack Henry.

In fact, after I retired from IBM, they hired me to write a book about their first 30 years in business, growing from two guys writing software on a door laying across two sawhorses in the back room of a machine shop, then driving all night from bank to bank for those same two guys to install the software. At the end of their fiscal year, ending in June 2021, Jack Henry & Associates had revenue of $1.758 billion with roughly 6,800 employees nationwide and nearing 9,000 customers. My working relationship and friendship with Jerry and Jack were highlights of my IBM career. (Like an idiot, I never bought any of their stock—IBM ethics kept me from investing in one Business Partner when I was dealing with several.)

Another quick short story...my immediate boss was a director whose experience was in dealing with the nation's largest banks, as was his boss, the VP responsible for all banking in the US. We were scheduled to present to the Fall Plan conference of IBM's top executives one October afternoon. They, of course, covered the big banks (about 90% of their revenue objective) and they told me to present my needs for community banks. Since they knew I knew my job, and seldom ever needed them for anything, they put off until the morning before the presentation for me to review my presentation with them.

I walked into their NY executive suites and the VPs secretary told me the VP had been called out on a large bank customer problem, and that my director boss was at the hospital where his wife was giving birth to a baby. She said, "Bob, you're on your own—I'm sure you will do great." Here I was, with a plan and funding request for the next year that nobody outside of my own organization knew anything about, and I was going straight to IBM's highest level approval board. To say I was sweating bullets would be an understatement.

I walked into the room where the Who's Who of IBM top level executives were sitting, to take my never presented or approved request for next year's budget direct to the final decision makers. In military terms, I felt like a second lieutenant presenting to generals. I took my seat at the big conference table. Anything said to me before it was my turn to present, I answered with a simple, "Yes, Sir" or "No, Sir." A legendary IBM executive sitting next to me, about to retire after his long career, tapped me on the knee, leaned over and said, "Bob, call me (whatever his first name was). You make me feel old calling me Sir."

That broke the ice—I let out a 'whew' of stored up breath. When called on to present, I blew them away and got approval for everything I asked for. It seems that everyone sitting at the table had called on community banks at some point in their career and each wanted to tell his banking story. Sitting around the back of the room were several same level as me manager friends, there to take notes for their bosses, who simply shook their heads and smiled as they saw me successfully survive my hot seat experience. My software marketing experiences of selling to many of these same executives several years before served me well. I had learned back then that no matter how much of a "big shot" you are, you still put your pants on one leg at a time and are human just like I am. Since then, I've never let rank scare me—civilian or military. They are in their positions because they are good, not because they are mean.

My Community Banking Executive time at IBM led me to my biggest IBM job. In late 1994, Wirt Cook, president of IBM's Small and Medium Business division, told me I had been selected to take the leadership of all sales and marketing for IBM's SMB Industry Marketing teams covering North and South America. My quota was to be $2 billion in revenue (gulp). Not bad for a boy with roots in Heavener, Oklahoma.

Life was good for Bob and Jan Babcock. We loved our new home, our neighborhood, and the church we had joined. I had become an usher there and Jan was taking Bible study classes. Unfortunately, some challenges with two teenage kids (Stephanie and Rob) forced Jan to make the decision to leave IBM and become a stay-at-home mom. Never one to let grass grow under her feet, she became an entrepreneur and became a successful consultant selling top of the line ladies clothing through Carlisle, an in-home New York City based clothing company catering to ladies desiring top quality in fashion. She became a trainer of new consultants at Carlisle and later started her own interior design company, JB Designs, where she worked one on one with customers wanting a new look for their home or office. It was tough for Jan to leave the job she loved at IBM, but we learned that when you are handed a lemon, it's time to make lemonade—which she did.

*****

It was during this time that my life outside IBM made a dramatic change that continues to this day to be my passion. I attended my first ever National 4th Infantry Division Association (4IDA) reunion in 1991, in Orlando, Florida. At that time, 95% of the members were World War II veterans with Vietnam vets like me just starting to show an interest. I had a fascinating time listening to the stories of our WWII vets over those three or four days. Among the vets I met was Joe Motil, who told me about another organization, the 22nd Infantry Regiment Society, which was made up solely of those who had fought across Europe in WWII with the same Regiment that I had fought with in Vietnam.

I contacted the president of the Society, Major General (Retired) John Ruggles, who invited me to their reunion in Jackson, Mississippi in November 1992 where I had another fabulous time sitting in silence and listening to the stories of our WWII vets.

Without going through all the details, I have only missed one 4IDA reunion since that first one in 1991. At the reunion in Washington, DC in 1994, my Vietnam battalion commander, Colonel (Retired) Len Morley and I roomed together. One night before going into the business meeting the next day, he turned to me and said, "Bob, I want you to become an officer in this Association." What does a Lieutenant do when his battalion commander tells him to do something? You do not hesitate, and reply with, "Yes, Sir!"

And in the summer of 1995, John Ruggles and Chaplain Bill Boice called and asked me to take over as president of the 22nd Infantry Regiment Society. They said, "If you don't take it over and open it to all 22nd vets from all eras, we are getting too old so will have to shut it down." Again, what could I say but, "Yes, Sir!"

Thus, for the next ten years, from 1995 to 2005, I was president of the 22nd Infantry Regiment Society, built it from a WWII only organization to one that now has only the few remaining living WWII vets, but is full of veterans from Vietnam and a growing number of veterans from Iraq and Afghanistan and other hot spots where the Regiment has been deployed. I remain on the board of this organization.

As for the 4IDA, I became a Junior Vice President in 1994 and have had an officer's job ever since. In 1998, I became president for a two-year term. When I became president, as I always did in my IBM life, I decided on "less than a handful" of key objectives to focus on during the next year. My four objectives as president of the 4IDA were 1) raise money for and complete the 4ID monument in Washington, DC that had been approved at the end of WWI and never built, 2) write a book of War Stories from 4ID WWII veterans who were dying far too fast, 3) appoint myself as liaison to the Commanding General of the active Army 4th Infantry Division to ensure we knew how we could best help today's Soldiers and Families, 4) appoint myself as historian to preserve our history for future generations.

I successfully completed all four objectives. God told me to name Gerry Howard, a Vietnam vet I hardly knew, to get our 4ID monument built—Gerry accomplished that in less than two years. Our 4ID War Stories book came out in 2001 with 325 WWII stories, 25 from the Cold War, and 100 from Vietnam veterans. I appointed myself Historian and still hold that job, now for 23 years. I also appointed myself liaison to the Commanding General of the active Army 4th Infantry Division, a job I held until 2017 and resumed in August 2021. I am on a first name basis with every 4ID Commanding General, and their wives, from 1996 through today.

Plus, I was elected president again and served from 2011 to 2017 and returned for my last term as 4IDA president in August 2021 through summer of 2023 when I plan to ride off into the sunset. My main objective is to turn the 4IDA over to our Iraq and Afghanistan vets, just as the WWII vets turned it over to us Vietnam vets, and our founding WWI vets turned it over to the WWII vets.

Another project I undertook was when I learned that the National D-Day Museum (now the National World War II Museum) would be opening on June 6, 2000, in New Orleans. I immediately took it upon myself to commit to have more

D-Day veterans from 4ID at the grand opening than any other division. To net this out, we had 104 D-Day veterans (plus an equal or larger group of Family members) from the 4ID in attendance—not only more than anyone else but far more than the second largest group. The smiles on their faces, the stories they swapped, and the memories I have from that long weekend will be with me the rest of my life.

Anyone who knows me well understands the passion I have for our military, our veterans, and our active-duty personnel, plus their Family members. I'll tell some more stories about that later in this book. Jan knows this passion and supports me daily in it.

My passion for military history and working with veterans came at a time when I was comfortable in my IBM career, knew that I wasn't going to move up any higher than I had already attained, and had surrounded myself with good managers running the day-to-day operations of the eleven Industry segments that I had overall responsibility for. I can honestly say that my military history love and working with my passion for veterans never got into the way of my IBM responsibilities. I've always been a multi-tasker, so this was just unrelated things I was focused on.

And speaking of good people running the day-to-day operations of our part of the IBM business, I would be remiss not to mention the great team that I had selected and kept me moving forward at IBM. Going back to my second Kansas City tour in 1982 to 1985, that is where I met Donn Atkins, David Glenn, Steve Scott, Kathy Schulte, Moe Cougher, Mark Roberts, and Mike Welbaum. These seven people did great things for IBM and for me personally and professionally. It's amazing how you get comfortable with people you know who share your work ethic and that you can trust.

Over the next twenty years until I retired in 2002, it seems one or more of these people (with Brian Lewis and An Brewer joining the group a couple of years later after I moved back to Atlanta) were always on my team, working for me or alongside me. We shared a lot of successes, experiences, funny stories, and are still friends today. And, of course, my original boss when I started selling at IBM, Gary Swanson, remains a good friend and is still my mentor.

* * * * * *

While 1995 was a good year for me as far as my IBM career blossoming and my military passion growing, it was also a tough year personally. My brother Jim, after surviving and thriving since 1969 dealing with being a quadriplegic, had gone as long as he could. Various health issues continued to pile on to his condition and on February 22, 1995, he died. I visited him the last few years as often as I could get to Miami (IBM reps in south Florida got great support from me). He was in the hospital in February 1995. I found a reason to visit Miami on my way to an IBM business trip in Washington, DC. I spent as much time as I could with him for the two days I was there. As I walked out of his hospital room late that afternoon to catch my flight to DC, I knew that would be the last time I saw him alive.

And it was. As I was ready to fly home to Atlanta that Friday, I received a call from my parents that Jim had died. He was buried in our hometown of Heavener, where our parents would later be buried next to him.

That wasn't the end of bad Family times in 1995. In March, while I was on an IBM trip to Denver, we learned that Daddy had prostate cancer and the prognosis was not good. By early July, we knew his days were numbered. I told my team at IBM that I would be gone as long as necessary and to call me if they needed me, I would be with my parents in Oklahoma.

Early on the morning of July 21, 1995, I woke up and walked into my parents' bedroom. Daddy was in a hospital bed pulled up next to their bed where Mother was sleeping. As soon as I saw him, I knew he was gone—Mother was still asleep. I went to the phone, called my brother Bill to break the news to him, then called the Dowden Funeral Home. Losing a parent is tough, but we knew that the loss of Jim in February had taken a lot of the fire out of Daddy over the past months. He was now with Jim in heaven.

On a personal note...July 21, 1966, was the date that I started the biggest adventure of my life, my year in Vietnam. July 21, 1995, was the date I lost the man I admired the most in my life. Every year, July 21 is a bittersweet day of memories for me.

In 2001, IBM decided to elevate and put a Vice President as leader of SMB Industry Marketing. As someone who was an "old guy" in IBM terms (58 years old at the time), the job went to a well-qualified woman in her 40s, who I was very supportive of. While somewhat disappointed, I understood I had peaked. The higher-level VP I worked for offered me a worldwide job as a one-man gang pushing a software product I knew nothing about, nor cared anything about. I asked him what my alternative was if I didn't take that job. He said, "I suggest you consider retiring."

Again, I realized IBM was changing, I was part of the old school, and under Lou Gerstner, our CEO since April 1993, we old timers weren't held in the high esteem we once were.

Since I had done zero preparation for life after retirement from IBM, I opted to take the job offered and started learning it and pushing the rope up the hill. Even my closest friends in IBM, ones whose careers I had helped move forward, told me that what I was responsible for, IBM's version of Linux, wasn't something they could afford to spend any time or resources on in their current jobs.

Memories of 9/11/2001

The Fall Plan—a ritual at IBM where all organizations put together their wish list of how much money they need to grow their business through the next year required a lot of work in September and October each year. On that fateful morning of 9/11/2001, the team I was on were on a conference call discussing our requirements for 2002. Since it was an early morning call, many of us were working in our home offices (IBM encouraged us to work from home). As we were talking, I got a call from our son, Rob, on my cell phone. "Dad, turn on the TV—a plane just hit the World Trade Center."

I quickly went into the next room and flicked on the TV, expecting to see a Piper Cub or equivalent had hit the building. In 1985, I had taken Kristen to New York City to celebrate her 16th birthday, just the two of us. One of our treats was to have lunch on the very top floor of the World Trade Center. This was a place I had been.

Instead of the small plane I had expected to see, it was obvious a full-sized passenger jet had hit the building. I was stunned, left the TV on, and returned to the meeting. One of our team members was taking the call from a phone booth in Midtown Manhattan, on her way to LaGuardia airport to take a flight out to call on a customer later that day. She commented, "There are people running around me like crazy. Does anyone know what is going on?" I told the group what I had just seen.

We attempted to get back to the topic at hand, but we were all distracted. Soon, Rob called me again and told me another plane had hit the other building. This was obviously not an accident but a terrorist attack. I came back to the conference call and said, "Folks, you can talk Fall Plan if you want but I'm signing off. We have much bigger problems now than an IBM budget." And I hung up.

Upstairs, Jan was finishing packing our bags for a trip we had planned to leave on that evening, a ten-day trip to Europe, just the two of us. Naturally it didn't happen that day, nor that year. We rescheduled for late May of 2002 and took Mark, and Jan's mother with us—that's another story for later in this section.

The Beginning of the End for Me at IBM

I was assigned to work for a hotshot new executive, probably in his late 30's, who had worked outside IBM and thought that we career IBMers were part of IBM's problems, not a wealth of knowledge on how to work through the maze of IBM.

Interestingly, I informally worked as an advisor to several high-level executives who were hired from outside IBM. Once they saw the complexity of the IBM system, the smart ones would find an old-timer like me and use us as an off the record confidential sounding board to help teach the system to them. I enjoyed doing that and spent several meetings, over lunch, dinner, or a drink helping these new to IBM executives learn the internal workings of IBM. But the young stud I was working for always cut me off when I offered him some advice or even options on ways to solve problems. It was obvious that he wanted to get rid of me. When the next downsizing came, I was at the top of his list to eliminate.

By then, the bloom was off the rose of IBM as far as I was concerned. I have frequently said that I should have retired after

30 years instead of staying on for the last four years. While Lou Gerstner saved IBM from major problems in the first five years he was there, he stayed another five and effectively killed the rich culture of devotion and commitment to IBM that thousands of employees had built over the many years since 1914. That was when Tom Watson, Senior joined the Computer-Tabulating-Recording Company (CTR) and in 1924 renamed it IBM. The Basic Beliefs that Tom Watson developed, and IBM lived by—Respect for the Individual; Provide the Best Customer Service in the World; and Strive for Excellence in Everything You Do, were left in the dust as Gerstner and other outsiders he brought in were determined to kill our culture. Sadly, they were successful.

A Fabulous Ten-Day Trip to France — May/June 2002

After being declared "surplus" by my illustrious manager, I knew my IBM days were over. Without letting that deter me, Jan and I decided to go ahead with our plans made the previous fall and head to Europe to take the trip we had planned to start on 9/11/2001. As things turned out, it was an even better trip than we had anticipated. Rather than just the two of us, we took along two Family members—Mark, our son, who had just graduated from Walton High School, and Jan's mother, Peggy Savage.

I am amazed at how the old adage, "Even a blind squirrel finds a nut" came true on that trip. God was looking out for me—read on to learn about that.

We flew out of Atlanta in late May 2002 on an overnight flight to London, took a train to the Chunnel terminal, and then took the Chunnel under the English Channel to Paris. From there, we boarded a fast train to Provence, in southern France. So far so good. We got off the train with all our luggage (you can imagine how much "stuff" Jan and her mother had—Mark and I both traveled light).

I casually walked up to the Hertz desk to rent a car. As I usually did in my extensive travels over my many years with IBM, I hadn't made a reservation. IBM was Hertz's biggest customer, so they always had a car for us. I asked for a car, and they informed me that no cars were available, it was a major holiday in France. Gulp! Without breaking a sweat, I pulled out my IBM identification card and, sure enough, suddenly Hertz had a car available. So far, so good. Unfortunately, I let Mark choose the car. He picked a "cute" small car that we could barely get the four of us and our luggage in.

We took off like I knew what I was doing (which I didn't) and drove through the ancient town of Aix-en-Provence. Streets were narrow, I focused on driving and Jan, Peggy, and Mark enjoyed sightseeing. They kept asking, "Where are we staying tonight?" Beats the hell out of me, I thought—I didn't have a reservation.

In the back of my mind, I remembered talking to Ron Marksity, a fellow Army officer and friend I had served with in Vietnam, who had worked extensively in Europe, told me about a great hotel in Aix-en-Provence. God was looking out for me; I saw a sign with an arrow pointing to that hotel. I followed the signs, pulled up into the parking lot like I knew what I was doing, and told my passengers to stay in the car.

I walked up to the desk, asked for a room for four, and they said they only had one—a chateau that I had walked by as I walked into the hotel. That was all since it was a holiday weekend coming up, and it was only available for one night. I let them show it to me—it was the fanciest place I had ever seen—and asked them what it cost. Expensive, but I was about to retire and had severance pay coming from IBM, so I booked it.

I went back out to the car, gathered our luggage, and told them we had a "barely adequate" room, but we'd have to make do with it. As I took them in, the looks on their faces were ones I wished I had captured on my camera. It was fantastic, and historic.

After settling in, I took Mark into the main hotel and bought him his "first" beer. He had turned 18 in February and legal drinking age in France was that. We sat and talked and enjoyed one or two beers, a great father/son experience. Over time, I realized I was fooling myself—odds are he had had a few (or more) beers during his high school days, as most kids do. But it was a great fantasy and I still remember it. (And when Mark read this as an early reader, he assured me he never did have anything to drink in high school. Neither did I (nor his mother)—like father, like son. Always proud of you, Mark.)

The next morning, we had a great breakfast, enjoyed the grounds of the hotel a bit, and then headed out to our next destination—Nice, France. Once again, fly by the seat of my pants Bob, had nothing reserved and was trusting his instinct and dumb luck to find us a good place to stay. I will admit, my pucker factor was up since I now knew this was a holiday weekend in France. We got to Nice, pulled into an overlook with a map of the area, and viewed the beautiful city and bay that it surrounded. My travel experience kicked in and I decided that there will be lots of hotels around the beach area. That was our next stop.

The car was so full of bags that we were uncomfortable leaving it, so Jan and I left Peggy and Mark to keep an eye on the car while we went into a hotel whose sign we had noticed—*Hôtel La Pérouse* (my favorite hotel I've ever stayed in). Like the IBM traveler that I was, I walked in like I owned the place and asked for a room for four people. They explained they were sold out, except for one room, and it was expensive.

By now, I wasn't going to embarrass myself by letting my fellow travelers know how stupid I had been with no reservations, so I asked to see the room. Up the elevator, we got out and went into a nice, but not overly impressive room. Then they opened the door and took us out onto the patio—which was the largest patio I'd ever been on in my life! It covered the top of a hill/mountain that sprang up just off the beach. The hotel was built around it. I paced it off, and memory says it was about 25 x 50 feet, or larger. It had a view overlooking the beach. I was sold—book it, Danno—for two nights.

Jan and I went back to the car to get Peggy and Mark and the luggage and, of course, told them how inadequate the room was, but we'd have to make do. When we showed them the deck, both of their eyes lit up and they were as happy as we were. A few minutes later, I saw Mark out on the deck, looking down at the beach with the binoculars we had brought with us. He told me, "Dad, I'm going to take a walk on the beach, I'll be back before long." I wasn't comfortable with that in this foreign country, but soon knew his reasoning when I picked up the binoculars and looked down at the topless beach. I think my next comment was, "Wait a minute, Mark, I'll go down with you."

By the time we got back up to the room, Jan and Peggy had checked out the beach and knew what we had been up to. After all, boys will be boys.

The next two days are full of great memories. We ate both nights in outside restaurants off the beach of Nice, fabulous food, took a daytrip to Monte Carlo and visited the casinos and saw the cleaning up from the Monte Carlo Grand Prix auto race which had run a day or two before we got there, then on to Cannes where their annual film festival had just concluded. It was another topless beach that Mark and I enjoyed. All in all, Nice and the surrounding area is a place I hope Jan and I can visit again—and I'd love it if our whole Family visited it with us. One of my favorite places ever.

From the south of France, we turned in our car and took the fast train back to Paris, changed trains, and went on to Normandy, where the next part of our adventure was.

Since I was a young boy, I had been enthralled with the history of WWII and especially the landing on the Normandy coast on D-Day, 6 June 1944. Now I was going to see it in person. Philippe Cornil, a European friend I had made over the internet a few years earlier, and had visited us in Atlanta, was our host. He owns a bed and breakfast in Ste. Marie du Mont, the first village off Utah Beach, the landing place for my 4th Infantry Division on D-Day.

It was a fabulous experience. For openers, Philippe had scheduled a book signing for me with my *War Stories* books, where I sold a decent number of books and met several locals who had been there on D-Day, 1944. Of course, we walked Utah Beach, visited the American Cemetery above Omaha Beach (after visiting Omaha, Sword, Juno, Gold beaches) and toured many of the battle sites of the 4th Infantry Division in the month of June 1944. On June 5, 2002, Philippe took me to Ste. Mere Eglise to pick up two American paratroopers (current generation) from the 82nd Airborne Division, who would be spending the night with Philippe and us; and making a parachute jump on June 6 to reenact the jump in 1944. That night, after lots of talking among us, Philippe asked if I'd like to go on a "patrol" to see what it was like the night of June 5, 1944, when the Airborne troops jumped in.

Of course, I jumped at the opportunity and Mark and the two active Army paratroopers did as well. We took off as a patrol of five unarmed guys, with none of them as excited about the experience as I was. We walked away from Ste. Marie du Mont, so the lights were to our back, and were walking into the darkness. As we walked down a road between the hedgerows, I could feel the alertness and anxiety of the paratroopers from 58 years before. As we walked along, Mark flicked his cigarette lighter as he lit a cigarette — damned near scared me to death. I told him to put that thing out. Having not experienced life in the military, Mark didn't know smoking and patrolling are not concurrent tasks.

At the book signing earlier in the evening, we had met some British re-enactors who were simulating American troops of the 4th Infantry Division in their re-enactment group. They had asked me if I would like to go with them to Utah Beach at 0600 on D-Day morning to be there at H-Hour, 0630. Naturally I jumped at the opportunity, Mark and Jan opted to let me tell them about it, they would continue to sleep. It was another experience I will never forget. At 0620 hours, I took my shoes off and started wading out into the cold Utah Beach surf until I was chest deep. By then it was right at 0630 hours, H-Hour on D-Day (plus 58 years), and I turned around and scanned the beach to try to envision what my ancestors in the 4th Infantry Division had seen in 1944.

Nobody was shooting at me, no explosions were going off inland from naval gunfire, but the experience gave me a memory that I will forever cherish. I have nothing but ultimate respect for all our WWII veterans (and all veterans) and will forever work to help preserve their memories.

From Normandy, we went to Paris for a couple of days (I had reserved a hotel room there), saw the normal tourist spots, and then took the train back through the Chunnel to London and flew back home to Atlanta. All in all, it was a great trip, I got away from my IBM "forced" retirement worries, and had a great experience with Jan, Mark, and Peggy.

I continued to do what needed to be done for my last three weeks at IBM. I got a lot of calls from friends I'd made over the previous 34 years. Most appreciated were two calls I got from IBM VP's who had worked for me on their journey up to the executive suite. Both Donn Atkins and Jim Gregory called and offered me a job if I wanted to continue at IBM for a few more years. I was honored they would make the offer but was comfortable that it was time for me to start the next phase of my life. I had no clue what it would be, but I knew that the bloom was off the flower of IBM for me. I will always cherish my IBM years. My focus will remain on the first 30 years and overlook the last few years of turmoil.

My last day at IBM was June 30, 2002

It was a melancholy and bittersweet day. My last official IBM function was to fly to Kansas City to host the Quarter Century Club luncheon for Steve Scott at Kansas City's historic Union Station, a block away from where IBM's current offices were. Steve was/is one of my long-time friends and employees who I had worked with in several jobs in my last ten IBM years. Assembled there was Gary Swanson, my mentor, who had hired Steve into IBM; David Glenn, another favorite employee that I had mentored; and a few others from Steve's career to date. After the luncheon I walked across the street to the grounds of the Liberty Memorial and World War I Museum, thought about my long and mostly very positive IBM career, and then flew back to Atlanta.

Ten days into July, I was still in my office, waiting to be processed out of IBM. I finally picked up the phone and called the Vice President that my boss worked for and simply said, "Is my

34-years that I worked for IBM so unimportant that my boss (for the life of me, I can't remember his name, which is probably good) can't take the time to process me out of the business?" And I shut up. The VP was apologetic, called David Glenn, by then an executive in a different department at IBM, and asked him to out-process me. That happened the next day. David told me that was the hardest job he ever did in IBM—he and I were and still are great friends. He did tell me, "I'm not going to ask you for your IBM identification card." I replied with, "That's good because I'm keeping that for my personal archives."

As I summarized my 34 years at IBM, I was proud that I always accomplished the missions given me, whether it was Hundred Percent Club as a salesman and sales manager, or whatever area I was assigned working internally with IBM, our Business Partners, and our customers. I counted eleven IBM executives at Director and Vice President level that I had helped train as they grew in the business. One who did very well was Dan Pelino, who I hired when I was a sales manager in Evansville and was looking for a technical person to hire. Technical was not Dan's strength, but I quickly decided after talking to him that he was too good to pass up. My decision was a great one—he retired over the past few years after fantastic successes within IBM, including working in the CEO's office.

Thus ended my IBM career. I drove home and wondered what in the hell was I going to do when I grow up? I was two months short of my 59th birthday.

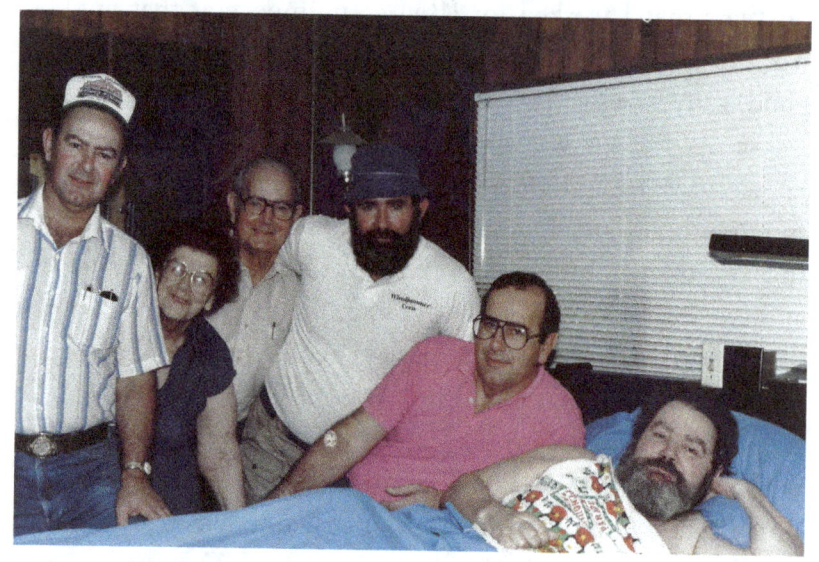

Our last Family picture, Jim's home in Miami, FL, early 1990s

Bob and Mark planting Ivy plants in honor of 50th anniversary of landing of 4th Infantry Division on D-Day in Normandy

Mark with his Granddaddy

Family church picture, early 1990s

Stephanie high school graduation — 1994

Stephanie, Jan, Peggy, High Tea at Ritz Carlton

Stephanie, Rob, Kristen, Mark, about 1994

Mark and Rob on butterfly chairs Rob made

What am I going to do when I grow up? "Follow your Passion."

Americans Remembered, Veterans History Project, Iraq War, Supporting our Military and Veterans — 2002 to Today

July 1, 2002 was the first time since I was in the 9th grade that I woke up without a job to go to, other than the first month after I got home from Vietnam. This was a major system shock to me — what was I going to do?

The first few days, I seemed to roam around in a daze. I did decide to start walking a minimum of 22 days per month (remember, I served in Vietnam with the 22nd Infantry Regiment — I love the number 22). The walking started in July 2002 and lasted until May 2003 when other priorities got in the way (my daily 4ID Update in Iraq project). I sometimes walked in the neighborhood, sometimes in the Chattahoochee River Park across the street from where we lived, and then more frequently further down the Chattahoochee River off Columns Drive where they had excellent, well-maintained, and fine graveled walking trails, and lots of people were always there. Being around people was something I had always done. Being at home without outside contact was not normal for me.

I did become the family "gofer" — Jan, Kristen, Rob, Mark all seemed to think that since I didn't have a job to go to, I would be happy to run errands for them at the drop of a hat. By the end of July, I let them know they could do like they had always done — run their own errands.

Finally, toward the end of July, Jan got tired of seeing me moping around the house and told me, "Follow your passion. IBM offered you a free week of transition training so take advantage of it." Great idea—and I jumped on it. Since IBM had eliminated so many jobs in the Atlanta area during the June 30 downsizing, transition classes were scheduled almost every week. While those younger than me who hadn't been able to retire were anxiously looking for their next job, I was looking for help in starting a totally new career as an entrepreneur.

I had applied for, and been accepted, as a Founding Official Partner of the Veterans History Project. This was a new federal law passed in 2001, hosted through the Library of Congress, where volunteer organizations would interview veterans on video about their experiences in wartime and have their stories preserved forever in the archives of the Library of Congress.

My purpose for the transition training week was to see what advice or resources they could provide for me as I started on this new adventure. I had two first projects to tackle—one was to create a 501(c)(3) non-profit organization so I could raise money to pay for my efforts over the coming years. The next was to create a corporation that would own the non-profit once it was approved. A friend of Jan's, whose husband was an attorney, liked my idea and her husband agreed to create the corporation for us and provide the paperwork that was ready to submit to the state of Georgia to make us official—pro bono.

That was done, I paid the fees, and the next step was to get the non-profit approval from the IRS. I started the process in mid-August, submitted it in late August, it was approved in record time by the end of 2002, and Americans Remembered, Inc. became our non-profit corporation, dedicated to preserving memories of America's veterans.

With the WWII generation starting to die off at an increasing rate, my initial focus was going to be on the "Greatest Generation." Gary Swanson, my first IBM boss and mentor, had told me at Steve Scott's Quarter Century Club luncheon at the end of June that he would like to work with me on this great project. Sure enough, early in 2003, Gary became the most prolific of all volunteers across the country of the Veterans History Project, interviewing over 1,200 WWII vets in about a ten-year period.

While I was doing interviews with (mostly WWII) veterans, Jan and I were trying to raise money for our non-profit, to pay for our cameras, recording tape, travel expenses, and hopefully someday before too far in the future a small salary for Jan and me. We found that the competition is fierce for non-profit money. We worked through individuals, corporate and private foundations, and other sources. More often than not, we hit a stone wall and did not get any money.

I continued to broaden my reach to veterans' organizations in the Atlanta metro area and had some excellent interview opportunities. One was Helen Denton, the WWII WAC who typed the D-Day orders for General Eisenhower while she worked on his staff in England (I later wrote and published her book about that). Another was a pilot who flew his P-47 for sixteen straight hours from England over Normandy, France patrolling his corridor to stop any German reinforcements on D-Day, landing only long enough to refuel and rearm before flying back across the English Channel. There were many more excellent stories I was hearing. I was in my element—my love of veterans and military history was being fed every day. Sadly, virtually all these WWII veterans are deceased now, but their stories will live on forever in the Library of Congress.

As 2003 came around, it appeared more and more obvious that war in Iraq was a real possibility. Sure enough, in January the 4th Infantry Division (4ID) was alerted that they would be deployed to Iraq. This was the first combat deployment of the 4ID since Vietnam. That was another turning point in my life. No, I didn't go to Iraq with them, but I did start devoting most of my time supporting the Soldiers and Family members of the 4th Infantry Division. The following piece that I've written for another book (yet to be published) explains my new challenge, opportunity, and passion that became all-consuming to me, frequently at the cost of ignoring other things…

When the 4ID was alerted for Iraq in January of 2003, I started surfing the internet and sending out some news items via email to fellow veterans, family, and friends who shared my interest in the 4ID. As the 4ID was deployed into Iraq, the updates became longer and more frequent, but still were limited to about 100+ veterans, family, and friends.

On May 18, 2003, a rainy Sunday afternoon, I happened to click on the National 4th Infantry Division Association web page and saw a string of notes on the guest book from wives and parents of 4ID Soldiers desperately looking for information about their Soldiers. After thinking about it for a few minutes, I sent a note to Roger Barton, our webmaster, and offered to make my informal update service available to 4ID Family members. My last comment in my note to Roger was, "I may be opening Pandora's box with this, but it seems like the right thing to do."

As that decision developed over the next months and years, I strongly feel that God tapped me on the shoulder that rainy Sunday afternoon and said, "I've got an opportunity to use the talents and passion I gave you, Bob. Are you going to do something or let it pass by?" I'll go to my grave thanking God for giving me that great life changing opportunity. I have many military friends around the world (active and retired) because of that simple note I sent to Roger Barton on May 18, 2003. (I still receive Christmas cards from many of those military Families).

Keep in mind, this was May 2003, the internet had not yet exploded to where it is today, cell phones were expensive and not owned by everyone, many people had slow-speed online communications into their homes, if they even had internet connections. All in all, I had to work with the limited tools available. I couldn't include pictures in my updates, too many people had the slow-speed lines that took forever to download anything other than text.

Little did I realize how that decision would change my life for the remainder of the 4ID's tour, and well beyond that as I update this in December 2021. Within the first four hours, I had requests from 85 people to be added to the list. My distribution list quickly crossed the 2,000 mark and grew daily as more people heard what I was doing. As things evolved, it made sense to add what became our most popular feature "What Our Families Are Hearing from Our Soldiers in Iraq." I shared, with discretion, messages/letters Family members had heard from their deployed Soldier.

Because of my keen interest in 4ID history, I always tried to educate others on what our great division had done in the past so that maybe they could extrapolate those experiences into the ones they were experiencing now, thus my "59 Years Ago Today about 4ID's service in WWII" feature was born (now it is 75+ years ago). And daily I tried to find the news articles that best summarized the 4ID actions in Iraq for the past day.

God gave me an ability to communicate, to be level-headed, and decide what needs to be communicated, and the drive to make my update service a reality for our Family members. To not use those God given talents in this time of national need would be wrong. As I said at the beginning, I am a patriotic American and this is a small way that I could help. I quickly had total buy-in from all the commanders and their wives, from the 4ID Commanding General and Chief of Staff on down.

With the above explanation, I became consumed with searching for information to send out to 4ID Family members, Soldiers in Iraq and at Fort Hood or Fort Carson, and to anyone else around the world who wanted to receive my daily "4ID Update from Iraq." For most of the deployment, they were sent out seven days per week. A normal day was for me to start work around 5:00AM and sign off around midnight. In addition to the daily update sent to everyone, I received several dozen individual notes and requests per day which I always tried to answer. My Family, fortunately, understood the value I was providing and put up with my ridiculous work schedule. Finally, in late fall of 2003, I started taking the weekends off and only sent the updates out five days per week.

One of the more interesting comments I got from a Soldier's mother was that "Our Soldiers aren't getting enough water to drink. My Soldier only gets one bottle of water a day." She went on to tell others reading my update that they should start shipping water to their Soldier. My response to that one note is probably what cemented my lifetime relationship with most of the commanders' wives more than anything I wrote.

I included in my next day's update that America has been sending troops to war since 1775 and they have never, nor will they ever, send them without the proper supplies, including water. Shipping water is ridiculous, don't do it. It is heavy and expensive. And I admonished the mother that her son was spoiled to plastic bottles of water rather than using the lister bags and water buffaloes (trailers) that the Army has used forever. Every Soldier has one or more canteens and whatever newer water vessels they were issued to carry with them. Several brigade and battalion commanders' wives sent me emails thanking me, with a note like, "I wish I could have written what you did, but we have restrictions that you don't have. Keep up the great work."

Ceilia Stratton, 4ID Museum Director, and I concluded that by the end of the first deployment in 2003-2004, over 30,000 people were reading the updates each day—either direct from me or from their own family members who forwarded them to their circle of influence. My intent is to create a book, something like *Best of 4ID Updates from Iraq* and publish it soon (hopefully in 2023). At the end of the first deployment, Major General Ray Odierno, the 4ID Commanding General, honored me with a Commander's Award for Public Service at the welcome home ceremony on the 4ID parade field at Fort Hood in April 2004. I treasure that award more than any I earned in the Army, other than my Combat Infantryman's Badge.

As the 4ID prepared to deploy again to Iraq in late 2005, I knew I couldn't afford to do the updates again, the drain it took on me personally and emotionally wouldn't allow it, plus I had started doing some other projects that actually paid me, my writing and publishing business had begun. With that said, I suddenly started hearing from 4ID Family members I had gotten to know, assuming I would once again start my update service with the second deployment. Thus, my patriotism kicked back in. If their Soldier (and them by default) was going to war again, I wasn't going to shirk doing what I could to help them out. This time I only did updates three days a week—Monday, Wednesday, Friday—which didn't tax me personally so much. Plus, new methods of communication were growing. The internet was becoming bigger and stronger, cell phones were becoming common, and the void of daily communications did not exist like it had in the first deployment.

The 2005-2006 deployment was our toughest as far as loss of

life was concerned, close to 250 killed and numerous wounded. This year proved that the war in Iraq was far from over. In another book, which I hope to get written in the next couple of years, I will include historical battle highlights from all four of the 4ID deployments to Iraq—2003-2004, 2005-2006, 2007-2009, 2010-2011—no rest for the weary Soldiers and Family members.

Suffice it to say, I supported our 4ID Soldiers and their Families during all four of their deployments to Iraq. The 2003-2004 deployment was daily, the 2005-2006 was three times a week, the 2007-2009 was weekly, as was the 2010-2011 deployment. My dedication and interest had not waned, but communications became better and better each year. High speed communications lines became common, cell phones and international communications at an affordable price allowed our troops and their Family members to talk to each other regularly, and the need for my 4ID Update from Iraq became less important.

I will say, instant communication is both a blessing and a curse. One morning during the 2007-2009 deployment, I received a panic call from the wife of a 4ID Soldier asking me if I knew if her Soldier husband was okay. My immediate thought was—how would I know that? She went on to tell me that she had talked to him the previous evening and he told her he was going on a patrol that night and would call her 'in the morning'. He didn't call and she started to panic—and called me. I did my best to calm her down. All the while, I was wondering why a Soldier would be so stupid as to tell his wife he was headed out on a combat patrol, and then tell her he would call the next morning. He overlooked one major thing—the enemy has a say in what happens on the battlefield.

I never heard why he didn't call her (he was okay), but I questioned the value of instant communications. Back during my tour in Vietnam, you wrote a letter, it took a week to get home and then it took another week to get a response. Thus, neither my wife, parents, nor I worried about what was happening daily on the home front or on the battlefield. I always said, and still say, "No news is good news, because bad news travels fast."

While these deployments were going on, I had contracted to write three books over a three-year period and had begun my Deeds Publishing company.

My interest in WWII and 4th Infantry Division history continued to get stronger. In 2004, on the 60th anniversary of D-Day in WWII, my Belgian friend, Philippe Cornil and I led a group of ten 4th Infantry Division WWII veterans and their Family members (a bus load) on a ten-day bus tour of Normandy, France—quite a memorable experience. And again, in early September 2010, Philippe led my first IBM boss, Gary Swanson, and me on another tour of the D-Day beaches and on into the Hurtgen Forest, Luxembourg, and other battle sites from WWII. A highlight of that trip was having the honor of folding the American flag at the American Cemetery in Normandy, overlooking Omaha Beach, at the end of the day.

In December 2014, on the 70th anniversary of the Battle of the Bulge, Philippe and I toured the key battlefields of that major series of battles, including the 4ID defending the southern shoulder of the Bulge in Luxembourg and visiting the besieged town of Bastogne, Belgium where the 101st Airborne Division were surrounded and the famous quote "Nuts!" came from the acting commanding general of the division when the Germans sent a message telling them to surrender.

On three occasions, in my role as president of the National 4th Infantry Division Association, I was invited to the White House to observe the award of the Medal of Honor to 4th Infantry Division Soldiers. The first one, awarded to SSG Clinton

Romesha for actions in Afghanistan on October 3, 2009, was awarded on February 11, 2013. I wanted so badly to be there, but it was just two months after I had open heart surgery on December 12, 2012. My common sense told me that to try to make that trip would have been foolish on my part. Thus, I sadly declined the invitation.

Six months later, on August 26, 2013, I was again invited to the White House for the Medal of Honor presentation to Staff Sergeant Ty Carter for actions in Afghanistan during the same battle where Clint Romesha earned his Medal of Honor. This time I was back in good shape and there was no way I would miss this honor. I sat in the audience as President Barack Obama awarded the Medal to Staff Sergeant Carter, an event I will never forget. After the ceremony, the reception in the White House allowed me to roam the area around the East Room and soak in the history of the building I was in.

On June 2, 2015, I was again in the East Room of the White House as Sergeant William Shemin, a 4th Division Soldier in World War I, was posthumously awarded the Medal of Honor by President Barack Obama for actions on August 7 to 9, 1918 during the Aisne-Marne offensive in France. His daughter accepted the Medal on his behalf. Sergeant Major of the Army Dan Dailey, a 4th Infantry Division veteran, attended the ceremony, along with Mike May and me, among others.

I will always cherish the opportunity to represent the 4th Infantry Division at these award ceremonies. I now could count four Presidents I had been in the presence of—President Harry Truman, President Gerald Ford, President Ronald Reagan (at the dedication of the 3-Man Statue at the Vietnam Memorial Wall in 2004), and President Barack Obama on two occasions.

Another memorable event in Jan and my life warrants a paragraph here. On Saturday, 24 April 2010 at 6:00AM, we were awakened by a horrific "BOOM" as lightning hit the chimney of our fireplace. The smoke alarms went off, we ran in and saw flames leaping from the fireplace wall. While I called the fire department, Jan ran upstairs to get the dogs out of the house. Long story short, over the next six months, we were out of the house, in a rental house, as it was being repaired. And it was that experience that made us know how great USAA Insurance company is. They covered virtually everything. When all their work was finished, we had almost all new furniture, a freshly repaired and repainted home, with a new roof, and will always sing the praises of USAA.

Americans Remembered, my non-profit organization for collecting memories from America's veterans and home front workers, had fallen by the wayside—not enough hours in the day. My three books were a big learning experience for me. You'll read more about them in my section on my publishing company, the next part of this book.

Annabeth at dedication of 4ID Monument in DC — 5 July 2002

Philippe, Ray, and Bob sample some Belgian beer.

Bob leading 4ID veterans in Normandy tour—June 2004

Flag folding ceremony on the 60th anniversary of D-Day

Bob and GEN Ray Odierno cut the ribbon on the 4ID Monument, Fort Benning, GA, July 2011

Bob with Army wives at Ft. Hood

Treasures in my office—guidon we used in Vietnam,
4ID picture Rob painted in 5th grade, American flag

Veterans Day 2020—Talking to Ava's class at school

Reflections on 16 Years as an Author and Publisher
2005 to 2021

Never in my early life did I consider becoming an author or publisher. "Now I are one..." and have loved doing both for the past 16 plus years and plan to enjoy continuing for years to come.

As I started writing the story of my life, it made sense that I wrote it in segments—this is the fourth segment I've tackled. The first piece I wrote was my time as an Infantry platoon leader in Vietnam in July 1966 to July 1967. That was the most exciting two years of my life and helped to form my adult life. I wrote that starting in 1986 and finally published it in 2007. Title of that book is *What Now, Lieutenant?* by Robert O. Babcock. The second piece was my memories of growing up in the small Oklahoma town of Heavener, where football and lots of other school memories were key elements. That second segment also includes my college years and my first job after I returned from Vietnam. The third segment was my 34-years working at IBM and raising our Family. Now, it's time to write about my author and publishing career.

The Army was my first career, only two years but the most focused and memorable years of my life. Something about getting ready and going into combat in Vietnam makes those years stand out. My second career was the longest—34 years as an IBM sales and marketing executive. This third career is where I have become an author, a publisher, an entrepreneur, and followed my passion and built a company that has grown far beyond any expectations I had when I started it.

All my life, I have enjoyed reading and writing. My brothers made fun of me when I sat inside with mother, reading and eating popcorn, while they were playing outside until they were called in after dark. I read all the book series that were prevalent in the 1950s—the *Buddy* books, the *Hardy Boys*, *Nancy Drew*, and many more. I was a regular visitor to the city library in my small hometown of Heavener, Oklahoma and read about every book for my age group through elementary school. It was never a problem for me to read 25 books a year, I passed that number early in each of my elementary school years.

I always made A's in English and enjoyed writing assignments. My first writing for others to read was as sports editor of our high school newspaper. When I went off to my freshman year in college, I was asked to come to an event during the summer to take a writing test to see if I qualified to "test out" of freshman English. I was handed my first "blue book" and given two hours to write about a 20th century invention that has changed mankind. I wrote about the airplane—and must have done well because they gave me six hours of A. (That was a nice offset to the five hours of "F" I got when I flunked biology the second semester of my freshman year—only time in my life I flunked a class).

Life went on, I graduated from college with an ROTC Army commission, loved my time in the Army, writing letters home from Vietnam regularly to my wife and parents, started my IBM career, wrote and typed my own customer proposals, and continued to enjoy reading—with military books taking a bigger part of my reading time. During the last half of my IBM career, I spent lots of time on an airplane and never boarded without a book, newspaper, or both to read.

On June 30, 2002, I retired from IBM and spent the month of July wandering around the house like a lost puppy with no clue what to do with myself. Since I was 14 years old, I had always had a job, now I was rudderless. After a couple of weeks of seeing how lost I was, Jan told me to "follow your passion." I took her advice and by the end of 2002 I had successfully applied for a non-profit 501(c)(3) organization through the IRS and became a founding official partner of the newly formed Veterans History Project, a subsidiary of the Library of Congress. (My non-profit company is Americans Remembered Inc.—temporarily allowed to lapse but now back into operation.)

My team and I enjoyed interviewing veterans, especially the WWII vets who were dying too quickly, and preserved many of their stories before they were gone. Then the war in Iraq started in March 2003 and my life took another turn (stay with me, I'm about to tell you how I became a publisher).

It's another story that is included earlier in this book, but I got very involved in supporting the Soldiers and Family members of the 4th Infantry Division during their first year in Iraq in 2003-2004. That consumed many hours of my time each day and I was considered a part of the 4ID team, both those fighting in Iraq and those on the Home Front at Fort Hood, TX, Fort Carson, CO, and around the country. The historian came out in me, and I sent a note to Colonel Don Campbell, the Chief of Staff of the 4ID as they prepared to return home from Iraq, telling him I wanted to write the history of this deployment to Iraq while it was still fresh on the minds of those who fought it, and the leaders were still available to interview. Major General Ray Odierno, the Commanding General, agreed with my proposal and in the late spring of 2004, I started interviewing many Soldiers of all ranks who had participated in that first year in Iraq (including the capture of Saddam Hussein) and writing their history.

The plan all along was for the first printing of the book to be a part of the Army Green Book series. I was also asked to print it commercially to sell to the Soldiers and their Families. I was working with a fellow Vietnam veteran who had his own publishing company and we worked well getting the book completed, turned over to the Army to print internally, and sending my commercial version to a printer. At the same time, I was pre-selling the book to those Soldiers and Family members who had made the history I was reporting. I wasn't surprised when I pre-sold 1,500 books in two or three months.

I used the money from the presales to pay my publisher and for him to pay the printer. Several weeks went by and I kept asking my publisher/friend when our books would be shipped. He kept saying, "Soon—the printer is slow." Finally, being the aggressive guy that I am, I called the printer myself and they said, "We're waiting on the publisher to pay for the books, then we will print them." My response was, "What??? You must be kidding. I paid the publisher for everything two months ago."

My next call, of course, was to my publisher (note friend has been dropped). He told me he had gotten into financial trouble and would have the money recovered "soon." My response was, "You have my money to me, in the form of a certified check, in 48 hours or I'm coming to you and take it out of your hide (or much stronger words to that effect)." He, a fellow Vietnam Infantry veteran, knew I meant business and sure enough, within 48 hours an overnight certified check was delivered to my home. It was short $500, which he still owes me, but there was more than enough to get the books printed.

I sent payment to the printer and began performing the job of a publisher as I worked with the printer on approving the proof copy, re-reading to be sure no errors were in the book, and approving and getting the books printed and shipped to me.

Since I was now a publisher, I asked Jan, "What do we call our publishing company? And I don't want it to be Babcock Publishing." She immediately came back with, "Call it Deeds Publishing." And that's how Deeds Publishing was born. Jan knew how much I loved the motto of the Regiment I had served in combat with in Vietnam. The motto of the 22nd Infantry Regiment, "Deeds not Words" has been in my signature block of every email I have sent out since IBM issued my first email address in the early 1990s.

Our local friends knew the challenges I had been facing with getting the 4th Infantry Division book published (by the way—title of that book is: *Operation Iraqi Freedom I: A Year in the Sunni Triangle* by Robert O. Babcock). One day a good friend who lived across the street from us asked if I would be interested in publishing the book her Daddy had written about his WWII and Korean War Navy flying experiences and his architecture business. With my frustrating book project off my back and time on my hands, I quickly agreed to publish his book. He asked what my charge was, and I told him I'd do it for nothing. He wouldn't agree to that, so I told him, "When it's done, pay me what you think it is worth."

I knew how to edit and to work with an author about improving where the book needed more or less detail and information, but I knew nothing about laying out a book for printing. My solution to that problem was the marketing department at Mt. Bethel United Methodist Church, where we were members. Ali Grasty and Jeff McKay were young college graduates working at the church and knew how to use the InDesign software to layout books and other things. They took care of that for me, I got a proof copy printed from a local printer, and asked Jim Warner, my first author, how many copies of the book he wanted.

His response was, "Print 20, I don't even know that many

people who would want to read my book." I knew he was wrong, so I pushed back. "Jim, print at least 50, and that is probably not enough." He said, "I'll never need 50 books and you're wasting my money, but I've got plenty of it so if you want to print 50, I'll take them." A week after I delivered the books to him, I got a panic phone call from Jim. "Bob, I'm out of books — can you get me some more?" And my journey and learning curve as a publisher continued. A few years later, Jim died. At his funeral, the discussion of the Family revolved around how great it was that he had written his story to preserve the memory of his life. And — just a week before he died unexpectedly, I had delivered a shipment of books that brought him up to 400 copies. Pretty good success for a guy who didn't think he could get rid of 20.

Word continued to spread and two friends from my first year on the high school football team contacted me separately and asked if I'd do a book for them. One was a nuclear engineer who wrote a historical short story fiction book, the other wrote a memoir of his life (by then, both were in their mid 60s age-wise). The nuclear engineer wanted to prove that engineers can write fiction, the other wanted to preserve his story for his Family.

Around this same time, the mother of a 4th Infantry Division Soldier who had been severely wounded in Iraq in 2006, came to me with a question. "Bob, I trust you and want your advice on whether this contract I got from a publishing company (who will go unnamed) is a good deal for printing the book I wrote about my experience with my son after he was wounded." As I read the 17-page contract, there was no question it was written to benefit the publisher and effectively was an insult to this new author.

With that, I offered to publish the book for her. We agreed to the first partnership, 50/50 split of costs and profits, of several I have done over the years. I over-estimated how many books we would sell and bought too many. As I kept pushing it through my large group of Army email contacts, an Army wife finally called me and explained it. "Bob, we know this can happen, but we don't want to read about it in advance." Bingo — that explained it. I have since donated copies of the book to Walter Reed Army hospital and to the Brooke Army hospital at Fort Sam Houston, TX. A good thing to read for people who were living through the pain of severe injuries sustained in combat.

Back in the summer of 2002 when I retired from IBM, my best banking software partner, Jerry Hall and Marguerite Butterworth of Jack Henry & Associates (JHA), flew into Atlanta and took Jan and me to dinner in recognition of my retirement and friendship. We stayed in touch and any time their business brought Jerry back to Atlanta, he would give me a call and we'd go out to dinner again.

Sometime in the spring of 2006, I mentioned to Jerry that they should write the history of JHA that he and Jack Henry had built from nothing, starting in 1976. Jerry acknowledged they probably should, but he had no idea how to do it. By then I had the 4th Infantry Division book about Iraq under my belt and told him, "I know how to write a book, hire me and I'll write it for you."

In a couple of weeks, I got a call from Jerry who told me that he and Jack had talked about how best to celebrate their 30th anniversary and they wanted me to give them a proposal to write a book for them. I took the proposal I'd presented to the Army for the Iraq book, modified it, and sent it to Jerry and Jack.

In less than a week, they had the signed contract back to me, along with payment in full (the Army paid me based on percent of completion, in multiple payments over a year). A few weeks later, they sent their corporate jet to Atlanta to pick up Jan and me to fly back to Monett, MO to get started. I worked feverishly on that project, and almost had it finished when Jack suddenly got sick and a month later, he died (on April 13, 2007). Jerry and the team at JHA decided out of respect for Jack to put the book on hold and not release it until 2008, which they did. That continued to build on my credentials as both an author and a publisher.

You've likely heard the saying, "The cobbler's kids have no shoes," meaning the cobbler is too busy taking care of customers to have time to take care of his own kids. I had been sitting on the book I wrote about my Vietnam experiences, starting in 1986 and finished in 1993, and never seriously considered publishing it. In the fall of 2007, I published *What Now, Lieutenant?* in time to give to Family members as Christmas presents.

2008 dawned and my 4th Infantry Division was once again in Iraq, for the third time, and I was actively engaged in support of them. I had agreement from the chief of staff and commanding general that as they went through the deployment was a good time for me to start writing their book to preserve the history. I was hired as a historian by the Department of Defense, assigned to write the 4th Infantry Division history of Operation Iraqi Freedom 2007-2009, a 15-month deployment. That job started in late 2008 and ended in 2010 when the Obama administration did a major cost cutting across the military, with historians being among the first to be let go. I did finish the book in late 2009. It is part of the Army Green Book series.

Our son, Mark, graduated from the University of Georgia in 2008. As you will probably recall, the economy was in the tank then, jobs were hard to find, and Mark was working as the morning manager of a Jittery Joe's coffee shop. He liked the morning shift because he was a bicycle racer and needed training time in the afternoons. As I was getting more business, and our church was growing, Ali and Jeff didn't have time to do the layout work on my books as quickly as they had done earlier.

So, I made a decision that propelled Deeds Publishing forward. I said to Mark, "Mark, if you'll come to work for me at Deeds Publishing, I'll let you train on your bicycle whenever you want, I'll pay you more than you are making now, and as long as you get the work done, you can choose your own hours."

His response was, "Dad, I don't know anything about the publishing business or the software it uses."

My immediate reply was, "Neither do I, we'll learn it together."

With that, Mark became employee #2 of Deeds Publishing. Now, thirteen years after he started, I will match Mark with anyone you can bring to me in the publishing business. He quickly learned the Adobe Creative Suite, learned the industry standards in book layout and design (and stays current as they change), always gets rave reviews on the book covers he designs, and has won numerous awards. While I continue as the lead guy bringing in new books to publish, and am lead editor, Mark owns the production side of our business and I never have to worry about it.

Not too long after Mark started working full-time for Deeds, he saw we needed more help, so he brought in Matt King, a friend and roommate from his UGA days. Matt quickly learned the software and publishing business and continues as a valuable member of the Deeds team.

As Mark, Matt, and I grew our business, more and more authors were wanting help with marketing their book. While I have a strong background in marketing from my IBM career, I was too busy finding the next books to publish, editing, working with authors, supporting the 4th Infantry Division and their Families during their deployments to Iraq, and later Afghanistan, to be able to add marketing support to my already full plate.

I quickly realized that my solution was right next to me—in

fact, I slept with her every night (and still do). Jan, my wife, had a job as director of marketing for a software company in the Buckhead area of Atlanta. While she made good money, her job satisfaction was lacking. The VP she worked for didn't appreciate what she did, even though the president regularly came to her with projects and for ideas. Plus, depending on traffic, she had anywhere from a 45 minute to hour and a half commute—each way—every day.

After listening to her dissatisfaction with her job many evenings as we relaxed from the day's work, I gave her this offer… "If you'll come to work for Deeds Publishing, I'll cut your daily commute to zero, I'll let you choose your own hours, I'll make you president of the company (I moved up to CEO), and you, Mark, and I will grow this company. There's only one downside—your pay is the same as mine—we work off profit, not a monthly salary. What do you say?" She jumped on the offer, put in her 30 days' notice at her current employer, and became a key part of the Deeds Publishing adventure, and our growth.

That was during the summer of 2010. Up to then, Mark, Matt, and I were publishing about one book a month. Over the next few years, we grew to where we were annually publishing between 40 and 50 books per year. As of this writing, we have published over 400 books with plenty more to publish in 2022, probably hitting the 425-450 books published milestone in 2022 (I hope to slow down in 2023—hope I'm successful.)

It is amazing what we have learned about publishing over the past sixteen years. I have had great experiences with authors, a few nightmare experiences, and I keep coming back for more. I could tell you tales that would make you laugh, make you cry, make you shake your head in disbelief. With each book and each experience over the first years of my publishing adventure, I learned more and stored it in my brain to use as I started working with my next group of authors. Now, sixteen years after my first book, I feel like there isn't a lot that will surprise me or fluster me—if I haven't seen it all, I've seen most of it.

In June 2016, Jan and I were invited to represent publishers at the 41st annual Southeastern Writers Conference at St. Simon's Island, Georgia. We spent a week speaking about publishing to groups of the 40+ authors in attendance and met one-on-one with most of them. As we drove home after a very enjoyable week, we were debriefing and concluded that virtually every author has the same questions about publishing. With that experience, we decided to write our *Deeds Author's Handbook*, to capture the many years of education we have gotten since I published our first book in 2005. We send it to all our new and prospective authors and get excellent feedback on its value. As the evolution of publishing changes, we update the handbook about twice a year. In December 2021, I came out with Version 12.

At the start of my publishing career, I would tackle just about anything that came my way. Too frequently, I listened to authors who convinced me that they had a best-selling book and that we'd both get rich if I would publish it as a "traditional" publisher. That means we (Deeds) put in all the work and money up front. As the book sells, we earn our money and pay the author a royalty once we have recovered our upfront costs. As more and more books that I funded lost money, I realized that I was a fool believing a first-time author was going to be the next Mark Twain, Ernest Hemingway, John Grisham, or JK Rowling. I was coming to the realization that most fiction authors have a very big ego, especially when they band with other authors in various writers' groups and tell each other how great they are.

Without going into detail, had I stayed on that disastrous course, we would have long ago gone out of business. The first few years I was funding Deeds Publishing from the book contracts I had with the Army and Jack Henry & Associates, and my personal IBM retirement income. With experience, I learned that authors who are unwilling to invest in themselves are likely writing a book as a "bucket list" item, or they have an ego that keeps them from dealing with the reality that over 5,000 new fiction books are published every day. Competition is fierce in the book business—especially in fiction.

We became what is known in the industry as a hybrid publisher—we have three contracts. In most cases (95+%), the author pays us for our expertise, we publish a book that is equivalent to the books published by the Big Five publishers, and the author makes all the money from sales of their book. Occasionally, I will partner with an author on a 50/50 split of costs and profits, and once or twice a year, I'll take all the risk and offer a traditional contract where I take all the risk and make most of the money—if the book sells. Before I do that, the author must convince me that this is going to be their vocation, not their avocation, and that they will work as hard on their book as I do on our publishing business (60+ hours per week, every week).

The highlights and what makes me smile is the thrill of watching an author hold his or her book in their hands for the first time (or hear them describe it since so many of our authors are scattered all over the country). I have made lifelong friends with some of our authors, some are like ships passing in the night that I seldom hear from again, and some, mostly traditional contracts, have become vicious and turned on me when their book doesn't sell like their ego told them it would. It obviously couldn't be that their book isn't that good—it's because the publisher (me) didn't spend enough time selling the book for them. One author who assured me she could easily sell 2,000 books in less than a year, has currently sold less than 200—and the book has been available over five years. Once she realized the hard WORK that is required to sell books, she lost interest and walked away to something that was easier and more enjoyable—she felt no obligation for the time and money I had invested in her.

As I write this, we have transitioned to focusing mostly on memoirs, military, a few coffee-table full color books a year, and fiction from authors that we've published for before and had good experiences with, along with a limited number of brand-new authors. Instead of 40 to 50 books per year, we plan to slow down to about 20 to 25 a year (if I can learn to say "no" better than I have in the past.)

I am also working on my love of writing—this book you are reading is one project that I have very much enjoyed getting immersed in over most of 2021. I also have several 4th Infantry Division history books that I plan to write over the next few years. This makes 12 books I have written and published, hopefully I'll hit at least 15 to 20 before I call it quits.

Mark has started a rapidly growing marketing company, Deeds Creative, and is still designing our covers and managing the production of our books. In Deeds Creative, he has attracted large customers in many industries unrelated to publishing that he is doing marketing work for. As I ease into retirement, he plans to continue running both Deeds Creative and Deeds Publishing. He doesn't want to let our Family business become a thing of the past. You can always find the latest information about Deeds Publishing at www.DeedsPublishing.com. Deeds Creative can be found at www.DeedsCreative.com.

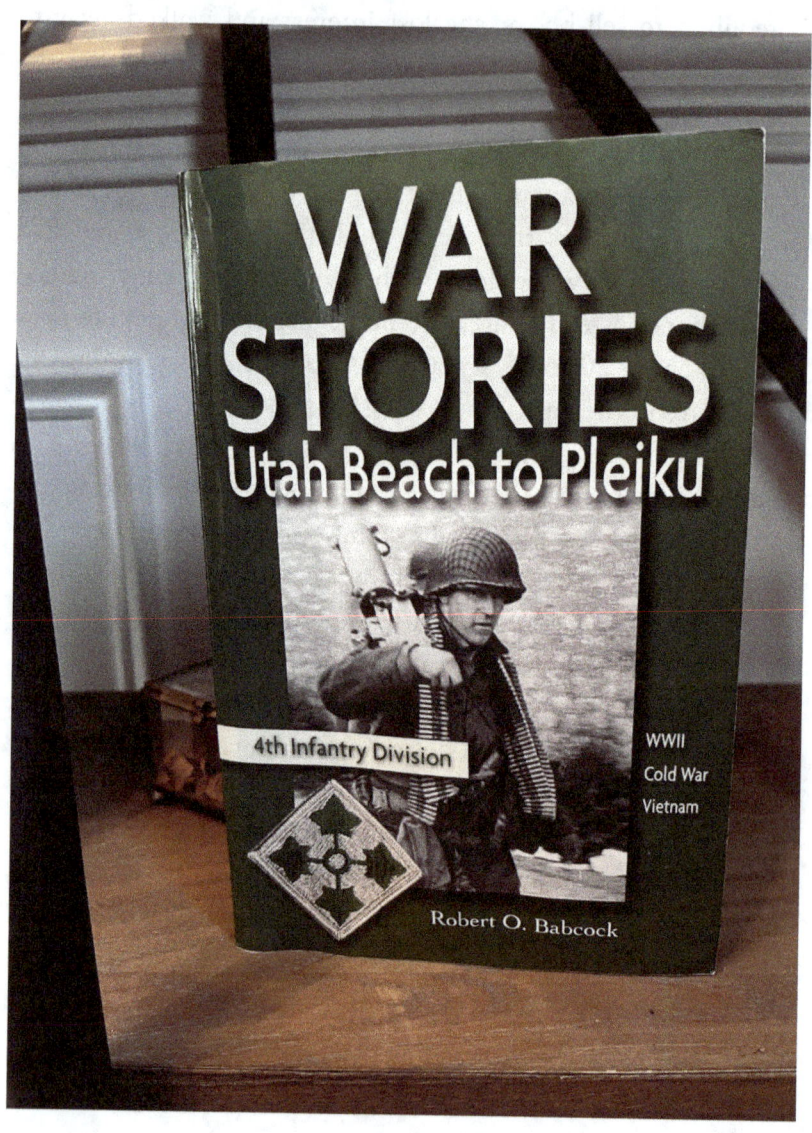

My first book as author/publisher, 2001

Republished into three books in 2014 for the 70th anniversary of D-Day

My Deeds Publishing office in Athens, GA from 2016 to 2020

Books written and published by Bob as of 2021—I'm still writing.

You get to sell your own books! Sundog Book Store, Seaside, FL

Moving to Athens to be close to Ava
2015 to now

In 2013, after Mark, Sarah, and Ava had moved back to Athens for Sarah to pursue her doctorate degree at the University of Georgia, Jan and I started talking about selling our home and following them.

With Mark continuing to be the most important piece of Deeds Publishing, it was inconvenient for him to be an hour and a half drive (best case) to three-hour drive (bad traffic days) when we needed to meet with an author, or with him, in person. Jan and I loved the dream home we had lived in since 1990, but it was too big for just the two of us. Many of the friends we had made in our neighborhood had moved away and there was no real reason to stay where we were, even though we were comfortable there.

We had friends that we had known many years through church, IBM, veterans' organizations, and other sources, but the pull of three-year-old Ava was very strong. With Kristen, Annabeth, and Rob long moved from the Atlanta area, our only Family left in metro Atlanta were Stephanie and Maxx.

By Christmas 2014, we had pretty much agreed that we were going to put our house on the market and move to Athens and rent a house until Sarah had completed her doctorate degree. We had no reason to be in Athens other than Ava, Mark, and Sarah and didn't want to be stuck there in case Sarah got an offer someplace else once she graduated.

After test marketing our home in 2014 with a 'friend' realtor who did a poor job trying to sell it, we shopped for a strong reputation realtor we didn't know and decided to put it on the market on January 30, 2015. Based on our previous experience, we were thinking the home would sell in late spring and we would move in the summer, with plenty of time to get 25 years of "stuff" disposed of and organized for a move.

How naïve could we be? The house sold to the first couple who looked at it on January 31. They offered full price with one caveat—they wanted possession on March 1. We got them to agree to give us until March 10, accepted the offer, and panic set in. The first two weeks of February, I was committed to be out of town working in my part-time IBM consulting job, teaching global sales school. I had three weeks to pack and move 25 years of life, with a good chunk of it going into storage because we knew we would be moving to a much smaller home.

Those who have done a move like that can understand why we have things that were packed in the last half of February 2015 that we haven't seen since. I know these things are important, that we may need them one day, so they remain packed in boxes, first in rented storage facilities and now that we have purchased our final dream home, in our basement.

Suffice it to say, it was late afternoon on March 10, 2015, when Jan and I threw the final things into our car and moving van and vacated 1588 Asheforde Drive in Marietta, GA, a home we had loved for 25 years, and drove to the start of our new adventure in Athens, a rental home at 88 Charter Oak Drive.

We acclimated quickly to our new home and to Athens, excited about our new adventure. With no room to run Deeds Publishing from our home like we had done in our previous much larger home, we decided to rent office space in downtown Athens. After ten years working from our home, we felt like we were moving into the big leagues when we occupied two offices on the sixth floor of the Fred Building on College Avenue in downtown Athens. We could look out our window and to the left a block and a half south was the Arch entering the University of Georgia. We felt we had taken a major step upward with our business. A few months later, we moved to a suite of four offices on the north end of the same floor and felt even more like a successful business. We hired our first two intern students from UGA to help us with our workload—Ashley Clarke is still working for us as a very valuable full-time employee.

IBM was looking for more consultants to teach their global sales school, which I had started doing part-time in 2014. Jan was an easy sell to get one of those jobs since she had managed IBM sales school several years earlier.

In the way of work, lots of good things were happening. We were regularly getting more books to publish than we had capacity for. We could pick and choose which ones we accepted. The IBM consulting work was fun for Jan and me—got us back into the IBM culture that we had been so comfortable with when we were full-time IBMers. And, we sometimes were assigned to the same classes, often in Atlanta which let us be at home every night, and other times in New York, San Francisco, Dallas, or Raleigh, which gave us evening time together over a nice restaurant meal, and maybe a day or two of vacation before or after the class. We had a great visit to California wine country after our San Francisco class.

After our first year's lease came up in the Fred Building in early 2016, we had a notice posted on our door that our lease would not be renewed. I quickly called the landlord and asked him why. He told us one of the other tenants on our floor wanted the whole floor, had been there a long time, and we were odd man out. The following Monday, a friend of Mark's came into our office and told us about some rental space where his office was. We walked over there, loved it at first sight, and rented it on the spot.

As of April 2016, we were the prime tenants on the first floor of 345 West Hancock Avenue, the former YWCA building, built in 1912, that had been converted to offices (and on the National Registry of Historic Buildings). Not only was the rent cheaper, we had free parking and free internet service included—a great deal that we loved until we let it go in May 2021. A year and a half working from home during the COVID pandemic showed us that we can be just as efficient at home as in an office, and we were by now in our own home, not a rented one.

But all was not rosy…It seemed that every week we spent consulting at IBM, we got home and were behind two weeks in our publishing business, making the next week or two non-stop work. We quit doing IBM consulting in early 2017—enjoyable while we did it. The other challenge was we had zero friends in Athens, other than Mark, Sarah, and Ava. Try as we would, we didn't seem to be able to link up with neighbors or have any other way of connecting. In our years in metro Atlanta, Jan and I had our couple friends, our individual interest friends, and never felt lonely. In Athens, a liberal college town, with us both being conservative and not graduates of UGA, we seemed to be strangers living in a foreign land.

Two years after we moved to Athens, our landlord sold our rental house and we had to move. We found another place, on the east side of town and closer to where Mark's Family lived, which we liked and planned to stay in for at least two years, built a fence for the dogs in the back yard (at our expense), and after the first year they sold that house out from under us. By then, Mark and Sarah had bought a home in Athens and convinced us they were going to stay, so we started looking for a place to buy. In the meantime, we assumed the lease on the house they had rented for six years and learned what it was like to move to an even smaller house than the two previous ones we had rented.

In early February 2019, we found a home we loved, bought it, and closed on it the end of March, and moved in mid-April (and we built another fence for the dogs around the wooded backyard). We will never sell this house because we love it so much.

Back to making friends in Athens, we started attending Athens First United Methodist Church, got into a Sunday School class that, once again, did not include we outsiders in their inner circle. After nine months of frustration, we gave up on Sunday School, but continued going to church there. In mid-December 2018, we were sitting behind Archie and Priscilla Carroll one Sunday morning, they turned, started talking to us, and invited us to the Disciples Sunday School class. We gave it a visit the next Sunday, were welcomed with open arms, and have been regular members of that class ever since. Sunday School has become a real highlight of each week.

We continue to look for local friends, and are happy having Mark, Sarah, and Ava living just over a mile from us. Maxx, our then 22-year-old grandson, came from Florida to live with us on February 1, 2020, a month before COVID hit. He has been a joy to have here. I am convinced that for many young adults, 22 is the key year where their teenage personality goes away, and they transition to become pleasant and productive adults.

As I write this the day after Thanksgiving 2021, Jan and I are content in our home, will be at a bonfire this evening at Mark and Sarah's home, and know that the next chapters of our life will come from living here in Athens, Georgia, in our final dream home. But that story is for another book—I'm closing this one out today. Sarah did send us a text this morning which read, "I had a dream that we were all at Disney world! Mark and Bob were in a Dick Tracey show. It was so much fun! Now I want to go." Within seconds after receiving her text, Jan and I responded the same—"Let's Go!" Thus, I think before spring of 2022, we'll have a Family Disney World trip to add to our life's memories. It's been at least 30 years since my last visit to Disney World. (Our Disney World trip didn't happen in 2022, maybe it will in 2023.)

Ava and Sarah in Washington DC

Ava at the Statue of Liberty

Ava at the Statue of Liberty

Mark, Sarah, and Ava explored DC by bike.

Sarah and Ava ride toward Sanford Stadium, Athens, GA, November 2022

Bob, Jan, and Ava in Lander, Wyoming

Sarah and Jan in Dubois, Wyoming for Annabeth and Nate's wedding

Sarah, Jan, Ava, spring 2022

Reflections on 40 Years with my Special Lady

When Jan and I started dating, a popular song was *Special Lady* by Ray, Goodman, and Brown. That quickly became our song, and it remains so today. It brings smiles and great memories to me every time I hear it, as it does with Jan. The lyrics describe the 40 plus year journey we have had as a team... "You gotta be a special lady, 'Cause you got me sittin' on top of the world, Sittin' on top of the world..."

On July 18, 2021, Jan and I celebrated our 40th wedding anniversary with a week's vacation on the beach in Seaside, Florida. We have been looking forward to that for a long time. On January 1, 2021, despite the COVID pandemic that engulfed our country and the world, we made our reservation—come hell or high water, or COVID—we were going to celebrate our 40th anniversary on the beach. And we did.

It was simply a different location to spend another week with the special lady that I have depended on, loved, and spent my life with since July 18, 1981. During the COVID days, weeks, and months from March 2020 to the time I'm writing this, we have grown closer, not that we weren't always totally close and in love with each other. Days and weeks in the past 22 months which have been spent mostly with just the two of us were and are a blessing. We have never tired of each other.

Fortunately, Jan and I have always had a strong relationship. We share the same conservative values, have the same positive outlook on life, share our Christian faith, and love of our Family.

We love each other completely and always, and always have each other's back.

One thing we started early in our marriage was Saturday night "date night." That was a sacred time for us, we had a regular babysitter who knew she had a job every week, and we insured we had those special hours together over a nice dinner or movie or both. We religiously continued that through the first 30+ years of our marriage, missing a date night only on rare occasions. The past several years, we have passed the tradition along to Mark and Sarah and have volunteered to be their free babysitters for as long as Ava needs a babysitter. That is always enjoyable, and one of the main reasons we moved to Athens.

As is the case with many blended Families, we have had stumbling blocks along our journey, but nothing that we couldn't work through as a team. For a long time, we have never considered we have "yours, mine, and ours" kids (now adults with kids of their own)—they are all "ours." Fortunately, they feel the same way about us and their brothers and sisters.

I reflect on losing our parents, first Jan's dad, far too early, then my dad, my mother, and finally, Jan's mother who spent her last two years living with us (I'm still driving the car, a 1999 Nissan Maxima that she gave me when she moved in with us). Those are sad memories we will never forget and couldn't have gotten through without each other to lean on.

I think about our blended Family, the challenges we faced as our kids adapted to us and the new "normal" for our Family. Jan and I both understood, this too shall pass. And it did. Neither Jan nor I, nor Kristen, Rob, or Stephanie will ever forget "Taco Tuesday", the place we always ate on the Tuesday nights in Evansville when all three kids were with us during our first year of marriage, before we moved to Kansas City. Today, we are in regular contact with all four of our adult 'kids' at least weekly, if not more frequently.

I remember how Jan, without complaint, took the disappointments of her IBM career when the organization she was part of fell under my chain of command, and she had to go elsewhere in IBM. When we reflect on that, we benefitted from the excellent growth experiences she had, despite the initial disappointment.

I also remember how Jan, in a prime IBM job that she loved, manager in sales training, selflessly did what was right for our Family, left IBM, and became a stay-at-home mom for our two teenage kids who needed her love and attention. Plus, Mark benefitted from having his mom at home rather than going to day-care as he previously had done.

With the kids all gone from home, and my retirement from IBM, Jan is the one who encouraged me and pushed me to quit wallowing in doubt and start my journey through my retirement years. And you can hardly call what I've been doing the last almost 20 years "retirement", with Jan supporting me every step of the way.

I remember my obsession/passion with supporting our troops in Iraq, and their Family members, tying up the single phone line in our friends' home, Diane and Steve Brace, getting out a "4ID Update from Iraq" when they and Jan were scurrying around getting ready for Di's 50th birthday party. Jan should have strangled me, but she understood my passion for what I was doing—my Special Lady.

Our Americans Remembered, non-profit business, and Deeds Publishing (mostly profitable business), are my passions, not Jan's. Without hesitation, Jan worked as hard in both as I ever did. Always I could (can) count on her when a job needed done, when I needed a sounding board to decide direction, she was (is) who I went to and thought through the options with me.

Any time I have something physically wrong with me, it is Jan who checks it out, makes a doctor's appointment, and stands by me to make sure I do what I've been instructed to do. My open-heart surgery in 2012 was the biggest challenge we have ever had, and she, along with our whole Family (especially our RN daughter Kristen), were always there supporting me.

Hopefully you get the drift by now—Jan is my very special lady, for 40+ years the love of my life, in sickness and health, in good times and bad, 'til death do us part.

Quite frankly, this is a tough chapter to write. A love letter to my wife, best friend, partner forever, is between the two of us, not something to try to explain to the world at large. Those who have the good fortune of having a "Special Lady" to share your life with understand what I'm trying to say. We have 40+ years of great memories, great experiences, some sad and bad times, but in the big scheme of things, I wouldn't take anything for the life I've had the great fortune of living with Jan.

Both of our parents had similar relationships. We learned from their undying love and partnership. We still fondly remember our days with them as our great examples as we reflect on how fortunate we were to grow up in similar home environments.

Jan is a fixer and I'm a leader. I've learned as I've had a few health challenges over the years that the fixer in her trumps the leader in me. When Jan takes over, I've learned to follow her lead and she always takes care of me (or anyone else who needs her help). Woe be unto me if I try to play tough guy and not do what she tells me to when she is in fixer mode. That's one piece of our unconditional love and partnership. And I'll stop there—and reflect on my Special Lady that I will love forever.

Our wedding day, July 18, 1981

Trip to Utah Beach, 2002

Jan completing the bicycle leg of a duathlon

Bob and Jan at Mark and Sarah's wedding, May 21, 2005

Bob and Jan at 4ID Memorial, Fort Hood, TX, April 2004

Annabeth, Maxx, and Jan with Rob's butterfly chair

Bob and Jan on the beach in Seaside, FL—our favorite vacation place

In front of the fireplace at our home for 25 years in Marietta, GA

Fall in the North Georgia Mountains — a favorite place

Jan and Bob on the beach in Seaside, FL, celebrating 40 years

A Deeper Dive
Three Stories Worth Writing More About

As I wind up this journey through the life and times of Bob Babcock, there are three stories that had a profound impact on me—first and very positive was participating in the 1996 Atlanta Olympics as a corporate volunteer—second was having open heart surgery in 2012, which was scary and profoundly brought out my faith in God—third is my valedictorian speech that I gave in 1961 that Jan miraculously found 60 years later.

Read on if you are so inclined …

Volunteering at the Atlanta Olympics
Written in July 2006 — Ten Years After the Event

Opening Ceremony

It was ten years ago this month that the Olympics came to Atlanta — July 1996. IBM was a major corporate sponsor and encouraged our employees to volunteer to help give the world a first-class impression of the United States, IBM, and Atlanta. I was among the first to fill out the paperwork, along with my wife, Jan. We didn't mark any preferences, just the box that said, "available for whatever is needed." I also volunteered to be available for the entire seventeen days of the Games. There was nothing at IBM that wouldn't wait for my return. This was an opportunity of a lifetime.

I was given two assignments — working for IBM as a sales/marketing executive, I was to be a host, helping take care of our big customers who came in from all over the world. My Olympics committee assignment was as a security guard, assigned to the main Olympics Stadium (now Turner Field, home of the Atlanta Braves) where the opening and closing ceremonies and all track and field events were held.

The weeks leading up to the start of the Olympics included fittings for uniforms, classes on what was expected of us, and generally getting this great volunteer force of Atlanta area citizens prepared to greet the world. Each time we met, you could feel the excitement and electricity in the volunteer force. We soaked up all the information provided, happily stood in lines to get our uniforms, and many of us started exercise routines to get into better shape for this adventure. Some Atlanta citizens worried about the traffic jams (which never materialized) and left town. Not me—I wouldn't ever miss this opportunity to participate in a world class event. Excitement continued to build across Atlanta as the day of the opening ceremony approached.

For the 9:00pm start to the opening ceremony, our job was to report for duty seven hours earlier. Jan and I showed up at the appointed time, she not quite as excited about this new adventure as I was. We volunteered to be a walking security patrol—our job was to walk from the middle of the stadium on the west side, around the inside north end of the stadium (on the walkway about halfway up the stadium), to the middle point on the east side and return. We continued to repeat the process for six hours. Our job was to do whatever was necessary to help the guests and maintain security.

We were an interesting looking patrol, me at 6'2" and 200 pounds (plus) and Jan walking beside me at 5'1" and 100 pounds soaking wet. If there was ever a Mutt and Jeff looking team, we were it.

The July Atlanta sun, humidity, and heat bore down on us as we walked our beat, greeting early arriving guests, watching the preparations on the field, and generally having a good time soaking in the experience. On the east side of the stadium was a cache of bottled water (this was the first time I ever drank water from a plastic, disposable bottle—a new product then, now they are everywhere), in a special place known only to the volunteers, to keep us hydrated. I made a pit stop at some point, and Jan continued the patrol, knowing I would catch up with her. As I approached her, she came to me with a concerned look on her face, asking for help.

The rules of Olympic stadium were that no smoking was allowed inside the stadium—this was in the days when smoking restrictions were just starting and were not universally accepted. An usher had seen a man smoking and called Jan, the nearest security guard, to take care of it.

You must picture this situation. Ushers were volunteers from the Atlanta area, just as we security guards were. They came from IBM, Coca-Cola, Delta, UPS, Home Depot, banks, and various other Atlanta area corporations and individual volunteers from all walks of life. It was the luck of the draw, or some specified the job they wanted, that separated the two groups of volunteers. We all had the same level of experience at our jobs and earned the same money—zero.

The usher uniform was sharp looking—Panama hats with a colorful sash around it, colorful shirts with the Olympics theme emblazoned across it, comfortable khaki shorts, and white tennis shoes. In contrast, we security guards had forest green long pants, black tennis shoes, white short-sleeve collared shirts with the appropriate badges and patches sewn on to make us look like a "rent a cop" at some office complex or professional sporting event. What set us off the most were the tan safari pith helmets that we all wore. To some our uniform was ugly, but me, I loved it.

If there was ever an obvious looking class system among volunteers—it was obvious that the ushers looked to be in a higher class than we security guards. And, even though most of them wouldn't admit it, the ushers probably considered themselves to be a notch above the security guards. Their job was to help guests find their seats, smile, talk to the guests, and call for help if anything out of the ordinary came up. And security guards were who they typically went to for help.

That was the situation that greeted Jan. The usher had politely asked the man to put out his cigarette, he had refused, and she had dutifully gone to Jan to solve the problem. When Jan walked up to the man, all 5'1" and 100 pounds of her, wearing that funny looking pith helmet, and again politely asked him to put out his cigarette, the man told her the same thing—he was not going to do it. That's where I entered the picture.

As Jan explained the situation to me, I reverted to my military experience and decided to fix that real quick. I stood over him with my tallest posture, a stern look, and was polite but very straight to the point. "Buddy, either put that cigarette out or you are out of here. If you don't want to do that, you can look at that Atlanta policeman over there (wearing a gun). His instructions are to back us up and do what we ask him to do. The choice is yours—quit smoking or leave." With a few expletives, he put out his cigarette. On each subsequent round on our patrol, I made sure to look into his eyes to make sure he understood that he wasn't to smoke—and he didn't.

The crowd started to build; we volunteers took turns with a break for a quick dinner in a tent outside the stadium, and then were back on our assigned tasks. Jan still wasn't feeling the excitement of the moment like I was, and the heat and constant patrolling was starting to wear her down. As for me, I was still fresh—sweaty, but still ready to tackle anything that came my way. I was having a great time.

Around 7:30pm, the dignitaries from around the world started to show up in the reserved area around the 50-yard line on the west side. Being a card-carrying IBM sales executive, I took it upon myself to greet them and welcome them to Atlanta and the Olympics. The looks on many of their faces were priceless. In their countries, lowly security guards didn't talk to heads of states or dignitaries. I knew that was the case, but I was a proud American volunteer (and military veteran), not a paid guard from their country. I continued to greet them as we patrolled—as much to see their reaction to my loud voice and smiling face as to welcome them to Atlanta.

As it came closer to the start of the night's events, we had finished our umpteenth circuit of the day and turned to start another one and then head to our stationary post assigned for the ceremony. As we walked back along our route, a man in a suit and tie blocked our way. "You can't come this way," he said.

"Whadda you mean?" I said, "We've been walking this route since 2:00 this afternoon—get out of my way."

He stood his ground and stared at me and repeated, "You can't come this way." I then noticed he had an earpiece with a clear tube running down his neck and into his suit. It then struck me—President Clinton must be coming in and they are sealing this area off. He was obviously a Secret Service agent. I told him my dilemma, "Our security post is at the top of the stadium behind you. How do you suggest we get to it?" His response was simple, "Not my problem, you can't come this way."

Being a man of reasonable intelligence, and with my wife standing beside me with a worried look on her face, I decided not to push the issue any further. We retreated, found a ramp that took us under the stadium seats, past the concession stands, and another ramp that brought us back up close to our assigned security post.

If you watched the opening ceremony of the 1996 Olympics, you will recall the dancers who performed on a platform around the northwest top edge of the stadium. All the entertainment was excellent but there was something about the dancers silhouetted against the night sky and Atlanta skyline that the crowd really loved. Our security post was at one end of that platform. My instructions were to not let anyone other than the dancers onto the platform. The breeze was nice at the top of the stadium, we wouldn't be walking for the next two or three hours, and I was looking forward to the assignment.

As we got to our post, we saw our good friends and neighbors sitting on the top row, right next to our guard post. I smiled to myself—they had paid top dollar ($625 per seat) for the four tickets for their family, and Jan and I had free admission and got a set of uniforms as well. Plus, once the dancers were off the platform, my job was to patrol the platform. I wasn't stuck in a seat. I could leisurely walk along the platform and had a great view of not only what was going on down on the field, but also could watch the staging of the next performers outside the stadium. Jan sat on the steps beside their seats on the top row of the stadium, glad to get off her feet after the long day of patrolling.

It was a great performance. Everything went off perfectly. Watching the excited athletes parade into the stadium was a thrill. From my walkway, I remember watching the Olympic torch as it appeared in the distance and quickly moved through the parking area and approached the stadium. Carrying the torch on a leg of the route was an honor which many people cherish still today. I could feel the history and the thrill of the Olympics experience as it came closer and closer and finally was carried right below my post and disappeared into a doorway leading into the stadium. The torch was passed while under the stadium and at least once after it came onto the field of play. We all know who carried it the final few steps and lit the big Olympic cauldron that burned throughout the games—boxing great and former Olympics champion (Cassius Clay) Muhammad Ali.

Jan rode home with our neighbors; I hung around to be available if needed and to soak in more of the excitement after the opening ceremony was ended. I walked across the field and came face to face with another boxing great—Evander Holyfield (man I wouldn't want to get into a ring with that big guy). I finally made my way back to the bus which took me to my car in a remote parking lot and got home after 2:00am. My body was tired, but my mind was racing as I replayed the events of the day.

My adventures were just beginning—at 8:00am that same morning I was to be in my IBM Olympics host uniform and begin that duty. Track and field events in the Olympics Stadium weren't to start for several days, so until then, I was focused on my IBM host duties.

IBM Host in Centennial Olympics Park

Although my night's sleep was short, my adrenalin was flowing as I drove to the SwissOtel, headquarters of the IBM Olympics volunteers in the Buckhead area of Atlanta, the next morning. IBM had reserved much of that hotel and the Ritz Carlton across the street to house our customers from all over the world as they flowed in and out of the Olympic Games. We would bring executives and their spouses in for three to five days and then they would leave and would be replaced by another set of executives and spouses.

With over 25 years of IBM experience at the time, I fully understood and believed in our Basic Beliefs—"Respect for the Individual," "Provide the Best Customer Service in the World," and "Strive for Excellence in Everything You Do." This was going to be an opportunity to do just that—look out for our customers and make this a memorable experience for them.

I was briefed on the day's events (IBM is big on briefings and making sure everyone knows what is expected of them). My first job was to ride the bus with our customers down to the large, air-conditioned IBM tent adjoining Centennial Olympics Park. Everyone was in a festive mood as we made the trip and were all impressed as they walked into the home-like atmosphere of the IBM tent. That was their place to return to when they got tired or needed a break or were ready to head back to the hotel. Plenty of food stations, comfortable overstuffed chairs, and a staff eager to help were always there. And it was air-conditioned—a welcome oasis in the Atlanta summer heat.

My assignment was a simple one. I was to stroll through the park, no specific route required, carrying a small white IBM sign on a three-foot long white stick. That sign, along with my purple IBM host shirt (much better looking than my security uniform—plus we wore khaki shorts instead of long pants) were what our customers were instructed to look for if they had any questions while out in the park. Effectively, I was an ambassador of good will for IBM and the Olympics, a job which I eagerly dived in to.

When I got hot or tired, I would return to the IBM tent, get something cool to eat or drink, sit for a while, and then go back out into the mass of people and answer questions. Many more non-customers than customers asked me questions and my extroverted personality was in full bloom as I again worked in the searing Atlanta sun and heat. I helped people find engraved bricks that they had bought (a large area of the park was covered with bricks, sold as an Olympics fund raiser over the previous two years) and took the time to find the ones I had bought in honor of Soldiers of the 4th Infantry Division and 22nd Infantry Regiment (my old Army units).

I learned where all the venues were and where things were in the park, directed people to where they needed to go, answered hundreds (sometimes it seemed like thousands) of questions, and often explained why I was carrying the IBM sign. My answer was always, "IBM put me here to help you. What can I do to help?" I'm sure lots of the general public walked away thinking that IBM wasn't the big stuffy giant that they might have previously pictured. Customers of other corporate sponsors also knew my purpose in being there, so they frequently came to me with their questions. Others like me from IBM and from the other corporate sponsors were constantly strolling through the park whenever our customers were there.

At the end of my shift, I made it back home and crashed into my easy chair before an early bedtime. The following day, I was down there doing it again.

That day, Sunday as I recall, did not have as many early volunteers as we had the previous day. I showed up and spent time in the IBM tent talking to customers before grabbing my IBM sign and headed into the park. As key IBM executives were having conversations with customers in the tent, they would grab one of us to take over for them as they moved from customer to customer and worked the room. I was talking with the "Who's Who" of IBM's largest customer executives and also with IBM's top-level executives. It was great to see these executives in this different environment, away from work and having a fun time.

That Sunday was also the day that all the negative press was hitting the news wires about the IBM scoring systems not working properly. Around 9:30 that morning, IBM chairman Lou Gerstner walked into the tent with a scowl on his face. He walked through the tent, spoke to only a very few people, and then stalked out. Even the casual observer would have known that he was not happy. We soon found out from the big TV sets in the tent about the computer problems. Fortunately, other key IBM executives were there, in good moods, making our customers feel special.

Jan had also volunteered to be an IBM hostess; her shift started at noon. She joined me in the strolls through the park and was also bombarded by people seeking information. That day was even hotter than the previous two had been and around mid-afternoon we decided to head back to the IBM tent for some ice cream, a cold drink, and a cool place to sit.

As we entered the virtually empty tent, we were approached by a lady, part of an outside events planning firm that IBM had hired, who said, "Purple shirts aren't allowed in here, this is for IBM customers only." I explained to her that I was an IBM executive, had been there the day before and that morning, had been talking to customers regularly, that several high-level executives (who I named to her) had thanked me for my good work that morning, and started to walk into the tent.

She stepped in front of me and said again, "Purple shirts aren't allowed in here." At that point, my blood pressure went through the roof. Nobody, especially a contracted events person who did not understand the IBM culture, was going to keep me out of an IBM location. I went to the back of the tent, the nerve center, and told her manager, also a contracted person (not an IBM manager), that the first basic belief of IBM is "Respect for the Individual" and that my wife and I had been working hard for IBM out in the heat and we needed a place to cool off.

The manager listened to what I had to say, saw that I was fuming, and told me to not get in the way of customers, to stay in the background, and we could stay in there as long as it wasn't too busy. That upset me even more—I was used to working with IBM managers who solved simple problems like that one. Jan finally had to take me out of the tent to let me cool off (in the 95+ degree heat). After calming down a little, I picked up my IBM sign, put the smile back on my face, and finished my shift in the heat.

When I got off the bus back at the hotel, I went directly to the great Atlanta based IBM Olympics management team, many of whom I knew, and expressed my shock and dismay that we IBM volunteers were not welcome in our own company's hospitality tent. To make a long story short, there was never again a problem with us "purple shirts" going into the IBM customer tent. The contractor event lady steered clear of me any time that I walked in after that.

Except for that one little glitch, my experience as an IBM host was very positive. Our shifts were of reasonable length and if spare tickets were turned back in by our customers, they were offered to us to use if our schedules allowed. I was able to take Rob and Mark, our two sons, to several track and field events during the seventeen days, plus their favorite event, the bicycle racing. We volunteers were treated with all the "Respect for the Individual" that I had always expected from IBM. The total experience—before, during, and after the Olympics—was a great shot in the arm and made me even more proud that I was working for IBM.

Bomb at Centennial Olympic Park

The night of July 27, 1996 will live in infamy in the annals of the Olympic Games. That was the night that a bomb exploded in Centennial Olympic Park, killing Alice Hawthorne, and injuring 100 others.

As fate would have it, that was the one day that I did not work during the Olympics. I had taken the day off to go with our sons to attend the cross-country bicycle races and spent the evening relaxing at home, preparing to put my security guard uniform back on the next day as my responsibilities moved from host duty at Centennial Olympic Park back to the main Olympic stadium to provide security for the track and field events.

I was sound asleep when my phone rang around 1:30am that

morning. "Daddy, are you okay!?" exclaimed the worried voice of our daughter, Kristen. She had been working the night shift as a nurse at a hospital in Oklahoma and had seen the news as it hit CNN. My grogginess quickly went away. I was wide awake and clicked on the television. I assured her that I was far away from the bombing, and she could quit worrying. The rest of the night I watched the raw, unedited film footage that was being run on CNN (this was when CNN was the only non-major news network—before Fox News) as they tried to piece together what had happened. Sleep was the farthest thing from my mind. I knew that my Olympic experience had taken a sudden change in focus.

As scheduled the next morning, I showed up at our check-in location to resume my work as a security guard. (With more than enough volunteers eager to work, Jan opted to let me have the fun as a security guard, she hadn't enjoyed it nearly as much as I did. Her next security duty was at the closing ceremony). Our briefing was longer than the one before the opening event and we all paid more attention to every detail they gave us. At that point we had no idea whether this was a random bombing or the first of many more to come. The killings of the Israeli team members at the Munich Olympics in 1972 crossed my mind.

Rather than being assigned a walking post, I was assigned to an entrance to the stadium, just under the Olympics torch cauldron that was the landmark of the Games. While staying very alert, I resumed my jovial greetings to all who approached me. I tried to keep a positive tone and act like everything was just fine. As the crowds started to come into the stadium, I stayed alert. What were the odds that someone would bring a bomb to this spot? Really pretty good, if they were so inclined. As stated above, the torch I was standing under was the landmark of the Olympics. If someone wanted to make a statement, what better target was there than the torch and those standing around it?

Around mid-morning, a man approached me, pointed to a small rectangular box covered in canvas sitting on a ledge on the outside of the stadium, near the very top, and high above my location. He identified himself as a retired New Jersey police detective and said it looked suspicious to him. My response was simply, "It does to me, too—I'll go check it out." I headed into the still sparsely populated stadium and up the steps, my heart pounding. I motioned for a couple of uniformed Atlanta policemen to come with me and explained what we were doing as we climbed the steps. The thought crossed my mind, "Babcock, why in the world are you doing this?"

As I got to the top and peered over the ledge, a feeling of relief washed over me as I saw what the canvas covered box was. It was part of the electronics of the public address system, not a bomb. The policemen were as relieved as I was—and we went back to our assigned posts.

On another day, we arrived around 2:00pm for the afternoon and evening shift. Events would start in the stadium around 6:00pm and the gates would be opened to admit guests at 4:00pm. Our first instructions were, "There has been a phoned in bomb threat, it is scheduled to go off at 4:00pm, and our job is to search the stadium to see if we find anything." All the security guards spread out and systematically searched the stadium. Our team was very focused as we walked through our assigned sections, eyes scanning everywhere to ensure no nook or cranny was left unsearched.

At about 3:45, we re-assembled under the stadium for our debriefing. Again, my common sense and military training came into play. I suggested to our team leader that if a bomb was scheduled to go off in fifteen minutes, didn't it make more sense for us to hold this meeting out on the field of play rather than under the stadium? He agreed with my logic, and we moved out to the track.

The time for the suspected explosion came and went and nothing happened. The gates were opened, the guests came in without ever knowing about the threat—the Games went on as scheduled.

The bomb put a higher level of concern on all of us at the Olympics, but it did not ruin the experience. Although we always kept alert throughout the Games, there were many more good memories than the few related to bombs.

Fun as a Security Guard in the Olympic Stadium

Since I had looked forward to the Olympic experience for so long, I wasn't going to let the bomb or threat of more bombs stop my work or cloud my enjoyment of this once in a lifetime experience.

Whenever possible, I volunteered to be a security guard near the finish line of track events. Right after the athletes finished their races, they came into a special area just off the track, walked past the always present NBC television camera to talk to reporters from around the world. Our job was to keep the reporters on one side of a metal crowd control fence and the athletes on the other side. That wasn't always an easy job. By nature, reporters are pushy and like to go into places where they don't belong. We were constantly telling reporters to get back to their designated area and not to get out onto the track or area surrounding it. As long as we kept an eye on them, most of them begrudgingly complied with our instructions. One reporter, however, was bound and determined that he was going to get onto the field of play to do his interviews.

Not all security guards were as aggressive as me and didn't take it as a personal challenge to do the job as it was supposed to be done. For some, they did their best and if that wasn't good enough, they accepted it. The reporter found one of those security guards and barreled his way past her. I saw what he had done and decided that keeping him off the field was going to be my personal responsibility. I saw it as a game, and the reporter probably did, too. I approached him on the field, told him he was not where he was supposed to be, and told him to get back with the other reporters. He eyed me up and down and said he wasn't moving. I moved closer and towered over him by several inches. My size and aggressiveness seemed to get his attention, so he retreated to the reporter area.

As soon as I turned my back and started scanning the area to see what else needed to be done, he headed back onto the field. I spun on my heel and cut him off at the pass. He tried an end run on me, but I had the angle and stopped him again. Maintaining my politeness, I again played my policeman card. I pointed out the uniformed Atlanta policemen standing nearby and explained that if I told them to, they would escort him out of the stadium and take away his press credentials (I don't think I had that authority, but I acted like I did). He again returned to the reporter area.

Each time I drifted too far away from him and if he thought he could elude me, he started edging toward the field. Since I had assigned myself as his one-on-one security guard, I stopped whatever I was doing and headed for him. He finally gave up and accepted that as long as I was on duty, he wasn't going onto the field. I enjoyed the experience, and he probably did, too.

Other memorable things happened around the finish line. I

found out that athletes from a lot of countries do not understand what deodorant is. The smell of many of the athletes was not something I like to remember.

Many world record holders and well known American and global athletes were within arms-length of me at the finish line area. It was obvious to see that they were at the peak of physical fitness — great specimen of humanity.

A German female athlete came to the reporter area after her race. She was good looking and very well endowed. Her spandex (or whatever material the uniform was made of) uniform left little to the imagination as to what was under it. I was standing behind her, looking at the reporters who were interviewing her. It was comical to watch their eyes — few, if any, were looking into her eyes. Most were focused on her obvious assets.

Olympic pin trading was a tradition that I knew nothing about prior to the Olympics. In a nutshell, corporate sponsors and others produced metal pins in various designs which were traded among the guests and athletes at the Olympic Games. I'm not sure when the tradition started but it became a great source of fun. As volunteers, we were given a supply of the various IBM Olympic pins and we pinned them on a cloth shoelace type necklace that we wore with our Olympic credentials. It was common for people to approach you, examine your collections of pins, and offer to trade for one or more of them. One of the rules for the volunteers was that we didn't harass or bother our customers trying to get their pins, but we were welcome to trade with them if they initiated it. I loved trading pins — it became like trading baseball cards. I got a few "Mickey Mantle rookie card" equivalents with my trading and kicked myself a few times when I traded one of those prizes for something that I later decided wasn't nearly as valuable. One of these days I'm going to dig those Olympic pins out of my memorabilia storage and admire them again.

The day of the closing ceremony finally arrived. In some ways, we were ready for it, in other ways, it ended all too soon. The newness and excitement of the opening ceremony was not felt by me during the closing ceremony, but I was still enjoying myself and staying alert in my security guard role. I was fortunate, along with Jan, to have been able to attend both the opening and closing ceremonies. The pageantry, pomp, and ceremony were carried off without flaw. My only memorable security event was when an IBM vice president I worked under in my everyday IBM job asked me to get him into the NBC hospitality suite in its prime spot overlooking the ceremony. I had to explain that NBC security guards at the door of their suite trumped us lowly "rent a cop" security guards and there was no way I could do that. He took it in good humor—at least he gave it a shot.

All in all, my work as an Atlanta Olympics volunteer was an experience I will never forget, will always enjoy remembering, and wouldn't trade for anything. I made friends, shared great experiences, and my IBM work was still there waiting for me when I returned to it after being gone for seventeen days.

As we celebrate the tenth anniversary of the Atlanta Olympics (now 25 years as I include this in 2021), I'm proud to be able to say that I was one of those thousands of volunteers who, in our opinion, made it the "best Olympics ever."

Bob and Jan—Opening Ceremony 1996 Atlanta Olympics

Open Heart Surgery
December 2012

Like many men do, in my early 50s, around 1995 as I recall, I developed high blood pressure. Since I had good insurance through IBM, I started going to see a cardiologist on an annual basis. He put me on blood pressure medicine which works for me. I religiously signed up for the next year's appointment and after about ten years of seeing him, he told me he noticed a "thickening" in something around my heart. I didn't fully understand it, he said it was nothing to worry about now, and he kept scheduling annual appointments, including various heart tests and treadmill tests to insure everything was okay. Each year he told me the "thickening" was still there but not a problem.

At my appointment in late August 2012, he told me I needed to go see a heart surgeon—my "thickening" had increased, and it was time to do something. Naturally, that got Jan and my attention (she always goes to the doctor with me) and we scheduled an appointment to see the surgeon that he recommended. I liked the guy immediately—he had been a doctor in the US Army, had served in Iraq, so I had full confidence in him. When we met, he had examined all the charts and tests that my regular heart doctor had sent him, and said I had an Ascending Aorta Aneurism (Triple A as he called it). He told me we needed to repair it.

Feeling totally okay, with no adverse symptoms, I wasn't overly concerned so I asked him if it could be put off until the following year. He looked me in the eye and said something to the effect,

"You don't understand. If that bursts, you are a dead man—even if you were on the operating table when it happened." That immediately got my attention, but I still pushed back and asked if we could wait until after Christmas and do it the last week of December. Again, he looked at me and said, "You're crazy—the week after Christmas the first team is on vacation. You won't have the best of the best working on you." With that, and Jan telling me we are doing it NOW, we scheduled the surgery.

Of course, there were more preliminary medical procedures that needed to be done to check it out further. It was 12 December 2012 (12/12/12) when the surgery was scheduled—at St. Joseph's Hospital on the northside of Atlanta.

Following are some emails I found on my computer describing the experience...

Before going into my memories of my surgery, Jan told me as I was writing this memoir that she had kept a diary during the day that I had my surgery on 12/12/2012. I had no idea she had done that, or if she had told me, I had forgotten it. I will start the story of my surgery and recovery with her on the spot writing on the actual day of the surgery. I will admit that I shed a lot of tears as I read this for the first time ever on March 30, 2021 (and am doing it again as I type what she wrote to and for me that day):

Tuesday, December 12, 2012

We both woke at 2:00 am. Ruthanne (our Rottweiler) had moved to my side of the bed causing Betty (our Beagle) to growl. From that point on, neither one of us slept. You held me and told me everything would be alright.

We left for the church at 4:35 am. Rob and Kris followed close behind. We all stopped in the parking lot, put our arms around each other and listened to Bob's prayer. Your calm demeanor washed over us.

When we arrived at the hospital, John Fraser (our favorite Methodist minister and retired Army chaplain) met us with his smile. It wasn't a surprise and was very definitely a comfort. He prayed with us before you were taken back. After you were prepped, the nurse said that other members of the family could come back. They said they would be taking you to surgery at 6:30. I called Mark to check on where he was. He said they were on Glenridge. Mark said, "Stall them!"

The man that was wheeling you to surgery was very kind and waited until Mark and Stephanie got to you. We all hugged and kissed you and went on to the waiting area. Diane Parrish (another favorite Methodist minister) was with us and thought she had missed the chance to pray with you. But she knew that John had.

Shortly after we were seated, the man that took you to surgery came and got Diane so that she could pray with you. She said she rubbed your feet as you fell asleep. (I remember her doing that vividly—a great comfort).

At 6:41 am, Maxx called to say that he was going to bring you the letter he wrote. Molly texted and said she was sending lots of prayers. Lindsey called to just check in. Lita texted and Di texted.

At 8:55 am, we were told the procedure was started at 8:15. Sarah came to the hospital and stayed until 11:19 am.

Ron Marksity called to check on you. He said he would call back later.

I wish we would get an update soon. Diane Parrish called to check in and said she would see us about 1:30 pm. Lindsey texted again saying, "You're almost there!"

At 11:37 am a nurse came out saying they were about done

and that we were to wait for Dr. Anderson to come talk to us. She had no details to share.

Evanne texted at 12:13 pm telling us they were praying for us.

It is 12:37 pm and we are still waiting to hear from Dr. Anderson. Very anxious to hear something. I can't wait to see you and touch you.

By the way, Diane said she doesn't get to do as many hospital visitations as she would like since she is working on her doctorate. But she said she really wanted to be the one to do your visitation!

Finally, Dr. Anderson came out:

- He did really good
- Had to go in a different way
- Clamping worked great
- Aneurism pretty large
- Blood pressure low
- Fluids volume given
- Epi and levifed for blood pressure—you have a Schatzki ring
- Came off machine very well—heart started up immediately

2:40 pm—we just saw you—all five of us. Eyes were open some of the time. You were shaking your head yes. You winked at me twice and squeezed my hand.

2:48 pm—Mike Boyce came by to get an update. He will talk to everyone tonight at Vet's meeting. They have Frank's arrangements taken care of.

Now I can't wait until 5:30 pm so I can see you again. We are all talking about how you were trying to let us know that you were OK. I wish you could see all of us together. You would be so happy! Rob and Krissie were talking about the sound you make when you walk. Rob said it's a very comforting sound. Krissie said she remembered the sound of your wingtips.

We just spent 30 minutes with you. Amazing!!! You remembered us coming in earlier. You were doing fabulous!

Bill Ziegler came by to check on you. He said to give you a hug. George Weinstein called, and I gave him the great news. He was so happy!

8:16 pm — Sandy Fiacco (my company commander in Vietnam in 1966) called from Seattle to check on you. Asked a lot of questions and was so happy to hear how well you were doing! Said he will call back in a few days.

You were happy to see us at 8:30 pm. You were very talkative. Maxx called while we were with you, and he got to talk with you. You told him not to worry, that you were fine.

After we left, we all settled down in our "beds" to try to rest. Steph had texted me asking me to call her. She talked about the day and how great it was to be with her brother and sister. Even when we were silent, we were still together. "It made me realize how much I had missed my family. All the silly little issues we've had in the past didn't matter. It was surreal for me!"

Wednesday, December 13 — I was up at 5:00 am, unable to sleep. I got dressed and did an update on your status. At about 6:23 am I got Krissie and Rob up. We walked to the ICU promptly at 6:30 and were welcomed by your waving arm.

You didn't sleep much but you were in great spirits! You told us about a Code 1 and all the excitement associated with it.

Just finished our 10:30 visit with you, you had been sitting up in a chair since 7:00 am. You had eaten Jello and drank some kind of red juice. They were still working on regulating your blood pressure.

Your spirits continue to be great. Ron Marksity called again to check on you. He said when they move you to a room, tell him to not milk this!

Kris and Rob left around 11:20 am to go home, shower, and rest a bit before the 3:30 pm visitation. Mackey Carson called, and I explained the situation. I told him we would be in touch in a few days. (End of Jan's diary notes—so happy to know these exist).

With the above diary, Jan had saved the hand-written in pencil letter that our grandson, Maxx had written to me—it also brings tears to my eyes:

Hi Granddaddy. Whether this gets to you before or after the surgery, I want you to have this. I want to let you know that I love you and you have always been a role model. You are an amazing person, funny, nice, I can always talk to you when I need to talk about something. You have always been there for me. I hope that your surgery goes outstanding. I want to live a long healthy life, just like you. And you're always gonna be the best Oklahoma fan ever! I always never want to let you down whenever you ask me to do something I try to put my full effort into completing the task. You are and always have been and always will be my favorite granddaddy ever. I am going to be praying for you on Tuesday and on the recovery days. I really hope this goes well. I also am going to promise you that I'm gonna get into a good college and be on the soccer team and live a successful life for the rest of my life.

You're the best, you have never made me mad, you always make me happy. Well, I love you, granddaddy.

Love, Maxx Hollingsworth

E-mail on 12/16/2012 (four days after surgery)

My lovely wife, Jan, has done her normal outstanding job doing whatever she needs to do—and that, to me, was to keep my friends informed of what my progress is in recovering from open heart surgery last Tuesday. So, now that I am home and sitting here in my easy chair watching pro football, it's time to take over the update responsibility and give you the latest progress report.

To net it out—last Tuesday morning at 0430 we left the house, stopped by our church, sat out in the parking lot and had a prayer with our son and daughter before heading to the hospital to "get 'er done." As we got to the hospital about 0510, there sat a good friend and retired Army chaplain, John Fraser—Vietnam combat vet who fought alongside and ministered to 2-14 Infantry and later 1-27 Infantry, 25th Infantry Division during his first of two tours in Vietnam. Seeing John there took even more of the little load I was carrying off my shoulders.

Our other son and daughter soon joined us, John led us in another prayer, and we said our goodbyes and I was wheeled into the prep room before the operation. As I was talking to the anesthesiologists, two more ministers from our church, Diane Parrish, and Glenn Ray, showed up and shared a prayer. Diane stayed with me, rubbing my foot, until I went under and was rolled into the operating room. I found out later that Wil Parker, another retired Army chaplain, had come to sit with my Family during the surgery. We were well covered by Methodist ministers that morning.

The next thing I recall was seeing a nurse hovering over me and then my whole Family came in and spent just a few minutes with me in the intensive care unit. They were told I probably would not remember their first visit to the ICU, but I did—it was a sight for sore eyes to see Jan and our four grown kids all standing there. The first 24 hours in the intensive care unit is somewhat hazy but what is clear as a bell is the great care I was being given by a special nurse, then another special nurse, and then another as shifts changed, but quality of service did not. I knew that my prayers, and yours, had been answered. I went into this believing in God, my surgeon, and the medical staff assisting him. In all cases, I was never disappointed.

My first night, Wednesday, outside the ICU was right at the top of the worst I had ever experienced, mostly because of the pain medication they were giving me not agreeing with me (or me not agreeing with it). Hallucinations, while never scary, made that a night I will hope to soon forget and never want to experience again if I don't have to.

As the days progressed on Wednesday, Thursday, Friday, and Saturday, I kept getting stronger and feeling better. I am a good patient and do what I'm told. That meant several laps—10-15 per day around the unit I was in, always with one or more of my Family members with me. Plus, I religiously used the breathing machine to cause me to breathe deeply and clean out the bad stuff in the bottom of my lungs. It was tough on Friday afternoon when our son, Rob, had to return to his home in Utah, but that was the best answer since I was obviously progressing well and in good shape and he needed to get back to his Family and work.

We had some visitors, not too many, and none of them stayed too long—each was a shot in the arm to me to see friends who care. A real shot in the arm was to see our 14-year-old grandson, Maxx, who made his first ever visit to a hospital. The letter he left with me is one I will always cherish.

As Jan told you in a previous update, our RN nurse daughter, Kristen, was a real Godsend to both Jan and me. Her experience and medical knowledge and great bedside manner (maybe a little better with her Daddy than with most patients, but I'm happy to accept it) took all the concern and questions from our minds. If Jan or I didn't understand anything, or even if we thought we did, we turned to Krissie and she gave us the answer. Krissie stayed with me Thursday, Friday, and Saturday nights and allowed Jan to get some much-needed rest. Again — prayers were answered and our concern was minimal.

My biggest entertainment was watching the Georgia high school football championships on Friday and Saturday. I believe there were seven televised games, all coming from the Georgia Dome where the Falcons play. That allowed me to stay off network TV and not get taken down by the heartbreaking news of the senseless massacre that happened in Connecticut on Friday.

The food sucked, to net it out. I'm not sure I've ever had good hospital food and this experience did not break that chain of terrible food experiences. Bad food is one of the driving forces in making you do what you're supposed to do to get out of the hospital sooner rather than later.

This morning the nurse practitioner made early rounds and confirmed that she was letting me go home today. After a morning of hurry up and wait, we finally were in the car headed home by 1300 and I was sitting in my easy chair by 1330 watching the Falcons whip the Giants.

I'm tired, know I have a long period of recuperation ahead of me, but I will continue to do what I started with — trust in God, trust the advice of my medical team, and continue to marvel at the power of prayer. Knowing that I could have not come off that operating table alive, the fact I did not worry made me realize the power of my Christian faith that I have known but never experienced as strongly as this before.

Thanks to all of you for caring about me, for your prayers, your notes back in response to Jan's notes, your calls, and making me know that I am a lucky man to be blessed with people like you.

Kristen will be here tonight then heading back to Oklahoma tomorrow to her job and daughter. Jan will pick up the load. She will be assisted by Mark and Sarah, our local son and daughter-in-law and Stephanie, our local daughter.

For those of you who know us through Deeds Publishing, we will still be running at less than full speed through the end of December, but we'll pull together to meet your needs as quickly and completely as possible.

For my 4th Infantry Division friends, I know I owe you some history updates. I missed four significant events in the life of our division. First—our birthday on 10 December 1917; second, the capture of Saddam Hussein on 13 December 2003; third, the dedication of the 4ID monument at Fort Carson on 14 December 2012 (two days ago—I had planned to be there before this came up); and finally, our division's great defense of Luxembourg as the Battle of the Bulge broke out on 16 December 1944. I'll get those history lessons pulled together and sent to you over the coming days.

For my other veteran friends from the various veterans' organizations I am an active member in, I love your notes and your hard hitting, caustic, and humorous comments that only we veterans can understand and appreciate. We are truly a brotherhood.

So—Family, authors, others who have helped Jan, me, and our Family out, fellow veterans of 4ID and all branches of the military—you are all my friends, and I am honored to call you that. God is great—never doubt that.

P.S. A fellow Mt. Bethel UMC vet friend stopped by our house this afternoon and brought me a balloon that reads "It's a Girl", some cookies his daughters made, and a heartfelt card that I will always cherish. Again, the bond of veterans is one I will always love—thanks, John. When Kristen asked me why the balloon said what it did—she started laughing when I told her it was from a Marine, he doesn't know any better. Semper Fi!

E-mail—December 20, 2012

I think many or most of you saw the update that Jan sent out on Tuesday morning. Net is, Monday afternoon about 1:30, my incision started draining and did so for about an hour and a half before stopping. When it started again, we did per the instructions we got from our doctor's nurse and headed into the emergency room at 3:00. That was a long ordeal—got there about 3:15 and finally was re-admitted to a hospital room at 1:15 on Tuesday morning—five doors down from where I was last week.

In the emergency room they gave me no water, food, I didn't have access to my breathing exercise machine, and generally showed why America's emergency rooms are places to avoid if you can do it. I spent Tuesday recovering the lost progress from the emergency room experience, the doc put a wound vac in to suction out the rest of the drainage, and he took that off yesterday afternoon after 24 hours.

I feel fine, am somewhat frustrated, but probably God put me back into the hospital to get a lesson on patience, not one of my strong points. Other than the expected pain in my chest when I cough, I periodically run a low-grade fever, which is common for operations like the one I had. All vital signs are good.

Doctor has not been in yet today and I'm going to try to talk him into sending me home. If he does, great! If he doesn't, compared to many of our wounded warriors from our nation's wars who spent months up to a year or more in hospitals, this is a very minor inconvenience.

When the doctor told me about the wound vac maybe going to cost me three more days in the hospital and what did I think, I told him, "I place my trust in God and you, so you give me the answer." I loved his answer…"You have your trust placed in the right order." Then he started putting the wound vac on me. That's my kind of doctor.

Rather than being my usual too windy self, let me summarize a couple of things. On Monday morning, our RN Nurse daughter, Kristen, had started the 710-mile drive from Atlanta to her home in Oklahoma. When the incident happened that afternoon, she was halfway home when I had Mark call her for instructions of what to do. Of course, we stayed in close contact with her while we were in the emergency room and after she got to Oklahoma. Tuesday morning, I called and asked if she was back at work. She said she was taking a mother/daughter day with Annabeth, our granddaughter. We talked throughout the day on Tuesday. Tuesday evening after I had been napping for a couple of hours, a knock on the hospital room door was followed with, "Night shift is here." I was blown away. Kris and Annabeth walked in the door, taking a huge load off all our shoulders. I›m pretty sure that young lady loves me. They will be here through the weekend, longer if needed.

The other item…Jan was running errands when the incident happened, so I hollered at Mark to come quickly. He came bounding up the stairs from his basement office (he is the Creative Director of our publishing business) and immediately started with, "Stay calm, Dad, you are all right and we'll get this under control." He grabbed a bunch of towels and kept reassuring me every step of the way. Interestingly, because of the faith I have mentioned all along the way, I wasn't overly concerned, thought this was just another bump in the road. Jan got home and took over, linking us up with commo with the doctor's nurse and I knew at that point I had zero say on what I would be doing the rest of the day. Net is, our entire Family is 100% into this journey with me and will do whatever they can to help me and reassure me. I'm not used to others taking over the lead from me, but that's what I'm doing now, learning how to be a good patient and follower.

When my drainage started again at 3:00, the Deeds Publishing president, Jan, and the creative director, Mark, piled the CEO, Bob, into the car and off we went to the hospital. Ten hours later, we had done zero productive work for Deeds or our authors. But, God being the great guy that He is, He opted to seat an aspiring author right next to us in the waiting room. We talked at length and by early next year we'll be back in touch with another potential piece of book business for 2013. (We never followed up with that author, hopefully he found a good publisher for his book).

I'll keep you informed as I can—Jan will do it if I can't. Keep your prayers coming our way. And keep your fingers crossed that I get sent home this afternoon.

Again, I explain my strength—total trust in God, my doctor, the medical staff, my Family, our friends, and the love that flows my way through your notes, calls, and other signs that you send our way. Now...it's time for me to work on my Patience.

Christmas E-Mail 2012

Merry Christmas to all of you. I continue to make progress in my recovery, most days are better than the one before it but with a few minor setbacks that are part of the recovery process. I got six solid hours of uninterrupted sleep last night—a first for me since my surgery. It is hard to believe that it was two weeks ago that I had my open-heart surgery.

My work on Patience continues, even making some progress along those lines. I must admit—I expected that I'd be well over 90% recovered by now, which isn't the case, but I'm moving closer to that mark every day. I've adjusted my target from Christmas Day to New Year's Day...and will move it further out if required. I didn't fully appreciate how major this surgery was when I went into it. I'm glad it is behind me instead of looming ahead of me.

My trust in God and my medical team has not wavered, nor has the continual thanks I give God for the support of Family and friends from all over this great country of ours—and those deployed overseas.

Our daughter, Kris, and granddaughter, Annabeth, went home on Sunday. Jan and I are learning to fill the big void she left and know that she's only a phone call away if we need her to talk us through anything. Again, I can't tell you enough the great gift she gave us by dropping her life and giving us a live-in private RN to take the load off us. And as is the case all over the world with our military and medical personnel, she is "on call" today to help her home hospice patients who may need her.

We will spend Christmas here at home with our Atlanta based Family members, including the first Christmas with our nine-month-old granddaughter, Ava, and another Christmas with our 14-year-old grandson, Maxx. Last night I missed my first Christmas Eve service in memory but opted to skip since lots of people have colds and all my advisors said to stay home—including a retired Army chaplain (first time I ever had a minister or chaplain tell me to stay away from church).

I have lots of anecdotal stories that I will never forget...of how so many of you are reaching out to us and lifting us up with prayer and encouragement, and good-natured jabs from my fellow veterans. But, on this day to share with your own Family, I'll spare you those stories and sign off.

Merry Christmas—thanks for your prayers and support—and I have your back, I'm praying for all my Family and friends as well as you are praying for me.

P.S. When I got up at 0400 this morning and turned on the TV, I was pleased the see the West Point Christmas Concert on Fox News Channel. I watched an hour of that—a beautiful way to start Christmas Day. It plays again at 1:00 EST this afternoon on Fox News if you want to watch it.

My private nurse, Kristen

Valedictorian Speech
May 1961

After going 60 years thinking the only copy of my speech had long ago been thrown away, in May 2021, 60 years to the month later, Jan was going through some keepsakes we have inherited from my parents and found this. She simply said, "Here, you might be interested in this."

WOW! I had no clue what I said during my valedictorian speech at Heavener High School in 1961. There may be a half dozen people besides me who care, but I am going to retype it and include it in the book in case my great-great-grandchild may someday be interested. And Mother, thanks a million for saving this and many more keepsakes we have discovered since your death in 2004.

People of today are looking toward space. Alan Shepherd plainly showed that fact in his historic flight of a few weeks ago. But we as seniors going out into the world have another space to be concerned about. It is the space which must be filled between our ears, and especially in our hearts. I read a poem by Henry van Dyke which might help us in filling this space. It reads as follows:

> Four things a man must learn to do
> If he wants to make his record true;
> To think without confusion clearly;
> To love his fellowmen sincerely;
> To act from honest motive purely;
> To trust in God and Heaven securely.

We are now making our record. Not only is our transcript being filed as a permanent record of our high school accomplishments, but our very life and character are being molded in this, our time of learning. Is our record a true one?

A friend of mine once told me of a tough math problem he had to work, but he wanted to play baseball instead of working the problem. He took the problem to his father and after a little thinking, his father gave him the correct answer. The boy wrote the answer down and went out to play baseball. The next morning in class, the teacher asked him to go to the board and work the problem. After scratching some illegible figures on the board, he wrote down the answer. When the teacher asked him to explain his work, he tried his best to think of an explanation, but he was at a loss. Finally, after some stammering and stuttering, he admitted that he had not worked the problem and did not know the answer. We must learn to do our own thinking without confusion.

Our second line of the poem suggests that we need to love our fellowmen sincerely. I think the residents of Leflore County have learned this love for their fellowmen. The recent tornado at Howe, Glendale, and Reichert has brought out all the love and goodness in the people of this area. The gifts of food, clothing, furniture, work, and other essentials have been given only out of the goodness of the people's hearts. This is a trait which most of the people in this area have, and we can be proud of having it on our records.

We can and do love our fellowmen sincerely and out of this love issues the power to act from honest motives purely. So many of our people today have a knack of twisting the truth just so that it will read just as they want it to. The newspapers are full of articles with headlines to attract attention, but which leave out some of the essential elements of the story because it takes some of the spice from it. Abraham Lincoln was an excellent example of honesty when he was just a young boy. A book which he had borrowed from a friend was ruined by a rainstorm. Instead of trying to lie his way out of paying for the book, he went to work in the man's fields to pay him back for the loss. We must learn to be like Abraham Lincoln and act purely from honest motives or we will not make the true record which we are striving for in our lives.

I would like to refer back to the poem by van Dyke. The last line reads: "To trust in God and Heaven securely." This country was founded on trust in God. As young people going out into the world, we must put our faith in God and Heaven. Only by doing this will we have something worthwhile to live for.

Again, I would like to refer back to our poem by van Dyke. (See top of this speech).

The first three things in making a true record will come more easily if we, the class of 1961, will concentrate on the trust in God and Heaven as our forefathers did. I have in my hand a silver dollar that my father gave me. On it and on all official documents are stamped the words "IN GOD WE TRUST." As the graduating class, let us resolve to make trust in God official in each of our hearts.

(I smile when I see my speech was focused on a poem. I have always made a big deal out of the fact that I do not like poetry of any kind—yet 60 years ago, my valedictory speech seemed to indicate I like poetry. Trust me, I don't.)

Giving my valedictorian speech, May 1961

Random Stories
From my 78 Years of Life

Dogs

I can't remember not having a dog. The first dog I remember is Butch. He was hit (and killed) by a car in the street in front of our house, with the whole family outside and saw it. It was probably my first big trauma in my life. Soon after, when I was in about the second grade, we got another dog, Spot, for Christmas as I recall. He was an inside and outside dog, lived to an old age, and disappeared when I was about to graduate from college. We never knew what happened to him.

Phyllis and I got a dog, Ralph, a Schnauzer, from our friend Grace Coggins Kidwell when she was headed to the Philippines so she could meet her husband when his Naval aircraft carrier came in for a break from flying bombing missions over North Vietnam. Ralph immediately took to us and when Kristen, our first child, was born in September 1969, Ralph started sleeping under her baby bed almost immediately after she came home from the hospital. He was protective of her, was gentle with her, and a great dog.

When Kris was about four, we bribed her with another dog if she would quit sucking her thumb. She quit in the month I gave her to do it and never did it again. Thus, we picked up another Schnauzer, Ping. Ralph was medium size; Ping was very small. They were buddies. On 4th of July in 1977 or 1978, Ralph was spooked by firecrackers and ran in front of a car, killing him.

Ping moved with Phyllis and the kids when we divorced and lived a long life.

Jan and I have had dogs since soon after we were married. Plus, Mark and Rob had to add their own dogs to the mix. April, Jeff, Ruth, Betty, Joey Martin, Gladys, Nick Chubb were/are ours—Rob had Grendel and Anchorage. Mark had Steve growing up, got Frank when he was in college, then Abbey (a former racing greyhound). Both Rob and Mark worked at the Roswell Animal Clinic when they were in high school. One day, Rob brought home a white wolf, maybe it was just part wolf but for certain had wolf in it, that someone had dropped off at the vet. At the time, Mark was about five years old, and Jan threw a fit…"Get that wolf out of here! And do it right now!" Though Rob and Mark were disappointed, I had to agree with Jan's logic and Rob grudgingly took it back to the vet.

After Frank and Abbey died after long lives, Mark, Sarah, and Ava have their two current dogs, Dale and Maggie, who are at our house several times a week with Gladys and Nick, our two current dogs. Rob and Amy have two dogs now—Zeus, a Great Dane, and Scamp, a tiny dog Rob carries inside his coat during winter months. Kristen and Annabeth have had Ricky and Sugar Pie, who have died, and their most recent dogs are Magnum, Brooke, Bea, and a long list of horses over the years (I won't include horse stories since I have shied away from horses since I broke my elbow many years ago. I have sat through many riding lessons with Kristen and Annabeth as their driver to lessons).

We always looked for rescue dogs—but two found us. Driving back from a bicycle race in Fayetteville, Arkansas several years ago, Jan, Mark, and Sarah saw a dog alongside a busy highway in Mississippi and stopped to pick it up. Their plan was to drop it off at a vet's office in the next town, but it was closed by the time they got there. Thus began our lives with a 12-year-old (guess) female beagle who had been used in a puppy mill. No telling how many litters of puppies she had before we got her. They brought her home, we fell in love with her, spent $1,200 on her at the vet the first week we had her, and she had about three more years living a great life with us.

The other one who found us was Nick Chubb, the smallest dog we have ever had. On 4 January 2019, he showed up on our back deck, had come through a picket fence (that's how small he is), climbed the steps to the deck and was standing at our back door shivering in 14-degree weather. Tough old Bob let him in, he rushed to the water and food bowls, and then jumped up into my lap and started licking me. I was hooked. In the Rose Bowl a few days earlier, Nick Chubb, the Georgia running back, had performed well in upsetting my Oklahoma Sooners, so we named the new dog, Nick Chubb. I, however, always call him Little Bit because that name just fits him. He's laying here beside me as I finish editing this, as he does most of the time.

With the exception of Jeff, a full-blooded English Sheepdog, every dog we have owned is a rescue puppy. And Jeff was the meanest dog ever—we had to get rid of him after he cornered Jan in the yard while I was on a business trip many years ago.

It is amazing the joy that a dog brings to a Family. It hurts to lose them, you never forget them, and when another one comes along to fill the void, you quickly fall in love with them. I doubt any members of our Family will ever be without at least one dog. Kristen and Rob both are attached to two dogs in each of their homes now and Stephanie has one.

And no life would be complete without a couple of cat stories. With an across the alley neighbor who had as many as 28 cats at one time, I was never a cat fan. But, when Kristen was about four years old, we came upon a kitten, can't remember the details, but do remember how she named it. I was laying in her bed as she was about to go to sleep and asked her what she wanted to name her cat. She looked up at her light fixture, which had flowers on it, and said, "Flower Light—we'll name her Flower Light." And that was her name. After we made our first move to Atlanta, Flower Light disappeared, never knew the circumstances. It was a real loss to Kristen and all of us, we loved Flower Light. Later in life, Kristen and Annabeth had a cat named Meow. Interesting names they came up with.

And our second cat story is...a neighbor took Mark to a park near the Atlanta Zoo with their kids to go roller skating. When they brought him home, he brought a cat in. They explained it was a stray, Mark liked it, and they brought him to us. (Thanks, neighbors). We had it for two or three years. That cat never got along with our dogs, spent a lot of time in the basement, and disappeared without us ever knowing how it got out of the house.

Firearms

Mother would not allow us to have a gun in the house, not even a BB gun. When all the neighbor boys were shooting birds and each other with BB guns, our instructions were to come home. Daddy, having grown up in a houseful of women, had no experience that I was aware of with a gun, so he pretty much let mother have her way.

I believe it was Bill who talked Daddy into buying a .22 caliber rifle, think it came from Sears. Bill took it out occasionally but mostly it was kept in Daddy's closet and seldom saw the light of day. I think it gave us all a good feeling to have a gun in the house if we ever needed it (except for Mother).

One day when I was in junior high, Daddy and Reeder

Thornton, Sr. took Reeder, Jr. and me to Blackfork River to fish and spend the night camping out—just the four of us. Reeder and I were sitting on the bank of the river, pulling in a nice batch of crappie on our cane fishing poles when Daddy loudly said, "Boys, do not move, stay still." We looked back over our shoulder toward where the two adults were pitching camp, and saw Daddy with the .22 rifle, aiming it in our direction. We looked closer and between him and us, a copperhead snake was headed our way. Before we could react, he fired one shot and hit the snake in the head, killing it.

I was shocked. I had no idea that he was that type of marksman. While I always was proud of him, that moved him up a notch in my mind. We cooked the fish we had caught, spent the night, and saw no more snakes.

Fast forward a few years to when I was home from college, either for Christmas or the summer. Joe was sitting in the dining room cleaning that same .22 rifle and failed to clear it—it fired, and the bullet went through the wall between the dining room and kitchen (where mother was standing at the sink washing dishes) and stopped in a cabinet after breaking a dish or two. You can imagine how that went over—nobody was hurt. My memory can't say where the .22 went, but I'm pretty sure that it was out of the house before the sun went down that day.

When I went to Vietnam, I heard stories of officers carrying their own personally owned pistols to augment their assigned military rifle. With advice and counsel of brother Jim, I ordered a Smith & Wesson .357 pistol. I packed it in my footlocker, we arrived in Vietnam, and about that time somebody had shot himself or someone else with a personally owned weapon and it became a crime for a Soldier to carry a personal weapon in Vietnam. Being the compliant young officer that I was, that pistol never came out of my footlocker the whole year. I probably didn't fire it ten times in the many years I owned it. Jim had made a leather belt and holster for it, and I'm not sure I ever wore it. About ten years ago, Rob, our son, asked if he could have it—which was fine with me. I'm sure he puts it to good use living in rural Utah.

But...I did buy another one. In today's world, we need to be prepared to defend ourselves.

Teaching Youth Sunday School

Mark, our youngest son, has stuttered since he was five years old. We did all we could to help with speech therapists, but to no avail. As he left elementary school and was starting middle school, Jan and I knew how concerned he was because of his constant fight with stuttering. Middle school kids can be the cruelest in making fun of people.

We made up our mind before Mark entered sixth grade that he was not going to be made fun of in Sunday School class at Mt. Bethel United Methodist Church—we were going to volunteer to teach his class. We did and were welcomed with opened arms.

Having raised our three older kids, we knew how to deal with young teenagers and enjoyed our teaching experience. As it has done all my life, my deep and loud voice was effective in keeping the kids focused and not too rowdy. Jan and I took turns teaching, along with Bill and Susan Ziegler, the other half of our teaching team.

One Sunday, the teacher of the seventh-grade class next door to us did not show up so we consolidated that class with ours. When Mark spoke up in class, one of the seventh-grade boys laughed at him. I was teaching that day and Jan immediately sprang from the back of the room, tapped the boy on the shoulder, and told him to come outside with her. When they came back into the room a few minutes later, I could tell by the expression on his face that Jan had gotten his attention about making fun of Mark, or anyone. We never had another incident.

As the next school year started, we were very much enjoying working with the kids and volunteered to move up with them to seventh grade. Bill and Susan Ziegler also moved up with us.

Long story short, we stayed with these same kids from sixth grade to twelfth grade, watched them grow physically, mentally, spiritually, and will carry fond memories of those seven years of teaching Sunday School for the rest of our lives. Bill and Susan feel the same way—quite an honor we had. I don't recall there ever being a Sunday when one of we four teachers, if not all of us, were there with our normal class attendance of about 25 to 30 youth, sometimes as many as 40. Each year the kids asked us to move up with them (we didn't force ourselves on them and were happy to keep teaching). When they had their graduating senior Sunday at church, nobody was prouder of the 2002 Walton High School graduating class than were Bill, Susan, Jan, and me.

Coaching

I have always been a baseball and football fan. When I was planning for college, my leaning was to become a coach. My mother vehemently argued against my doing that, saying she didn't think I wanted to depend on the skill of a bunch of boys I hardly know to be the source of my income. I can't say that I am sorry I didn't go into fulltime coaching, but I did enjoy the many times I coached during my lifetime.

As an IBM salesman in Kansas City in the early 1970s, I coached the son of Hank Stram, head football coach of the Kansas City Chiefs and winner of Super Bowl III. It was 7th grade weight limit football where players over a certain weight couldn't play in the backfield but had to be linemen. Stu Stram fell into that category, about five pounds too heavy to be in the backfield. Weigh in was at the beginning of the season, in August. If a player made the weight, he was good for the season. Unbeknown to me, the day of weigh in, he was out most of the day running in the hot Kansas City heat, wearing winter-weight running gear. When he stepped on the scales, he was dripping wet from sweat, looked pale, but made weight—he could play in the backfield.

He was the fastest and most talented athlete I ever coached. He seldom got the ball without making yardage, and many times ran the length of the field for a touchdown. He was also a great passer at quarterback. On defense, he was so fast that no opposing back could outrun him. He was one of a kind—and later played quarterback for University of Louisville during his college days.

Stu's mother religiously brought him to practice and sat quietly on the sideline while we practiced, and on game days his dad showed up unless the Chiefs were playing out of town. It was somewhat intimidating to have such a world-class NFL coach watching me coach his son, but he never gave me advice nor complained in any way. It was a memorable start to my coaching experiences.

My next coaching challenge was much different—coaching Kristen's softball team when she was in second or third grade. None of the girls knew the rules, had ever played before, and would look at me when they hit or caught a ball, waiting for me to tell them what to do next. Same with base running, they wouldn't take off on a ground ball until I gave them a shout to "run."

My next coaching was Rob in 7th grade football. He was

very talented but lacked the desire to play. He was only there because I pushed him. One of my favorite pictures of Rob is of him during a game, sweating and looking very serious. After that one year, he told me, "Dad, I don't like football so is it okay if I don't play next year?" I agreed and that was the end of my coaching him. (Rob was a very talented skateboarder and bicycle rider, which resulted in Mark, his ten-year younger brother, loving those two sports).

Stephanie had no interest in sports, instead was an avid cheerleader. Since I had no experience in that, I didn't coach Stephanie in any sport. But she was a great cheerleader the short time she did it. I covered in an earlier story her disappointment when we moved to Kansas and kept her from being the cheerleader she wanted to be.

Next up was Mark. As a first or second grader, I wanted him to play weight limit football. Since he was so big for his age, he ended up playing with third and fourth grade boys. I didn't realize the age difference and maturity difference would ruin him in ever wanting to play football. Each week all players had to weigh in. Most of the players stepped on the scale, made weight, and went on to warmup. Mark, even two or three years younger, always had to strip down to his shorts and barely made the weight limit. After that one year, I realized I was doing a dumb thing by pushing him, so he never played football again.

He did play baseball, with me as his coach. That was probably his 3rd and 4th grade years. I think he enjoyed it and was a decent player. One of the problems I had as head coach was finding somebody to play catcher. One foul ball that hit off a boy's arm or hit his face mask would scare him and he took off the catcher's gear and headed to the bench. I bribed Mark to play catcher by promising him I'd get him a GI Joe figure if he'd stay behind the plate. He always did, never quit, and we enjoyed those few years of baseball. I was an aggressive third base coach, most of the times when a player got to third base, I would send him in because most catchers at that age either couldn't catch the ball or avoided getting hit by the runner coming in.

My next coaching gig was coaching our grandson Maxx and granddaughter Annabeth in soccer when they were five years old (they are six weeks apart in age). I didn't know soccer, was an inept coach, and my role was mostly keeping the kids under control. Keeping them focused was an impossibility. If an airplane flew over (we were in the landing pattern of Dobbins Air Force base) they stopped to look at it. If they saw a dandelion on the field, they would stop and pick it. The onlooking parents and we coaches on the field all got lots of laughs from that one season I coached soccer.

My final coaching was Maxx in T-ball and then in coach pitch baseball at our church. Maxx has great hand/eye coordination and is a natural athlete. He could hit the ball, catch the ball, throw the ball, and is a lefty—a coach's dream. Whatever sport he wanted to play; he could excel at. I'll never forget when one of our coaches was pitching to Maxx and he hit a big-league level line drive back to the pitcher's mound, hit the coach in the face, and the coach sported a black eye for a couple of weeks. From then on, all pitchers were very alert when Maxx was batting.

In my day in small-town Oklahoma, boys played all sports, usually with no adults around. Today, with organized athletics starting at a very young age, too many kids focus on just one sport and never try the others. That is what happened with Maxx. His dad had played soccer, so he convinced Maxx to only play soccer. It broke my heart, but Maxx started on his high school soccer team as a freshman and remained a starter throughout high school. Had he played multiple sports, no telling what he could have enjoyed.

The Bob-mobile

In 1984, a few weeks before Mark was born, I bought a brand-new dark blue Audi 4000 automobile. I never was one who cared much about cars, except for my 1965 Mustang. Dependable transportation was good enough for me. But for some reason I really liked that Audi 4000, drove Mark home from the hospital in it, and drove it for the next ten years.

Like all high school kids, Stephanie really wanted a car to drive. Going back to my high school days, I bought my own car. My first one was not worth the $95 I paid for it, the second one was a gem (to me), so I decided since I knew the history of my Audi 4000, and I had my eyes on my first ever used Ford pickup truck for myself, I was going to give Stephanie my Audi.

Many of her friends had been given new, or almost new, cars by their parents. To say she was disappointed to be driving my old Audi would be an understatement. After explaining to Stephanie, with Jan's agreement, I told her, "It's the Audi or nothing," she decided even that old Audi beat walking. It had a few things wrong with it, like the back left window wouldn't come back up when you put it down, there probably were a few small dents or dings in it, but it ran great. Oh, and it was five-speed standard transmission, which she had to learn how to drive.

Unknown to me until after she had been driving it for several months, I found out that my Audi was the talk of Walton High School. She and her friends had named it the "Bob-mobile." I took it as a compliment, it got her where she wanted to go, and gave her some bragging rights to be driving such an old car. A picture of it, with its name, even made the Walton yearbook her senior year of 1994. Stephanie even grew to like her "Bob-mobile."

One day she came home and said the car wouldn't start and it was left sitting somewhere. A friend brought her home. I was in non-stop travel time in my IBM job, so I waited until it was convenient to go have the car towed to get it fixed. I waited too long…I received a notice from the county impound lot that the car had been sitting too long, they had hauled it to their impound lot, and I could have it back for $250. You know the rest of the story…the "Bob-mobile" was likely crushed into a cube and sold as junk. It wasn't worth $250.

Taking Annabeth, Our Granddaughter, to Washington, DC

Annabeth Pauline Babcock has always been an adventurer and patriot. She and Kristen, her mother, never let a year go by during her growing up years that they didn't take a trip somewhere to learn more about this great country we live in. In 2019, as her 21st birthday present, I took her to Washington, DC for a grandfather/granddaughter visit.

Our first stop was the 4th Infantry Division monument on the road leading into Arlington National Cemetery. In 2001, when we dedicated the monument, she attended as a three-year old with her mother. Back then, we spent the 4th of July on the steps of the Capitol in DC listening to the annual Independence Day concert—in a constant rainstorm. Both Kristen and Annabeth loved dancing in the rain—a story Kristen and I will never forget, Annabeth was probably too young to remember it, except from our stories and the pictures we took. The next day, we dedicated the monument in bright sunshine.

After our time at the 4ID monument and the Vietnam Wall, we toured as many of the key tourist attractions as we could in DC. It was great fun visiting DC and a privilege to share my stories of my times visiting our nation's capital over the years with Annabeth, an interested listener.

Annabeth's senior year in high school, she was selected to attend Girls' State in her home state of Wyoming. She participated extensively and was beaten in her run for governor (you may remember that in 1960, I attended Oklahoma Boys' State). Among other things she did in her Wyoming hometown was to organize and run a Christmas dinner for the homeless during her senior year and first year out of high school. Mark my word—this proud Granddaddy expects to see Annabeth continue, probably as a public servant, to do what's right for this country of ours. It would not surprise me to see Annabeth as the first elected official of our Family.

Part-time Metalworker

Our son, Rob, is an extremely talented metal artist. During his high school years, he took a class in welding and immediately fell in love with what could be done with metal. Starting in a small shop in Roswell, Georgia, he rapidly advanced to where he was making high dollar and top-quality items for multi-million-dollar homes—kitchen hoods, stair railings, whatever the owner wanted. I was in awe of what he could make. I offered to help him during the making of the items, but other than occasionally being an extra set of hands, I wasn't much help.

But when it came time to install whatever he had made, that's where he needed help to carry and install his artwork into the home. As a guy who worked at no expense for Rob (and all my kids), I had the privilege of going into multiple high dollar value homes to help Rob install what they had ordered from him. When I was doing that, I was still in decent shape in my late 50's and early 60's age-wise. I totally followed his lead, did what I was told, and often wondered how much longer I would have to hold something while he got it fastened into permanent place. I always walked away (sweating from the hard work), shaking my head in awe at the great metal and functional art that our son had created. There are pieces of his metal artwork in several prestige places in Atlanta, and around the country, but I won't say where since part of his agreement with his customers is maintaining their confidentiality.

Several years ago, Rob and his Family moved to Utah. He has established his business there and has become a certified welding inspector who worked in the oil fields making top dollar before the leadership of our country effectively shut down our petroleum business. But he continues to thrive with his metal artwork. He no longer has his dad to be the part-time metalworker to help install what he makes.

Bicycle Races

No, I never participated in a bicycle race. But our two sons, Mark and Rob, gave me many weekend days of enjoying the sport, and sweating it out that they didn't get hurt as they raced around city streets in a pack of 50 to 100 (or more) other racers.

Both of our sons were avid bicycle and skateboard riders from elementary school to today as I write this. The first race they participated in together was in Rome, Georgia, probably around the 2005 timeframe. It was a hot, 100-degree day in July. Jan and I did not know what to expect as we watched them start the race. Rob had raced before; it was Mark's first. Halfway through the race, Mark was cut because he was too far behind the leaders. The look of disappointment and determination on his face showed me that he was going to double down and master the sport of bicycle racing. And he did.

Until Rob moved to Utah, they raced together, both usually finishing in the middle of the pack. Jan and I were always there watching. There are three types of bicycle racing (that I understand)...A criterium (or crit) is a pack of riders who do multiple laps around city streets in what is normally a downtown area of a city. As noted above, packs are huge, or at least they are to parents watching their son or sons. When a rider wrecks, odds are pretty good that those riding close to him will also go down. Crits are my least favorite type of races—but I've watched dozens of them. The biggest annual race we watch each year is Twilight, through the streets of downtown Athens, GA the last Saturday of April.

We've made a few emergency room visits with Mark from wrecks—but he always comes back for more.

Then the most boring races (to me) are road races. The riders start off in a rural area, ride a course of 25 to 100 miles, and later that day either come back to the starting line or end at another finish point. As spectators, you can ride along in your car behind them but that gets old quickly as the pack spreads out. After a few road races, I typically found an excuse of why I couldn't be an observer at those races. I will admit, most years I spend a lot of TV time watching the annual Tour de France races, run in 21 stages over 23 days, mostly in France. The race always ends in Paris. During Mark's prime racing days, we knew who the best professional riders were (a few that Mark knew from races he participated in) and loved watching the daily racing and talking about it.

My favorite type of bicycle racing is cyclo-cross. Cyclo-cross races typically take place in the autumn and winter and consist of many laps of a short course featuring pavement, wooded trails, grass, steep hills and obstacles requiring the rider to quickly dismount, carry the bike while navigating the obstruction, and remount. Races are multiple laps around a closed course and are very spectator friendly. Jan, Sarah, Ava, and I have spent many enjoyable Sunday afternoons in the fall and early winter watching Mark race cyclo-cross. In February 2013, two months after my open-heart surgery, we (Deeds Publishing) had the concession to sell programs at the World Cyclo-Cross Finals held in Louisville, KY. It was bitter cold and wasn't a money maker, but with our love of bicycle racing, I'm glad it was something we experienced.

Mark and Rob have retired from racing, but they still enjoy time on their bicycles. Mark tries to ride every day and Rob does when his work schedule allows it. Amy often rides with Rob out in Utah, and Sarah and Ava typically do at least one weekly ride with Mark. Jan and I miss the cyclo-cross races. I have many great memories from bicycle racing weekends over the years.

Mark at a cyclo-cross race in Macon, GA

Household 6

This memory relates to my strong relationship with Army leaders over the past 20+ years. I've mentioned Linda Odierno, wife of General Ray Odierno, earlier in the book. We became friends during the 4th Infantry Division's first tour in Iraq in 2003-2004 and have remained friends since.

As I was providing daily support to 4ID Family members and Soldiers during that year in Iraq, Linda told me that if I ever needed any help on anything, to give her a call or send an email. She gave me her cellphone number, which I still have. I knew she meant it, so any time I felt I needed to go to the commanding general's wife to help solve a problem or overcome an obstacle, I never hesitated to contact Linda. We jointly fixed whatever needed fixing.

Along the way, I picked up the fact that while all Army commanders call sign ends with the number 6, such as Ironhorse 6 for MG Ray Odierno, and Oscar 6 for my company commander in Vietnam, all Army wives were (and still are) called Household 6. While their husband commanded a military unit of various sizes, his wife commanded their household—and him when she needed to.

As I got to know more and more ranking Army officers' wives and became friends, I always knew I had another important asset in my bag of tricks when I needed to get something done to support my Army passion. While the commanders had an aide, a secretary, and some level of staff supporting him and protecting him from being hit with things they didn't think he needed to deal with, I knew that Household 6 would always get me to the high-level officer I needed to contact. I never abused that privilege, thus I never failed to get to the man I needed to talk to, including four-star generals.

My favorite Household 6 story was late in the Iraq war when I received a call on my cellphone that went something like this…

"Bob, this is Steve Russell (retired Lt. Colonel, commander of 1-22 Infantry when Saddam was captured in 2003), I'm in Baghdad and being held captive." I was shocked and went into warrior mode. "Who has you, Steve? Where are you being held?" was my reply. "I'm in Camp Victory. The American Army is holding me captive. Because I'm an Oklahoma State Senator (by then he had retired from the Army), they won't let me off the base because they are afraid something might happen to me. Can you get to General Odierno and have him tell these people to release me?" was Steve's unexpected response.

General Odierno at the time was the III Corps Commander in Iraq; Steve and I knew he could make things happen. My dilemma—how in the hell do I get to him in Iraq with me being in Georgia? Then it hit me, Household 6. I had Linda's phone number in my cell phone (still do) and called her. She answered immediately, I explained Steve's problem, and she said, "I'll pass it on to Ray."

A few hours later, I got a call, don't remember if it was from Steve or from Linda, but he had been released and was out into Baghdad, headed north to Tikrit where he had served a few years earlier, with an Iraqi driver taking instructions from him. (Later I published a book for Steve—*We Got Him!*—about the hunt for and capture of Saddam Hussein.)

On two subsequent occasions, when Ray was Chief of Staff of the Army, when I needed him to participate in the dedication of the 4th Infantry Division monument on the Walk of Honor at the National Infantry Museum at Fort Benning, and when I needed him to participate in the presentation of 1SG David McNerney's (Medal of Honor recipient from Vietnam) stamp collection to the US Postal Museum in Washington, DC, I called

Household 6 and she, Ray, and I made it happen. I had told the staff at Fort Benning several months before, when we were planning our 4ID monument dedication, that I was going to have the Chief of Staff of the Army as our speaker. Their response was something like, "Yeah, right. No way will you make that happen."

About two weeks before the event, Ray's staff told the Fort Benning staff that he was going to be there to attend the dedication and observe training. Suddenly my phone lit up with calls from the staff at Fort Benning offering to help. It's amazing how well you are treated by staff members when the boss and his wife are your key contacts.

Fast forward to June 5, 2014, the day before the 70th anniversary of D-Day in Normandy, France. I was working as a consultant at IBM's Global Sales School and got a call. I looked at my phone and it said Linda Odierno. I knew she was in Normandy so was shocked to get a call from her. I answered with, "Linda—what are you calling me for? You're in France." The male voice on the phone said, "This is Ray. Where is the plaque that we dedicated back in 2004 (60th anniversary of D-Day) in Ste. Marie du Mont? I want to go visit it."

I recovered from my shock and replied, "Where are you—are you going into Ste. Marie du Mont from Utah Beach?" Ray responded, "Yes, we just got to the town square." I directed him to where the plaque was on Philippe Cornil's house, he saw it, and said, "I'm going to knock on his door, and we'll get some pictures with him." And they did. How many people in France have the Chief of Staff of the US Army knock on their door and remember details from ten years earlier—bet this was a one-time occurrence. (Shows the class act that Ray and Linda Odierno are, and many high-level Army commanders I've gotten to know are. Sadly, GEN (Retired) Ray Odierno died of cancer in October 2021.)

Earlier this year, in late June 2021, I needed to get in touch with MG Pat Donahoe, the commanding general of Fort Benning, Georgia. I have known his wife, Theresa, since 2006 when Pat commanded 1-67 Armor, part of 4ID, in Iraq. I met Pat when he returned home at the end of the year's tour. We've been friends since. With this issue to resolve, I sent a note to Pat's civilian email address, but more importantly, I sent it to Household 6—Theresa. Within hours, I received an email back from her, assuring me Pat had seen my note and would get back to me—and to get back to her if I didn't hear from him. We resolved what I needed to resolve, and Theresa stayed on top of it throughout the process.

Net of this story is—we have a great military standing up every day to protect us and our nation and the world. These are people like you and me—but willing to do whatever is required to keep our nation free. I write this to let whoever is reading it know that it is not only the Soldiers serving in our Army, but also the wives and other Family members who stand with them and support them, and us, the Americans who benefit from their sacrifices every day of every year. Because of my great respect for our American military and their Families, I always spell Soldier and Family with a capital letter. And I understand that all across the world, we have many Household 6's looking out for their husband, their Family, their Soldiers, and our country.

Volunteer Duty, Hurricanes Andrew and Katrina

Late August is always a busy time for hurricanes in the southeastern United States. Twice, I ended up as an early volunteer, two days after the hurricane hit—Hurricane Andrew in Miami, FL in 1992 and Hurricane Katrina in Gulfport, MS in 2005.

Both were Category 5 hurricanes and caused massive deaths, injuries, and property losses.

Our son Rob and I headed to Miami to help my quadriplegic brother, Jim, a day after Hurricane Andrew hit. We loaded my Ford Ranger with as much water, tarps, two brand new chain saws we bought at Home Depot, and whatever other emergency supplies made sense to us. Arriving late afternoon on the second day, the devastation had barely begun to be cleaned up. For a week, we started with Jim's home and property, working non-stop from daylight to dark. Then we fanned out to help Jim's daughter, Tami, whose home was also devastated. For a novice, I became pretty good with a chain saw.

We had laughed at Jim for buying a large generator a couple of years earlier. I don't know what the capacity was, but it took up most of the space in his storage shed. That was a life saver, not only for getting electricity to Jim's home, but to as many neighbors as could bring a long extension cord to tap in and bring the precious electricity to their homes.

While Jim weathered the storm in Baptist Hospital because of his quadriplegic condition, we were able to get his home back up to speed so he could return to his comfort area.

Rob, age 18 at the time, and I worked great as a team and bonded well as a father-son team helping Family members. This is a memory we will both cherish the rest of our lives, bad as it was to be in that mess.

* * * * *

Thirteen years later, in late August 2005, Hurricane Katrina smashed the Gulf Coast, with New Orleans being the center. 2005 was among the worst, if not the worst, hurricane seasons in United States history. Katrina was a large Category 5 hurricane that caused over 1,800 deaths and $125 billion in damage. I was glued to the TV set watching its path from the Gulf of Mexico as it slammed into New Orleans and many miles of coastline east and west of the city.

A day later I got a call from Mike Boyce, retired Marine colonel and head of the men's ministry at Mt. Bethel UMC. He asked, "Bob, will you go down to Gulfport, Mississippi with a team of fellow veterans from Mt. Bethel UMC to help with hurricane relief?" I quickly said, "Sure—but why me?" He responded with, "Mt. Bethel has decided this is a mission we want to take on for as long as we are needed. On this first of many trips, we want to send a team of military veterans. No telling what you will find down there, but we know we veterans will know how to deal with whatever it is."

Thus, the next day a team of eight veterans, led by Howard Long and Wayne LaRue, two Vietnam Air Force pilots, drove south and spent several days as first responders. We hauled a large trailer of supplies that Howard and Wayne had built up over the past several years, waiting for just such a disaster.

We slept on the floor in the Trinity United Methodist Church in Gulfport, spent our first half day cutting up and cooking donated frozen chickens from Perdue Poultry—the first hot meal most of the hurricane victims had in the past several days. My first reaction was, "I didn't come down here to cut up chickens, I came to help people in their homes." As the crowd started through the line getting chicken hot off the grill, we knew God acts in strange ways. The thanks we received for such a simple act as providing a hot meal will never be forgotten. (And, for the first time in my life, I know how to cut up a chicken).

That afternoon, until dark, we went to various homes to do whatever we could to help residents and continued it for the remainder of our time there. We always ended the day with a devotional and singing and fellowship with other volunteers who came from various places, near and far. We were worn out, we saw and did things we never dreamed we would do, and each night we slept on the floor like we did when we were young kids—too tired not to sleep.

A day before we returned home, another crew from Mt. Bethel UMC came in so we could orient them and show them the routine we had established. These weekly trips by one or two 10-12 person teams, men and women, from Mt. Bethel continued for over a year. I led a team to Gulfport in early October, still slept on the church floor, and we spent that week tearing moldy wallboard out of homes and trying to recover what we could two months after the hurricane had hit. It made an imprint on my memory as much as my first trip did—glad I did it.

Working as Hurricane Katrina relief crews must rank among the best long-term mission projects that Mt. Bethel UMC ever did. We got to know and made friends with people that we saw in church for months and years but never took the time to talk to. That was a long-time plus in addition to the immediate value we provided in helping the residents of Gulfport.

On my trip down to my second mission trip. Dr. Randy Mickler, senior minister of Mt. Bethel UMC, called me on my cellphone and said, "Bob, I want you to become the leader of the Mt. Bethel Mission Committee." Flabbergasted, I said, "Why me???" in typical minster response, Randy said, "Why not you?"

Long story short—I took on the job for a year, worked with a fellow IBM retiree, and we turned the focus and funding formula for Mt. Bethel missions around to one that was totally merit based. Plus, I learned the internal politics of churches—quite a surprise, not unlike corporate America.

A year later, Randy called me and asked me to start a Veterans Ministry at Mt. Bethel UMC. After some pushback, I did it and it is still thriving and active, with me still leading it as this is written in 2021.

And it all started with Hurricane Katrina…

Bill, Bert, Elicia celebrating 25th anniversary with Bill and Joan

Our current dogs, Gladys and Nick Chubb (aka Little Bit)

Time to slow down ... or not?

My first job (a drug store soda jerk) was the summer when I was between my freshman and sophomore years in high school. I have always had a job since then. I can't imagine not having a job and a purpose to make me want to wake up and face a new day every day.

I know many people my age tackle volunteer work, enjoy travel and leisure time, take care of their grandchildren, or do hundreds of other things to keep them busy in their retirement years. A fair number, maybe even a larger number, are content to not have a fixed purpose in each day and are happy doing whatever seems to be what they want to do that day.

My Daddy worked, doing what he loved to do with woodworking, trophies, and engraving, and traveling, until cancer caused him to stop at age 82, and he died four months later. My five-year older than me brother Bill, now 83, is still working for himself every day, and happy as he can be staying busy.

I think there must be a gene in my Family bloodstream that won't let us slow down. I am doing work I love to do — publishing books, especially memoirs and military books; working as a leader in several veterans' organizations; and serving as president and historian for the National 4th Infantry Division Association. Jan and I are as happy and as much in love as we've been in our lives (if not more so). We enjoy our local Family that we see almost daily, and talking to and occasionally visiting, or being visited by, our Family that lives across the country. Over Labor Day of 2022, we attended the wedding of our granddaughter, Annabeth, out in Wyoming. We welcome her new husband, Nate Koger, to our Family.

Thus, I guess the answer is…I don't see me slowing down as long as my health and brain stay good. I'm looking forward to going strong for several more years, and then maybe write another memoir about being "old."

Jan's bird feeder that we enjoy every day

Joe and Mona—sadly Joe died September 7, 2021

Final Thoughts and Reflections on the Life I've Lived

Writing your memoir is something each of us should do. I've been thinking about it, casually, for several years. As I got older, and COVID hit, I decided to quit putting it off and make it happen. I will say, I am very surprised at the emotions, good and bad, it evoked in me, the satisfaction I have from doing what I wish my ancestors had done for me, and how satisfied I feel now that I have gone through the process. After I had put this book on the back burner in late summer of 2021, to "finish in 2022", the death of my younger brother, Joe, in early September 2021, and a heart scare I had in late October 2021, prompted me to quit putting it off and get this finished. I plan to live much longer—but the vote on how long I live is not mine.

Our immediate Family—Jan, Kristen, Rob, Stephanie, Mark—and our grandkids—Meghan, Sullivan, Maxx, Annabeth, Ava—will all get a copy of this book for a late Christmas 2022 present (hope to have it in their hands in January 2023). My brother Bill and his three kids Bill, Bert, and Elicia; my brother Jim's daughter Tami and her two daughters, Rebecca and Mary; and my brother Joe's widow Mona and kids, Michelle, Michael, and Nick will also get a copy; and so will my cousin Mike Mason, and his son Kevin.

They know many of these stories, but not all of them. But what is more important to me is when their kids and grandkids, and their kids and grandkids, many years from now after I am long gone, can look back and read some of the background that makes up their DNA and who they are. The beauty of writing something down is that future generations can dig it out of the online and printed archives that are so prevalent (and will become more so) and learn from their ancestors.

I will be the first to admit that I have lived a blessed life. That is why I love the title of this book that Jan came up with for me — *Looking Back & Smiling*. My parents took great care of my brothers and me, we all went our separate ways and lived our own lives, very different from each other. My path through college, the Vietnam war, corporate America with IBM, a publishing business, and my complete love for history and working with active-duty military and veterans is totally different from the paths Jim, Bill, and Joe took. Our common thread is our parents and growing up in Heavener, Oklahoma.

All of us have the ties to our parents, their parents, and many previous generations. We should never forget our ancestors and the family tree that is behind us. I only wish that my grandparents, born in the 1880s, and my parents, born in 1912 and 1913, had taken the time to write about their lives and the totally different world they lived in. I have snippets of memories from stories they told me, but it is nothing I know enough about to write down and preserve.

For you reading this, whether a Family member or a total stranger, I encourage you to put into your plan of things to do before your life ends…write your memoir. For anyone over age 60, now is a great time to get started. As I said at the front of this book, to think that nobody cares about you is ridiculous. It is human nature to want to know where you came from, your ancestry. Don't be the one who lives and dies and doesn't leave a written record behind for your ancestors to learn from.

I've never in my life heard someone say, "I knew too much about my parents and grandparents and great-grandparents"…and the list goes on. Human nature is to want to know about your ancestors. I never have a month go by when I don't hear from a grandson or granddaughter of a 4th Infantry Division WWII or Vietnam vet who are seeking information on their relative who died and took their stories with them.

My ancestors can read this and know that Bob Babcock, linked genetically to them from earlier times, cared enough about them to have the foresight to tell them how I lived my life. Who knows, I may even have another memoir book in me—if I live long enough to be able to write about the life of an old man. My plan is to live to be 90 or more. With that said, on November 19, 2021, I had a pacemaker installed to regulate my heart. I'm planning on that keeping me going a long time, but we "old timers" never know how much longer we have. Quit putting off writing your memoir—your loved ones and American history will be sorry in the future if you don't do it.

I remain—Steadfast and Loyal—Deeds not Words. (The mottos of the 4th Infantry Division and the 22nd Infantry Regiment—two of the most memorable years of my life were when I served with them, and I will continue to serve many more years.)

Mother and Daddy 50th wedding anniversary, 1982

60th wedding anniversary of Mother and Daddy, 1992

Our permanent home sweet home, Christmas 2021

Our Immediate Family, with Kristen missing, spring 2022

Bob and Kristen — Charleston, SC, spring 2021

Rob, Amy, Meghan, Sullivan in Utah

Annabeth and Nate on their wedding day, September 3, 2022

Giving Maxx his first (used) MacBook Air

Palm Sunday, 2022, the day we joined Athens First UMC

This Is the Year I Wrote My Memoir
(A how to guide from someone who did it)

As the "high risk" age group, none of us over the age of 60 can say we "don't have time" now to write our personal memoir that we've thought about but have never actually stopped and done.

COVID-19, starting in mid-March of 2020, brought our world and us to a screeching halt, and while things are opening up now, most of us still stay close to home more than we'd like to, and we find ourselves looking for something to occupy our time. Watching sports reruns, the daily bad news, and the political chaos on TV became boring and depressing a long time ago.

Thus, this is the perfect time for each of us to write our life's story—our memoir or autobiography.

Don't say that nobody cares about your life story. Stop right there—Yes, they do. Ask yourself the question, do you wish that your parents and grandparents had taken the time to write down their life stories so you would have something to remember them by now that they are gone? Of course, you do—and your kids, grandkids, and great-grandkids feel the same about you…they want to read your story. I know that many of your long-time friends and acquaintances would love to read it as well.

I challenge everyone reading this who is 60 or older to decide that this year will be the time when you at least start, if not finish, your memoir. This is a great New Year's Resolution. None of us are getting any younger. As Nike would say…Just Do It! If you are under 60, it's okay to start on your memoir as well. Be a leader in your age group and set the example for others. It's great to write while things are fresh on your mind.

Your immediate response will likely be—I don't know how to even start doing that.

Fortunately, I have been a publisher for over 16 years and have a lot of experience preserving life stories for many people. Read on for some basic lessons on how to write your memoir or autobiography…

What is the difference in an autobiography and memoir? An autobiography is a chronological history of your life, in order as you move through life. A memoir is a series of memories that you want to preserve. A memoir doesn't need to be your complete life story—just snippets that are important to you and that you think your Family and friends will enjoy reading. Mine will be a combination of the two—I will walk through my whole life up to now but will stop and write specific expanded stories that I think are memories that others will enjoy reading—or learn things about me that they didn't know. Now…how do you get started?

1. Ideally, you will have a computer that you are comfortable using and will start 'typing' on your computer, using Microsoft Word as the vehicle to preserve your thoughts and writing. That is the universally accepted software—use that, not some out of date or less than mainline software. If you aren't a computer person and prefer to write by hand, then do it that way. If you do write pencil or pen on paper, be sure your writing is legible so others can read it. Many of us, including me, don't have the quality of penmanship that we had in our younger days. If you do use the old pen and paper approach, get one of your kids or grandkids or your spouse or a close friend to take your

work on a regular basis (weekly or monthly) and key it into a Word document on their computer and save it with a file name that can be remembered and thus easily found when you go back to it. Most publishers, including me, won't work from anything other than a document in Microsoft Word format. Another way to "write" your memoir without touching a keyboard is to look into some of the audio to print software that is available. Lots of doctors, lawyers, and others use dictation software which then converts their words to Microsoft Word so it can be used just like it had been typed on a computer.

2. Sit down with your favorite beverage and start with a list of chapters that you will flesh out. You can hand write it or put it on your computer—key is have it easy to find so when you get ready to flesh it out, you have the benefit of this list of chapters that you need to write.

Think about your life from birth to now—and what are key chapters that deserve being preserved for the future. There is no right or wrong way to do this—each person has a different life and thus their own unique story to tell. Some parts of your life can be handled in summary form, other parts you will want to elaborate on and dig deeper into the times in your life that helped mold you into what you are now.

My final Table of Contents—after quite a bit of tweaking since I first started writing: *(Check my table of contents at the front of this book—no need repeating it here).*

In your case, keep tweaking your Table of Contents until you are through with the book. You will always come up with something else you want to write about, so don't feel locked into a table of contents that looked good when you started your project. I have moved enough over the years that I use different moves and locations as break points in my life. You maybe haven't moved, and you will use other milestones as chapter break points.

3. Once you get your chapter outline done to your satisfaction, ask your spouse or one of your kids, or a good friend, to give it a look and tell you if you've left out anything that should be included. This is a working document so feel free to add things you forgot about when you started. I tweaked my outline frequently during the writing process.

4. Still with your favorite beverage in hand, start filling in short one line memory joggers that you will later turn into a story. A key memory of your life—could be "playing on the high school football team," "my first cars," "deciding to work at IBM," "volunteer work at the 1996 Atlanta Olympics," "supporting the 4ID during the Iraq War," "open heart surgery memories," etc.

   Again, this is a place to always refer to when you decide to work on your memoir. Keep adding to it regularly. When I was writing my book about my Vietnam experiences, I kept a pad of paper in my car and jotted down ideas as I drove back and forth to my IBM job each day—plenty of think time in Atlanta traffic. Since I don't drive to and from work like I did then, I keep my computer handy and keep updating my list on that—and I keep paper/pen handy to write an idea down if I'm not close to my computer. Ideas can be fleeting—capture them before they escape you.

5. Schedule time each day, or at least a few days a week,

when you are focused on writing your memoir. Some of us are morning people, others write best at night, or during the day, just plan to religiously spend some time each day or week working on writing your memoir. Make your memoir a priority to complete this year—or at least get a strong start on it. As you scan down your chapter and memory jogger list, something will hit you and you'll decide "I want to write about (fill in the blank) today."

Feel free to jump around and write the piece parts, you can glue them together in the proper sequence when you get close to completion. I remember one time I was on an IBM trip in New York, woke up early one morning and had my Army Airborne School experiences fresh in my brain—I wrote it that morning and it is one of my favorite chapters in my What Now, Lieutenant? book—then I went to work and did IBM stuff the rest of the day.

6. Tell your spouse, your kids, your grandkids, and your close friends what you are doing. Then, they become part of your support team. We all think of reasons to procrastinate when we don't feel like doing this and think that nobody cares about the memoir of my life. By letting them know what you are doing, you will be reinforced and encouraged—they can't wait to read it when it is finished. Also, if you want to share individual stories or chapters you've written, feel free to share them with someone you know will continue to encourage you. Put me on your list, I am becoming a pretty good expert on this subject.

7. Be sure to save and backup your work regularly—critical step. Nobody wants only one copy of something as important as the time you will spend working on writing

your memoir. I can give you a lot of ideas on backing up files—both handwritten pages and computer files. Don't risk losing this important work you are doing. Also send it periodically to a close friend or Family member to store electronically on their computer. This is a future Family jewel, be as careful taking care of it as you do your most precious possessions.

8. Be consistent with naming computer files. Believe me, it is much easier to start naming your files that will make up your book so you can easily find them. The alternative is to spend hours trying to find a file you know you've written but can't find on your computer because you can't remember the file name.

    As a publisher for 16 years, I have established a naming system that I ALWAYS use. That saves me much time in finding all the files I need for the multiple authors we are working with at any time. My system is simple—last name_first name_book title_other identifier_date. For example, all my memoir files start with Babcock_Bob_Memoir_and then any other identifier and the date the file was created. That works. You can create your own system, just make sure you remember it and it works for you.

9. There is no right or wrong way to write your memoir. This is YOUR memoir of your life. Write for your satisfaction and standards, as something you want to live long after you are gone. Don't let someone with a different point of view make you veer from what you want to write as your Family heirloom to leave to posterity. You decide if there are skeletons in your closet that you don't want to write about—that's okay. And don't be afraid to brag about

your biggest accomplishments. Modesty is not a requirement—you are writing about what is important to you as you reflect across your lifetime.

10. Emotions—don't fight them...Now that I have spent countless hours and days with heads down focus on writing my personal memoir, I have been amazed at the amounts of emotions and melancholy that I'm finding in me.

Don't fight it, it goes with the territory. It's called life. I'll tell you personally some of my emotions—writing about my deceased parents and brothers brings back tears to my eyes, happy emotions come as I write about some great memories of special times in my life (it's nice to relive it by writing it down), deciding how to write about the major transition in my life as I was divorced and started a new life with a new wife—and the impact on all Family members, and other things along this journey called life that jumps out of nowhere and opens up as sad or happy emotions.

I was somewhat shocked at how much I've focused on those emotions caused by reliving memories. It's tough, it's soothing, it's something that is worth having as you write the story of your life to leave as a legacy for your ancestors and American history. Suck it up and push on through—even we tough old guys are shocked with our emotions at times, but it's worth reliving them to get your story preserved. Don't be afraid to write about them, an emotionless story is a boring story. And don't be surprised if you feel tears running down your cheeks with some regularity as you think back into your life's experiences. And there will be plenty of smiles as well.

11. Pictures—start finding them now...The thought hit me recently that you will most likely want to include a cross section of pictures from your life in your memoir. The time to start looking for them is not when you are finished with the book and end up scrambling to find pictures that you know are 'somewhere around here' but can't be found. (I'm in that predicament now, I didn't practice what I preach, so my publishing is delayed because I don't have the pictures located that I want to include).

As part of your process from the beginning of your memoir project, start collecting pictures and put them in one place where you can find them when you are ready to select which ones to include. If you're like most of us, many of those great pictures are in 35mm slides that we haven't looked at in years, as well as random printed black/white and color pictures stored somewhere in your home, a box in the basement, and (if you are well organized) scrapbooks. But do you know where those scrapbooks are? Time to find them. And since about the year 2000, odds are most of your pictures are in digital format, stored on your cellphone and/or your computer, and have never been printed.

When you start adding pictures to your memoir (and don't do it until the end—they make computer files real large and hard to send to reviewers via email), I believe it is best to put all the pictures into one place in the book rather than scattered randomly throughout. Readers will quickly locate where the pictures are and will enjoy flipping through several picture pages. In the future, you will want to be able to go to one place to find a picture rather than trying to remember which part of your book you put that specific picture in. Second best choice is to put pictures at the end of a chapter or a section of the book that they pertain to. Trying to match a picture to a particular page or story in the body of a book is time consuming, wastes space in the book, and will cost you more money when you pay a publisher to put pictures in specific places in the body of a book.

12. Random thoughts…if you write annual Christmas letters, find old copies of those (probably on your computer) and they can be good reminders of specific years in your history. Do some "data mining" of your old computer hard drives, paper file cabinets, letters, relics, etc.

    Recently I dug back through my backup hard drive device for several old computers and found a ten-page paper I wrote in 2006 about my experiences as a volunteer in the 1996 Atlanta Olympics. You can bet that will be included in my memoir—work is already done. In fact, I will send that along when I send this document so you can see how I wrote about that memorable event. I'm sure I have more stories I've written and forgotten about and bet you do as well (I also found stories I have written about my high school football days and the experiences of my open-heart surgery in 2012, written as it happened—they also will be used). Don't forget to go through old paper file cabinets (remember those)—no telling what you will find there that you can reuse, or old letters, or other relics from your life that sparks a story to include in your memoir.

13. What's this going to cost me to do it? A favorite response I learned in the Army is, "It depends on the situation and the terrain…" There are a lot of variables. How long will your memoir be? How many copies do you want printed?

Are you okay with it being only in electronic form and not printed (I don't recommend that)? Do you want it to look like a professional book or are you comfortable with a simple Word document that you can print at a local copier store and have bound to pass out to those who are important to you? Do you want a professional editor and publisher to help you with the book to make it as professional looking as possible—a book you can put on a bookshelf with other books you treasure? Will you have pictures, family tree, drawings, other types of media other than words?

As a full-time publisher for 16 years, we provide all the services you need to produce a professional document—editing, recommendations on what else to add or maybe something to leave out, layout, font selection and book size, cover design, inclusion of pictures and other graphics, marketing (if you want to sell it to an audience bigger than your family and friends), and even worldwide distribution if you need or want it. We can do hard cover, paperback, e-books, or all three. Also, you can print as few or as many as you want. If you need more, we can get more printed when you run out.

My first memoir book I did, back in 2005, was for the father of a good friend, covering his WWII and Korean War-era Naval Aviator time and his lifelong architect career. I asked him how many copies he wanted. He said, "I don't have 25 people who would care about this." When I came back and suggested he print 50, he pushed back with, "I don't even know 50 people, but I can afford it so go ahead and get me 50 copies."

A week after the books were delivered, he called me in a panic, "Bob—I'm out of books. Can you get more?" I did, and before he died a few years ago, we had printed

400 copies of his book. At his funeral, some of the remaining books were passed out and many of his stories that he had preserved by caring enough and taking time to write his memoir put smiles on the faces of his Family and friends as we celebrated his life.

So, what does it cost? As little or as much as you want it to. But always be aware, there are a lot more people than your immediate Family who care about you and the life you lived. If you want a quote from a professional publisher, contact me and I will give you a price once I learn more about what you plan to write. If you want to do it on your own, I can also help you with ideas of how to do it so it doesn't get lost once you are gone and so it can be replicated for future generations. One copy stuck up on a shelf in your bedroom closet is a good way to get your memoir thrown away and never read by future generations, or even by those near and dear to you now.

14. I will continue to update this as I think of more topics, get more questions and experiences from fellow memoir writers, and think of ways to help encourage you to start and finish your memoir this year.

More questions... Ask me, I'm happy to help. Remember — *This is the year I'm going to write my memoir.* And feel free to share this with others who need to write their memoir.

Email bob@deedspublishing.com

Acknowledgments

This has been an interesting experience. First, thinking about whether and when I would slow down and write this book. I guess that is one good thing that came from COVID—it gave me time to reflect and write. I got early encouragement from Archie Carroll who let me read his memoir soon after it was finished. While we took different paths, we both started our journey in 1943. And fellow Vietnam veteran, Duke Doubleday, unknowingly encouraged me to take the plunge.

My special lady (and wife), Jan, was my first reader, followed by our daughter Kristen—both encouraged me and helped me smooth some rough edges. Mark, our son and partner in Deeds Publishing, not only caught some factual errors, but used his great skills in publishing to make this a book we can be proud of.

Other early readers who encouraged me are Gary Swanson, Michael Belis, John Fraser, Donn Atkins, Archie Carroll, Jim Henderson, Steve Scott, Jean Ann and Janis Franklin (I'll always call them the Franklin girls, along with Nancy).

To all who read this, I encourage you to quit putting off writing your own life story. Despite what you may think, lots of people will love to read it, especially your Family, friends, and future generations.

About the Author

Bob Babcock was born and grew up in the small railroad town of Heavener, Oklahoma. He graduated from Kansas State College in Pittsburg, KS in 1965. He served as an officer in the United States Army from 1965 to 1967 where he was a rifle platoon leader and executive officer in Vietnam with the 4th Infantry Division.

After a year with Phillips Petroleum Company, Bob was a Sales/Marketing Executive with IBM from 1968 to 2002. In his last IBM job, he was responsible for Industry Marketing for Small and Medium Businesses in North and South America.

Since 2002, Bob has been a founding official partner of the Veterans History Project, part of the Library of Congress, preserving memories of America's veterans.

As a lifetime writer with experience writing in school and military newspapers, newsletter editor for his military organizations, and much writing experience in his IBM sales and marketing career, Bob established a publishing company, Deeds Publishing LLC, in 2006 to pursue his passion for preserving excellent stories. In their sixteen years as a publisher, Deeds has published over 400 books of many genres. You can learn more through their web site: www.deedspublishing.com.

Bob has written twelve books, including one under contract to the founders of Jack Henry & Associates, a $4 billion banking software company; two under contract to the US Army about the Iraq War; and one for the World War II WAC who typed the D-Day orders for General Eisenhower. His personal books include three in a series of War Stories from World War II through Vietnam, one about his personal experiences in Vietnam, and three that are collections of military stories from members of veterans' organizations. This personal memoir is Bob's twelfth, but not last, book.

www.ingramcontent.com/pod-product-compliance
Lightning Source LLC
Chambersburg PA
CBHW070747230426
43665CB00017B/2283